100 PARADOXES + PARADOX MODELS

THE LIMITS OF REASON THAT DEFINE HUMAN AND MACHINE INTELLIGENCE

100 PARADOX MODELS

BY DAN WAITE

- LOTTERY INSURER PARADOX
- FAT MAN VARIATION
- OMNIPOTENCE PARADOX
- CHEATING HUSBAND PARADOX
- BIRTHDAY PARADOX
- SLEEPING BEAUTY PARADOX
- HAIRY BALL THEOREM
- TARSKI'S UNDEFINABILITY THEOREM
- SEMANTIC CLOSURE PARADOX
- CATCH-22
- BOOTSTRAP PARADOX
- SAYRE'S LAW
- PARRONDO'S PARADOX
- HILBERT'S HOTEL
- BARBER PARADOX
- BASE RATE FALLACY PARADOX
- GRANDFATHER PARADOX
- INFINITE MONKEY THEOREM
- TWO-CHILD PARADOX
- TWO ENVELOPES PARADOX
- JEALOUS HUSBANDS PROBLEM
- CHEAP TRICK
- TWIN PARADOX
- AND MANY, MANY MORE

100 PARADOXES

AND

PARADOX MODELS

100 PARADOXES

AND

PARADOX MODELS

BY DAN WAITE

Published by LOCO TEMPUS LIMITED 2025

Copyright Dan Waite 2025

Cover design by Dan Waite

All rights reserved. Apart from brief extracts for the purpose of review, no part of this publication may be reproduced, stored in a retrieval system, or transmitted in any form or by any means, electronic, mechanical, photocopying, recording or otherwise without permission of the publisher.

Dan Waite has asserted his right under the Copyright, Designs and Patents Act 1988 to be identified as author of this work.

British Library Cataloguing in Publication Data

A catalogue record for this book is available from the British Library

ISBN: 978-1-917784-21-4

Dan Waite here, CEO of Better Noise Music.

PARADOXES are something that I have become interested in over the last couple of years after listening to several of Rory Sutherland's videos.

When I went to try and learn more, I realised that there were so many paradoxes, some still unsolved, and I wanted to learn more. Perhaps you are hear for the same reason.

I started looking into **PARADOXES** and quickly realised that there was a lot more to it than I realised and I have enjoyed researching this book very much.

I hope you will also enjoy and be able to think deeply about these 100 **PARADOXES AND PARADOX MODELS** within the book.

Good luck on your journey of self-education.

My best,

Dan Waite

OTHER BOOKS IN THIS 100 SERIES – SCAN HERE

100 COGNITIVE AND MENTAL MODELS TO HELP YOUR CAREER: Mental Shortcuts for Smarter Choices, Sharper Thinking, and Success

-

ANOTHER 100 MENTAL MODELS TO HELP YOUR CAREER - VOLUME 2: Another 100 Powerful Mental Models for Clarity, Confidence, and Climbing the Career Ladder

-

100 HEURISTICS AND HEURISTIC MODELS: The Hidden Rules of Smart Thinking Used by Experts, Entrepreneurs, and Machines

-

100 GAME THEORIES AND DECISION MODELS FOR RATIONAL DECISION MAKING IN COMPETITIVE SITUATIONS: 100 Winning Strategies for Rational Thinking in High-Stakes Scenarios

-

100 BUSINESS STRATEGIES PROVEN TACTICS FOR GROWTH, INNOVATION AND MARKET DOMINATION:

Actionable Strategies to Scale, Disrupt and Lead in Any Industry

-

100 LEADERSHIP MODELS AND STRATEGIES FOR EFFECTIVE DECISION-MAKING FOR ORGANIZATIONAL SUCCESS: Empowering Your Leadership, 100 Proven Strategies and Models to Enhance Decision-Making & Drive Success

-

100 BUSINESS GROWTH HACKS AND STRATEGIES TO GROW PROFIT AND INCREASE YOUR COMPETITIVE ADVANTAGE: Proven Techniques to Scale Faster, Boost Revenue, and Dominate Your Market with Actionable Growth

-

100 ECONOMIC THEORIES DEMYSTIFIED : A Guide To The World's Most Influential Economic Ideas From Keynesian Economics To Debt-deflation Theory

-

100 PASSIVE INCOME STREAM SIDE HUSTLES, MASTERING SIDE HUSTLES AND SMART INVESTMENTS: How to Make Money While You Sleep and Secure Your Financial Future

This is dedicated to my wife Irena, my family & friends and work colleagues, present and past.

With thanks to Ade Adeluwoye, Nicolas Bate, Sir Richard Branson, Allen Kovac for your trust and guidance as a boss and mentor and Napolean Hill for the advice in spotting opportunity in hard work.

Thank you to inspirational contacts who as a result of their books and classes have me thinking differently, they are Rory Sutherland and Will Page.

In memory of my father David Waite.

100 PARADOXES AND PARADOX MODELS

CHAPTERS

🔄 Logical & Self-Referential Paradoxes

These involve contradictions from definitions or self-reference.

1. Curry's Paradox
2. Buridan's Bridge
3. Tarski's Indefinability Theorem
4. Sorites in Colour
5. Jealous Husbands Problem
6. Preference Reversal
7. Recursive Definition Paradox
8. Yablo's Paradox
9. Richard's Paradox
10. Quine's Paradox
11. Knower Paradox
12. Kaplan's Paradox
13. Specker's Paradox
14. Frege's Puzzle
15. Knowability Paradox (Fitch's)

16. Goodman's Grue Paradox

17. Lottery Insurer Paradox

18. Brandenburger–Keisler Paradox

19. Skolem's Paradox

20. Infinite Monkey Theorem (in formal logic terms)

21. Semantic Closure Paradox

22. Turing's Halting Paradox (self-referential computational logic)

🕰 Temporal & Time Travel Paradoxes

Arising from contradictions in time travel or temporal logic.

23. Grandfather Paradox

24. Chronology Protection Conjecture

25. Newcomb's Paradox

26. Prediction Paradox

27. Temporal Causal Loop Paradox

28. Omnipotence Paradox

29. Abilene Paradox (indirectly temporal)

30. Unexpected Hanging Paradox

Ethical & Decision Theory Paradoxes

Involve conflicting choices, utilities, and moral dilemmas.

31. Prisoner's Dilemma

32. Trolley Problem

33. Fat Man Variation

34. Mere Addition Paradox (Population Ethics)

35. Tragedy of the Commons

36. Catch-22

37. Voting Paradox (Condorcet)

38. Doestoevsky's Paradox

39. McNamara Fallacy

40. Bootstrap Paradox

41. Utility Monster Paradox

Epistemological & Information Paradoxes

Relate to knowledge, belief, or the nature of truth.

42. Paradox of the Court

43. Surprise Examination Paradox

44. Meno's Paradox

45. Information Bottleneck Paradox

46. Anthropic Principle Paradox

47. Russell's Paradox

48. Two-Child Paradox

49. Cheating Husband Paradox

50. Sayre's Law

51. Paradox of Inquiry

52. Löb's Paradox

Probability & Statistical Paradoxes

Statistical reasoning leads to counterintuitive outcomes.

53. Simpson's Paradox

54. Two Envelopes Paradox

55. Raven Paradox (Hempel's)

56. Ross–Littlewood Paradox

57. Birthday Paradox

58. Newcomb-like Variants

59. Zeigarnik Effect

60. Law of Small Numbers Paradox

61. Parrondo's Paradox

62. Sleeping Beauty Paradox

63. Base Rate Fallacy Paradox

Mathematical & Set-Theoretical Paradoxes

Formal reasoning in math leads to surprising conclusions.

63. Burali-Forti Paradox

64. Diagonalization Paradox

65. Hilbert's Hotel

66. Banach–Tarski Paradox

67. Peano's Arrow Paradox

68. Paradox of Cheap Trick (economic valuation)

69. Paradox of Value (Diamond–Water)

70. Bolzano–Weierstrass Paradox

71. Hairy Ball Theorem

72. Borel's Paradox

Linguistic & Semantic Paradoxes

Language and meaning create contradictions.

73. Liar Paradox

74. Barber Paradox

75. Recursion Paradox

76. Sorites Paradox (general form)

77. Grelling's Second-Order Adjective Problem

78. Meaning Holism Paradox

79. Vagueness Paradox

80. Referential Opacity Paradox

81. Performative Contradiction Paradox

🚀 Physics & Relativity Paradoxes

Stem from extreme or theoretical scenarios in physics.

82. Twin Paradox

83. Zeno's Paradoxes (Achilles, Dichotomy, Arrow)

84. Einstein–Podolsky–Rosen Paradox

85. Schrödinger's Cat

86. Quantum Zeno Effect

87. Information Paradox

88. Wigner's Friend

89. Ether Paradox

90. Delayed Choice Quantum Eraser Paradox

91. Firewall Paradox

Game Theory & Economic Paradoxes

Game mechanics or incentives misfire.

- 92. Grelling–Nelson Paradox
- 93. Braess' Paradox
- 94. Arrow's Impossibility Theorem
- 95. Ellsberg Paradox
- 96. St. Petersburg Paradox
- 97. Monty Hall Problem
- 98. Cooperator's Reward Paradox
- 99. Resource Paradox
- 100. Von Neumann–Morgenstern Stability
- 101. Dutch Book Paradox

Philosophical & Ontological Paradoxes

Challenge fundamental ideas about existence, identity, or reality.

- 102. Ship of Theseus
- 103. Paradox of the Stone
- 104. Boltzmann Brain
- 105. Identity of Indiscernibles Paradox
- 106. Paradox of Tolerance

107. Quantum Suicide

108. Many-worlds Paradoxes

109. Gödel's Incompleteness (reinstated as a core ontological puzzle)

110. Sorites (Vagueness)

111. Dialetheism

🔄 Logical & Self-Referential Paradoxes

These involve contradictions from definitions or self-reference.

1. Curry's Paradox

Theory Overview

Curry's Paradox is a logical paradox that arises in **naive set theory**, **formal logic**, and **semantic systems** when self-reference is combined with conditional logic (i.e., implications). Named after logician **Haskell Curry**, the paradox reveals that certain systems which allow **self-referential statements and unrestricted logical rules** become **inconsistent**—that is, they can be used to prove **any proposition**, including contradictions.

Unlike the Liar Paradox, which uses negation and contradiction to create trouble (e.g., "This statement is false"), Curry's Paradox avoids explicit negation and instead uses **implication** to derive absurd conclusions. This makes it especially dangerous because it **does not rely on falsity**—yet it still causes logical collapse.

Example

Let's examine the paradox using a self-referential sentence:

"If this sentence is true, then 2 + 2 = 5."

Let's call this sentence **C**. So:

$$C \equiv \text{"If C is true, then } 2 + 2 = 5.\text{"}$$

Now consider the implications:

1. **Assume C is true.**
   Then, by the content of C, **if C is true, then 2 + 2 = 5**.
   Since we've assumed C is true, we now conclude **2 + 2 = 5**.

2. Therefore, if C is true, then 2 + 2 = 5.
   But wait—that's **exactly what C claims**! So C is indeed **true**.

3. And since C is true, we again conclude: **2 + 2 = 5**.

Thus, using only implication and self-reference, we have derived a **false conclusion** from apparently harmless premises. Even worse, if this form of reasoning is accepted, we could prove **any arbitrary statement**, collapsing the consistency of the logical system.

Why It Works

Curry's Paradox works because of an uncritical acceptance of:

- **Unrestricted self-reference** (a sentence referring to itself),

- **Material implication** (the idea that "if A, then B" is valid whenever A is false or B is true),

- And sometimes, **naive comprehension in set theory** (e.g., defining a set of all sets that satisfy a certain condition).

These features, when combined, make it possible to **embed an arbitrary conclusion** into a seemingly valid logical structure.

The problem isn't that the reasoning is invalid in form—it's that the **premises allow self-reference without restriction**, making the entire structure vulnerable to collapse.

How It Works

In formal logic, Curry's Paradox uses a rule called **Modus Ponens**:

1. If P → Q (if P implies Q), and

2. P is true,

3. Then conclude Q.

Curry exploits this by constructing a self-referential sentence **C** that says:

"If C is true, then X," where X is any arbitrary claim (like 2 + 2 = 5).

Applying Modus Ponens leads you to accept X—**regardless of its content**—as long as you accept that C is true. And since C's truth condition is itself, the loop **short-circuits logic**, permitting any conclusion to follow.

Application

Curry's Paradox plays a central role in:

- **Formal logic**: Forcing systems to be constructed in ways that **restrict self-reference** or **limit implication**.

- **Set theory**: Motivating the development of **axiomatic systems** like Zermelo–Fraenkel set theory, which avoid naive comprehension.

- **Type theory and lambda calculus**: Areas where functions can refer to themselves (as in functional programming), requiring constraints to maintain consistency.

- **Philosophy of language**: Especially in semantics, where truth and reference must be carefully controlled.

Key Insights

- Curry's Paradox proves that **implication + self-reference = logical explosion**.

- Unlike the Liar Paradox, it **requires no negation**, making it more insidious.

- It exposes the **fragility of logical systems** that try to be both expressive and unrestricted.

- To preserve consistency, systems must **limit how statements can refer to themselves** or redefine implication more carefully.

- The paradox remains a key concern in designing **consistent formal systems**, both in mathematics and computer science.

2. Buridan's Bridge

Theory Overview

Buridan's Bridge is a medieval logical paradox attributed to the 14th-century philosopher **Jean Buridan**. It presents a compelling challenge involving **self-reference**, **truth conditions**, and **conditional obligations**, and anticipates modern developments in **semantic paradoxes** and **deontic logic** (the logic of duties and permissions).

The scenario involves **Socrates** and **Plato** on a bridge, with Plato acting as a judge or ruler who makes a conditional statement about Socrates' fate. The paradox arises when Socrates gives a response that creates a **contradiction** if Plato attempts to carry out the condition logically.

At its core, Buridan's Bridge highlights the difficulty of reasoning about **conditional actions** in the presence of **self-referential truth claims**, making it a cousin to the **Liar Paradox** and early examples of **logical indeterminacy**.

Example

Here's the classic version:

Socrates wants to cross a bridge. Plato, who controls the bridge, tells him:

"If you say something true, I shall let you pass. But if you say something false, I will throw you into the water."

Socrates replies:

"You will throw me into the water."

Now the dilemma:

- If Plato **throws Socrates into the water**, then Socrates's statement was **true**. But Plato only throws people who lie—so he **shouldn't** throw him in.

- If Plato **lets Socrates pass**, then the statement "You will throw me into the water" becomes **false**. But Plato only allows people to pass if they tell the **truth**.

In both cases, Plato's condition leads to a contradiction: **no consistent action he can take satisfies the original rule**.

Why It Works

The paradox works because it uses **self-reference** to create a logical trap. Socrates's statement sets up a conditional that reflects directly on the outcome it is meant to influence. In this way, the truth value of the statement depends on Plato's decision, and yet Plato's decision depends on the truth value of the statement.

This circular dependency creates a logical contradiction—**any action Plato takes invalidates the condition for that action**. The result is a situation where **no consistent resolution** is possible, exposing limits in our ability to reason through **truth-dependent conditions**.

How It Works

Buridan's Bridge operates through:

1. **Conditional logic**: Plato sets a rule based on the truth or falsehood of a statement.
2. **Self-referential content**: Socrates's statement directly refers to the action Plato will take.
3. **Contradictory implications**: Carrying out the condition negates the premise, and vice versa.
4. **Inescapable loop**: The outcome both affirms and negates the conditions set for it.

This is similar in structure to the **Liar Paradox**—"This statement is false"—but adds the twist of **external consequences** governed by conditional action.

Application

Buridan's Bridge anticipates challenges in:

- **Deontic logic**: Modelling obligations, permissions, and punishments when conditions are self-referential or paradoxical.

- **Legal reasoning**: Where judgments can sometimes be circular or depend on the truth of statements about legal consequences.

- **Programming and AI**: In rule-based systems, where self-referential commands can create logical deadlocks or contradictions.

- **Game theory and ethics**: Where predictions about actions change those very actions, creating strategic paradoxes.

Key Insights

- Self-referential conditions can undermine **logical rules** based on truth values.

- Actions conditional on statements about those same actions can result in **logical impasses**.

- The paradox reveals the fragility of systems that tie **truth**, **action**, and **prediction** too tightly together.

- Like other semantic paradoxes, Buridan's Bridge shows that **rules need boundaries** to prevent feedback loops that erode consistency.

- It's a precursor to more formal paradoxes in **logic, computation, and philosophy of language**, demonstrating that even simple language games can yield profound complications.

3. Tarski's Indefinability Theorem

Theory Overview

Tarski's Indefinability Theorem is a foundational result in **mathematical logic** and the **philosophy of language**, formulated by Polish logician **Alfred Tarski** in the 1930s. It states that **truth cannot be consistently defined within the same formal language** to which it applies. In simpler terms: a sufficiently expressive language (such as arithmetic) **cannot define its own truth predicate** without running into paradoxes like the **Liar Paradox**.

This theorem builds on earlier work regarding **semantic paradoxes**, formal languages, and self-reference, and it parallels **Gödel's Incompleteness Theorems**. It forms part of a broader discovery in the 20th century that **truth, consistency, and completeness** cannot all coexist comfortably in formal systems capable of basic arithmetic.

Example

Consider a formal language capable of expressing arithmetic, such as **Peano Arithmetic (PA)**. Suppose you try to define a predicate **"True(x)"** within this language that correctly identifies which statements are true in that very system.

Tarski's theorem shows that **you cannot define such a truth predicate within the system itself**. If you attempt to, you can construct a sentence that says:

"This sentence is not true."

This is a version of the **Liar Paradox**, rendered in formal logic. If the sentence is true, then what it says is correct—it is not true, and hence false. But if it is false, then it must be true. This creates a contradiction, showing that **internal definitions of truth lead to inconsistency**.

Therefore, the system cannot consistently include a function or predicate that captures the notion of "truth" for its own sentences. Truth must be defined in a **meta-language**, a language that stands **outside** the object language being evaluated.

Why It Works

Tarski's result works because it formalizes the **dangers of self-reference** in logical systems. When a language tries to describe its own semantic properties—especially truth—it **inevitably enables constructions** that mimic paradoxes like the Liar.

His proof uses **diagonalization**—a method similar to Gödel's technique—to show that any sufficiently rich language that tries to define its own truth predicate will become inconsistent or incomplete. In this way, Tarski provides a

semantic limit theorem, complementing Gödel's **syntactic limit** result.

How It Works

The theorem relies on:

1. A formal language **L** that can express basic arithmetic.
2. The assumption that **truth in L** can be defined within L itself using a predicate **True(x)**.
3. Construction of a **self-referential sentence** that says, "This sentence is not true," via diagonalization.
4. Demonstration that any such construction results in **logical contradiction**, unless the system is inconsistent or incomplete.

Therefore, **truth** for L must be defined **in a richer language**, often referred to as the **meta-language**.

Application

Tarski's Indefinability Theorem is crucial in:

- **Formal semantics**: Establishing that semantic notions like truth and satisfaction must be handled at the **meta-theoretical** level.
- **Foundations of mathematics**: Influencing how truth and proof are separated and understood.

- **Computer science**: Guiding the design of formal systems, programming languages, and logical frameworks.

- **Philosophy of language**: Shaping debates about meaning, reference, and the hierarchy of languages.

It also has practical implications in **AI and logic programming**, where rules about truth, inference, and consistency must be carefully designed to avoid collapse.

Key Insights

- **Truth cannot be captured internally** in expressive logical systems.

- **Self-reference and diagonalization** are powerful tools that expose the limitations of formal languages.

- The theorem complements Gödel's work by adding a **semantic boundary** to syntactic incompleteness.

- It emphasizes the need for **meta-languages** to discuss truth, validity, and meaning.

- Tarski's result is a profound reminder that **not everything meaningful or real can be captured within a system's own rules.**

4. Sorites in Colour

Theory Overview

The **Sorites Paradox** (from the Greek *sōritēs*, meaning "heap") addresses problems of **vagueness**, especially in predicates that lack clear boundaries. The classic version asks how many grains of sand make a heap—removing one grain seems to leave a heap, yet repeating this logic leads to the absurd conclusion that a single grain (or none) is still a heap.

The **Sorites in Colour** version applies this idea to **gradual colour change**, challenging our assumptions about when one colour becomes another. It underscores a central issue in **philosophy of language and perception**: how can we meaningfully use terms that refer to properties with **no sharp cutoffs**, such as "red," "orange," or "blue"?

This variant brings the paradox into the realm of **perception and classification**, where colour categories are both **continuous and discrete**—continuous in nature, but discrete in language.

Example

Imagine a colour gradient that moves imperceptibly from **red to orange**. You are shown 1,000 colour patches, arranged so that **each one is only slightly different** in hue from the one before. The first is clearly red. The last is clearly orange.

Now, you are asked:

"At what point does red become orange?"

Most people would say, "I don't know," or, "There's no clear cutoff." However, the paradox emerges when we apply **transitivity and tolerance**:

1. Patch 1 is red.
2. Patch 2 is only *slightly* different from Patch 1, so it must also be red.
3. Patch 3 is slightly different from Patch 2, so it must also be red.
4. Continuing this logic, Patch 1,000 must also be red.

But Patch 1,000 is clearly orange.

So: **If each small change doesn't suffice to change the colour, then no number of changes should. Yet they clearly do.**

Why It Works

The paradox works because it exploits our reliance on **tolerance to small changes**—the belief that a minimal shift in a property does not affect its classification. However, when this principle is applied repeatedly, it leads to **absurd or contradictory conclusions**.

It also highlights a deeper issue: **language and logic struggle with vagueness**, while the world (and especially human perception) is inherently fuzzy.

How It Works

The Sorites in Colour Paradox relies on:

1. **Vagueness of predicates**: Terms like "red" or "orange" have **fuzzy boundaries**.

2. **Tolerance principle**: A small enough change should not alter category membership.

3. **Transitivity**: If A is red, and A is similar to B, and B is similar to C, then C should also be red.

4. **Iteration**: Repeating tolerance reasoning step by step creates a cumulative shift that eventually breaks the category.

This results in a **logical contradiction between perception and classification.**

Application

This paradox has wide applications:

- **Philosophy of language**: Forces reconsideration of how words relate to the world.

- **Cognitive science**: Explores how we form categories and boundaries in the mind.

- **Artificial intelligence and computer vision**: Challenges how machines are taught to classify gradual inputs (e.g., colour recognition).

- **Law and ethics**: Where gradual changes (e.g., becoming an adult or accumulating harm) create definitional gray zones.

Key Insights

- The Sorites in Colour paradox shows that **precise logic breaks down in vague contexts**.
- It reveals the **limits of classical reasoning** in describing continuous phenomena.
- It encourages the use of **fuzzy logic**, **probabilistic reasoning**, or **degree-based predicates** to handle vagueness.
- It underscores that many real-world categories—especially in perception—are **inherently approximate**.
- The paradox teaches that the **boundaries of language and logic are not always aligned with human experience**.

5. Jealous Husbands Problem

Theory Overview

The **Jealous Husbands Problem** is a classic logic and constraint-based puzzle from recreational mathematics. It explores themes of **combinatorial reasoning, state space navigation**, and **constraint satisfaction**, often framed similarly to the Missionaries and Cannibals problem. The challenge involves transporting several couples across a river under strict social and logical conditions that prevent specific combinations from being left alone.

The paradox lies not in any contradiction, but in the **complexity of constraints** which can lead to **non-intuitive, counterproductive, or paradoxical-seeming decisions** that must be made to reach a viable solution.

The typical scenario includes **three married couples**, with the stipulation that no wife can be in the presence of another man unless her husband is also present. The goal is to get all individuals across a river using a boat that can carry only two people at a time.

Example

The setup:

- Three husbands (**H1, H2, H3**) and their wives (**W1, W2, W3**) must cross a river.

- The boat can hold at most two people.
- At no point may any wife be in the company of a man other than her husband **unless her husband is also present**.
- The boat cannot move by itself—it must be rowed by at least one person.

A naive approach, such as trying to shuttle couples over one by one, quickly fails due to constraint violations. For example, if W1 and W2 are left with H3, it violates the rule unless their husbands are present.

Thus, the problem forces a careful sequencing of moves where **state transitions** must always respect the condition of no "unaccompanied wives with other men."

Why It Works

The problem works because it illustrates how **simple-sounding constraints** can create **combinatorial complexity**. Human intuition struggles when logic involves **negative constraints** (rules about what cannot happen), particularly when they're **non-local**—meaning, the legality of a situation depends not just on who's present, but who's absent.

The tension of the problem arises from the **fragility of acceptable states** and the need to **backtrack or revisit prior states** to make future progress. It's a test of **logical foresight and memory**.

How It Works

The problem operates through:

1. **Constraint satisfaction**: The need to avoid illegal groupings on either bank or in the boat.

2. **Finite state transitions**: Each move can be mapped as a state, and the challenge becomes finding a valid sequence from the initial to the goal state.

3. **Symmetry and reversibility**: Many legal moves can be undone or mirrored; the logic must avoid dead ends while optimizing boat usage.

4. **Dependency management**: The safe movement of one person often depends on the position of several others.

These components combine to create a situation that feels paradoxical because **legal moves often look temporarily worse or counterproductive**—like taking someone back across the river to reposition.

Application

Though a theoretical puzzle, it has wider applications in:

- **Computer science**: Especially in **AI planning, constraint programming**, and **state machine modelling**.

- **Security and access control**: Where systems must ensure safe group compositions (e.g., authorizations, segregation of duties).

- **Cognitive psychology**: As a tool to study human problem-solving and reasoning under rules.

- **Logistics and transport planning**: Managing constraints where cargo or personnel cannot be mixed without certain conditions.

Key Insights

- The Jealous Husbands Problem highlights the **importance of sequencing and planning** under constraints.

- Problems that seem paradoxical may simply reflect **hidden complexity**, not actual contradictions.

- Logical puzzles like this develop **disciplined, step-by-step reasoning** and the ability to think in **state transitions**.

- It shows how **non-quantitative problems** can still require rigorous formal logic to solve.

- The puzzle teaches that sometimes progress requires **temporary regress**—a key insight in many dynamic systems.

6. Preference Reversal

Theory Overview

The **Preference Reversal Paradox** arises in behavioural economics and decision theory when individuals **reverse their preferences** between two options depending on the **method of elicitation**, even though their fundamental values or circumstances remain unchanged. It demonstrates a clear violation of **rational choice theory**, which assumes that individuals have consistent preferences across contexts.

First studied extensively by researchers like **Sarah Lichtenstein and Paul Slovic** in the 1970s, the paradox challenges the classical view that people's preferences are **stable and internally coherent**. Instead, it reveals that **context, framing, or evaluation criteria** can shift how choices are made—especially when involving **risk, probability, or time**.

This paradox plays a crucial role in **challenging expected utility theory**, suggesting that human preferences are more **constructive and context-dependent** than previously believed.

Example

Imagine a person is asked to choose between two bets:

- **Bet A**: 80% chance to win $100 (high probability, moderate reward).

- **Bet B**: 20% chance to win $300 (low probability, high reward).

When asked to **choose** one of the bets, the individual selects **Bet A**, preferring the higher probability. However, when asked to **assign a price** (i.e., how much money they'd be willing to pay for each bet), they might assign **a higher price to Bet B**.

This **preference reversal**—choosing Bet A but valuing Bet B more—contradicts the notion of stable, transitive preferences and exposes the **malleability of human decision-making**.

Why It Works

The paradox works because people rely on **different cognitive processes** depending on how a choice is framed. When choosing between two options, they may focus on **probability of winning** (favouring Bet A). When assigning value, however, they may focus more on **potential payoff** (favouring Bet B).

This inconsistency occurs because:

- People are influenced by **salient features** of each task.

- They often use **heuristics**—mental shortcuts—rather than calculating expected utility.

- Contextual cues **shift attention** between dimensions like risk, reward, and fairness.

Ultimately, it reveals that people often lack **internally consistent utility functions**, especially under uncertainty.

How It Works

The paradox typically appears when:

1. Two options are presented involving trade-offs between **probability and reward**.
2. Individuals are asked to **choose** and then to **price** the options.
3. The choice and pricing results **don't align**, despite involving the same underlying options.

The reversal suggests that preferences are not fixed but **constructed in real-time**, depending on which attributes are highlighted or how the question is posed.

It also undermines **procedural invariance**, a principle in rational decision theory stating that preference should remain unchanged across different elicitation methods.

Application

Preference Reversal has real-world relevance in:

- **Marketing**: Consumer preferences can flip depending on how products are described or bundled.

- **Policy design**: Citizens may support a policy in theory but reject it when asked to assign tax dollars.

- **Behavioural finance**: Investors may choose conservative funds but value high-risk ones more when asked to price them.

- **Healthcare**: Patients might prefer one treatment when explained probabilistically, but change their minds when asked for a utility valuation.

In all cases, it highlights the importance of **framing and presentation** in shaping choices.

Key Insights

- Preferences are often **context-dependent and constructed**, not retrieved from a stable internal map.

- The paradox demonstrates that **choice behaviour does not always follow logical consistency**.

- It challenges foundational assumptions of **expected utility theory** and **classical rationality**.

- Recognizing preference reversals helps design better **decision-making environments** and avoid **choice architecture biases**.

- Ultimately, it shows that to understand human decision-making, we must look beyond abstract models and account for **cognitive, emotional, and contextual factors**.

7. Recursive Definition Paradox

Theory Overview

The **Recursive Definition Paradox** refers to a class of logical and mathematical problems that arise when a concept is **defined in terms of itself**, leading to **infinite regress** or **circularity**. While recursion is a powerful and legitimate tool in logic, computer science, and mathematics, if not carefully constrained, it can produce paradoxes or undefined behaviour.

In many formal systems, **recursive definitions** are used to define sequences, functions, or sets by referencing earlier stages. However, a paradox occurs when the definition lacks a **base case** or termination rule, causing the definition to **never resolve** into concrete meaning. This paradox challenges assumptions about **self-reference**, **foundational logic**, and **computability**.

It relates to broader concerns in logic such as **Russell's Paradox**, **Gödel's Incompleteness Theorems**, and the **Halting Problem**, each of which exposes vulnerabilities in systems that reference themselves without clear limits.

Example

Consider the classic example of defining a function like this:

- Let **F(x)** be defined as **F(x) = F(x)**.

This definition is clearly **circular**—it tells us nothing about what F(x) actually is. It refers only to itself without additional information. Unlike proper recursion (e.g., factorials, Fibonacci sequences), which build on smaller, well-defined values, this definition doesn't bottom out—it **recursively references itself infinitely**, creating a paradox of meaning.

Another example in language:

"A 'recursive word' is a word that defines itself."

This seems self-explanatory but provides **no usable content**—its definition loops back into itself, producing **semantic emptiness** or confusion.

Why It Works

The paradox works because it **exploits the powerful yet dangerous tool of self-reference**. In formal systems, recursion can elegantly solve problems—like defining natural numbers (e.g., Peano arithmetic) or processing data structures in programming. However, without **base conditions**, recursion becomes **non-terminating**, leading to **undefined or paradoxical outcomes**.

Our intuition breaks down when we encounter definitions that are **self-justifying** but **unresolvable**. The paradox lies in the appearance of a meaningful statement that **fails to produce meaning** when unpacked.

How It Works

Recursive Definition Paradoxes arise when:

1. A concept is **defined in terms of itself**.
2. There is **no base case** to anchor the definition in concrete terms.
3. The evaluation leads to an **infinite regress** or circular logic.
4. The process **fails to yield a meaningful or computable output**.

In computer science, this leads to functions that **never halt**, causing stack overflows or infinite loops. In logic, it results in **non-well-founded definitions** that resist formal resolution.

Application

The Recursive Definition Paradox is relevant in:

- **Mathematics and logic**: To test the validity of formal definitions and systems.
- **Computer science**: Particularly in programming languages, algorithm design, and recursive function calls.

- **Philosophy of language**: When analysing meaning, reference, and definitions.

- **Artificial intelligence**: Where improperly defined recursive rules can result in non-terminating behaviour or failure to learn.

It also plays a role in theoretical discussions about **self-replicating systems**, **consciousness**, and **semantic paradoxes** like the Liar Paradox.

Key Insights

- Not all recursion is paradoxical—**well-founded recursion requires a base case**.

- Self-reference can be powerful but becomes paradoxical **without limits**.

- Recursive paradoxes illuminate boundaries between **syntactic form and semantic content**.

- They help identify **logical inconsistencies** in definitions, programs, or proofs.

- The paradox reminds us that **infinite regress is not always productive**—systems need **grounded axioms** or termination rules to be meaningful.

8. Yablo's Paradox

Theory Overview

Yablo's Paradox is a self-referential logical paradox devised by philosopher **Stephen Yablo** in 1993. It resembles the classic **Liar Paradox** ("This sentence is false") but with a crucial twist: it avoids **direct self-reference**. Instead of a single statement referring to itself, Yablo's Paradox involves an **infinite sequence** of statements, each referring **only to statements that come after it**.

Yablo created the paradox to demonstrate that **self-reference is not necessary to create paradoxes**—a challenge to previous assumptions in logic and philosophy. The paradox raises important questions about **truth, reference, and circularity**, particularly in formal logic and semantics.

Example

Consider an infinite list of sentences:

- S_1: "All of the sentences after this one are false."
- S_2: "All of the sentences after this one are false."
- S_3: "All of the sentences after this one are false."
- ... as so it continues to infinity..
- S_n: "All of the sentences after this one are false."

Each sentence S_n refers only to later sentences—S_{n+1}, S_{n+2}, and so on. There is no sentence that refers to itself, but each indirectly contributes to a **system-wide contradiction**.

Now suppose **one of these statements is true**—say, S_k. That would mean all later statements (S_{k+1}, S_{k+2}, etc.) are false. But if S_{k+1} is false, then not all sentences after it are false—meaning **at least one of them is true**, contradicting the assumption that S_k is true. On the other hand, if **all** statements are false, then S_1 is saying "all of the following statements are false"—which is **true**, contradicting the assumption that it's false.

Thus, we get an irresolvable conflict: **every possible truth assignment leads to a contradiction.**

Why It Works

Yablo's Paradox works because it **distributes the paradox across an infinite chain** of statements, cleverly avoiding the need for direct self-reference. Each statement makes a claim about **the truth of others**, and that collective structure loops back **indirectly**.

This breaks the traditional belief that paradoxes like the Liar only arise through **self-reference**. It suggests that **circularity can be implicit**, hidden within the logical interdependencies of otherwise harmless-looking statements.

How It Works

The paradox unfolds through:

1. **Indirect reference**: Each sentence refers only to others—not itself.

2. **Uniform structure**: Every sentence is identical in logical form.

3. **Infinite regress**: The dependencies never terminate—each sentence depends on the next.

Assuming any one of the statements is true causes a cascade that eventually **violates the condition** of that very truth. Assuming all are false makes at least one of them true (because its claim that "all following are false" would be accurate), again resulting in **contradiction**.

Logical systems that attempt to assign truth values to the entire sequence encounter **incoherence**, much like in the Liar Paradox.

Application

Yablo's Paradox has important applications in:

- **Philosophical logic**: It challenges assumptions about the necessity of self-reference for paradox.

- **Formal semantics**: Influences theories of meaning and truth conditions in language.

- **Mathematics and set theory**: Relates to circularity and hierarchy in foundational systems.

- **Computability and recursion theory**: Models indirect recursion, where definitions depend on other future definitions.

It also intersects with studies in **non-classical logics**, like paraconsistent logic and fixed-point theories of truth.

Key Insights

- Paradox does not require **explicit self-reference**; it can emerge through **indirect dependency**.

- Yablo's construction reveals that **truth and reference can be unstable** even in seemingly well-behaved systems.

- The paradox deepens our understanding of **logical circularity**—suggesting it can be **structural**, not merely syntactic.

- It serves as a valuable tool in re-examining **semantic and logical assumptions** about language, reference, and consistency.

- Yablo's Paradox invites rethinking how we design **logical hierarchies and truth frameworks** in formal systems.

9. Richard's Paradox

Theory

Richard's Paradox, also known as the Richard-Berry Paradox, is a semantic and logical paradox named after the French philosopher Jules Richard, who first formulated it in 1905. It emerges from the attempt to define certain numbers or objects using natural language, particularly in relation to the concept of definability and self-reference. At its core, the paradox highlights the contradictions that can arise when language, especially self-referential language, is used to define mathematical or logical entities.

The paradox stems from considering the set of all definable real numbers — that is, real numbers which can be described in a finite number of words. Since the English language (or any formal language) has only countably many finite descriptions, there are only countably many such definable numbers. However, the set of real numbers is uncountable. So, most real numbers are *not* definable.

Now here's where the paradox begins: consider the phrase *"the least real number that cannot be defined in fewer than twenty words."* This description itself uses only a finite number of words (in this case, fewer than twenty), so if such a number exists, then it must be definable — contradicting the premise that it cannot be defined in fewer than twenty words. This contradiction lies at the heart of Richard's Paradox.

Example

Suppose we try to define: *"The smallest positive integer not definable in under twenty words."* This sentence clearly contains fewer than twenty words. If such a number exists, then we have successfully defined it using fewer than twenty words — contradicting the definition. But if it doesn't exist, then the set of numbers definable in under twenty words must include every number, which it cannot.

Why It Works

The paradox functions by exploiting self-reference and the vague boundary between meta-language (a language used to talk about another language) and object-language (the language being talked about). It creates a definitional loop: defining something in terms of it being undefinable, which leads to a contradiction. This is akin to the liar paradox ("This statement is false."), but applied to definitions and set theory.

The paradox also subtly involves the concept of *diagonalization*, used by Cantor and later in Turing's halting problem. By attempting to define an object that lies *outside* the scope of all definitions, we accidentally create a new definition that includes it.

How It Works

Richard's Paradox reveals inconsistencies in naive formal systems — especially those that treat natural language as a perfectly rigorous method for defining mathematical objects. It arises from:

1. Assuming that all linguistic definitions are valid.

2. Treating self-reference as harmless.

3. Overlooking the hierarchy between the language used for description and the content being described.

The core issue lies in allowing natural language to define objects while also reasoning about the limits of such definitions *within* that same language, leading to a form of semantic circularity.

Application

One application of Richard's Paradox lies in the foundations of mathematics and logic, particularly in demonstrating the need for more rigorous frameworks. It influenced developments in formal logic, particularly in work by Gödel, Tarski, and Turing. Gödel's incompleteness theorems, for example, use a similar kind of self-reference to show that in any sufficiently complex formal system, there are true statements that cannot be proven within the system.

Key Insights

1. **Limits of Language**: Natural language, though powerful, is imprecise and can lead to paradox when used in self-referential ways.

2. **Definability is Countable**: Not every real number can be defined, even though some are quite simple to describe.

3. **Self-Reference is Problematic**: Self-referential definitions can create contradictions if not carefully handled.

4. **Need for Formal Systems**: The paradox underscores the importance of developing strict formal systems with clearly defined rules to avoid semantic paradoxes.

5. **Semantic Hierarchy**: It suggests a need to distinguish between object-level statements and meta-level commentary to maintain logical coherence.

Richard's Paradox remains a foundational thought experiment in logic and philosophy, emphasizing the limitations of language and the care needed in foundational reasoning.

10. Quine's Paradox

Quine's Paradox: A Breakdown

Theory

Quine's Paradox, formulated by the philosopher and logician Willard Van Orman Quine, is a self-referential paradox that challenges our understanding of truth and reference in formal languages. Unlike more famous semantic paradoxes like the Liar Paradox ("This sentence is false"), Quine's Paradox is unique because it constructs a paradoxical sentence *without* using direct self-reference or a truth predicate. Instead, the paradox arises entirely within the structure of quotation and reference.

At its heart, Quine's Paradox involves a sentence that refers to its own quotation — creating a circular definition — but it does so in a grammatically valid way that seems to evade the usual safeguards against paradox. This raises deep issues in the philosophy of language and logic, especially concerning how meaning and reference work.

Example

Consider the sentence:

"yields falsehood when preceded by its quotation" yields falsehood when preceded by its quotation.

This sentence appears innocent at first, but it's cleverly constructed. If you take the sentence in quotes — "yields falsehood when preceded by its quotation" — and put it in front of itself, you get:

"yields falsehood when preceded by its quotation" yields falsehood when preceded by its quotation.

Now the sentence talks about what happens when its own quotation is placed before it. If it's true, then what it says is accurate — that the result yields falsehood. But that would make the sentence false. However, if it's false, then it does *not* yield falsehood when preceded by its quotation, so it must be true. This logical loop produces a contradiction.

Why It Works
The paradox works by ingeniously sidestepping the need for overt self-reference or the use of a truth predicate like "This sentence is false." Instead, it uses syntactic reference — quoting part of the sentence and then applying that quoted part to the whole — to sneak in a form of indirect self-reference. The result is a sentence that refers to a syntactic operation on itself, producing the paradox without any obvious logical misstep.

This subtlety makes Quine's Paradox more troubling than many similar ones, because it highlights how self-reference and reference in general can produce inconsistencies even in apparently well-behaved formal systems.

How It Works
The paradox hinges on the dual role of quotation in language: as a syntactic operator (which turns expressions into names of expressions) and as a semantic device (which allows

statements about statements). By manipulating this dual role, Quine creates a sentence that indirectly refers to itself in a way that collapses the distinction between syntax and semantics.

The sentence has no standard way to be evaluated as true or false — whichever way you lean leads to a contradiction. This shows that certain types of language use, especially involving self-reference and quotation, can destabilize truth-value assignments in formal logic.

Application

Quine's Paradox has important implications for formal semantics, logic, and theories of truth. It plays a role in developing Tarski's hierarchy of languages, which attempts to prevent paradoxes by separating object-language (statements about the world) from meta-language (statements about statements). Quine's construction demonstrates how even without explicit truth predicates, paradoxes can still emerge from linguistic structure alone.

It also informs modern discussions in computer science and philosophy about self-reference, code-as-data (e.g., in compilers or interpreters), and how formal systems can safely handle self-descriptions.

Key Insights

1. **Self-Reference Can Be Implicit**: A paradox doesn't need overt self-reference; structural self-reference is enough.

2. **Syntax and Semantics Interact Dangerously**: Mixing quotation and evaluation leads to instability in truth assignments.

3. **Formal Languages Need Guardrails**: Tarski's hierarchical approach gains more justification due to such paradoxes.

4. **Truth Is Fragile**: Even well-formed sentences can resist classical evaluation under certain conditions.

5. **Semantics Must Be Carefully Defined**: Systems dealing with reference and meaning must strictly separate layers to avoid contradiction.

Quine's Paradox, while subtle, opens profound questions about language, logic, and the boundaries of meaning — reinforcing that in both philosophy and formal systems, self-reference remains a powerful and perilous tool.

11. Knower Paradox

Knower Paradox: A Breakdown

Theory

The Knower Paradox is a logical and epistemic paradox that explores the problematic intersection of knowledge and self-reference. It arises when we attempt to analyse knowledge using formal logic, particularly statements about what is known or unknown. The paradox challenges our assumptions about what it means to "know" something, especially when that knowledge refers to the knowledge status of the statement itself.

The paradox typically involves a sentence that says of itself, "This sentence is not known to be true." It mirrors the Liar Paradox ("This sentence is false") but replaces truth with knowledge. The contradiction emerges when we try to assign a truth value to such a sentence and determine whether it is known.

The Knower Paradox has important implications in epistemology (the study of knowledge) and modal logic (logic involving necessity and possibility). It reveals limits in our ability to consistently reason about knowledge within a single formal system.

Example

Consider the sentence:

(K) Sentence (K) is not known to be true.

Now, let's analyse whether (K) is known to be true:

- **Suppose (K) *is* known to be true.** Then what it asserts — that it is *not* known to be true — is false. So if it is known to be true, it must be false. That's a contradiction.

- **Suppose (K) *is not* known to be true.** Then what it says is true. So (K) is a true sentence that is not known to be true. But now we've found a true statement that is not known — yet we seem to have deduced that it's true. Shouldn't that count as knowledge?

We are left in a state of epistemic instability: the sentence seems both knowable and unknowable, true and untrue in a way that defies consistency.

Why It Works

The Knower Paradox works because it exploits a form of *epistemic circularity* — a sentence that makes a claim about its own knowability. The paradox hinges on how we treat the knowledge operator ("it is known that") and how that operator interacts with self-reference.

When formalizing such sentences in modal logic or epistemic logic, we run into contradictions unless very careful restrictions are placed on how self-referential knowledge statements are allowed. The paradox forces us to reconsider whether we can fully analyse knowledge within a formal system that can talk about its own knowledge.

How It Works

In formal terms, we can represent knowledge using a modal operator, typically denoted as **K**. So "Kφ" means "it is known that φ." The paradox then considers a sentence φ such that:

$$\varphi \leftrightarrow \neg K\varphi$$

This creates a loop: φ is true if and only if it is not known to be true. But then, by standard modal axioms (especially in systems that include positive introspection: if Kφ, then KKφ), we're forced into contradiction when we try to evaluate or formalize φ. The contradiction arises from trying to apply normal epistemic logic rules to statements that refer to their own knowledge status.

Application

The Knower Paradox has significant consequences in formal epistemology, computer science (particularly in AI reasoning systems), and the foundations of mathematics. It challenges systems that aim to model agents who can reflect on their own knowledge. For instance, in designing automated reasoning systems or artificial agents, the paradox shows that agents cannot freely reason about their own knowledge without risking inconsistency.

In philosophy, it pushes back against overly confident assumptions about self-knowledge and internalism — the idea that knowing one's mental states is straightforward or error-free.

Key Insights

1. **Self-Reference Undermines Epistemic Logic**: Statements about their own knowledge status create contradictions.

2. **Not All Truths Are Knowable**: The paradox hints that some truths, though valid, may be inherently unknowable.

3. **Limits of Formal Epistemology**: Knowledge can't always be fully captured in a formal, self-referential system.

4. **Knowledge and Truth Are Distinct**: Knowing a truth is different from a truth existing — and treating them as interchangeable leads to paradox.

5. **Philosophical Implications**: The paradox challenges assumptions about transparency of thought, infallibility of knowledge, and our ability to "know what we know."

Ultimately, the Knower Paradox reveals a deep tension between knowledge, language, and logic — suggesting that even our most basic epistemic concepts must be handled with care when formalized.

12. Kaplan's Paradox

Theory

Kaplan's Paradox is a lesser-known but deeply important paradox in the philosophy of language and logic, formulated by David Kaplan. It deals with indexicals — expressions like "I," "here," and "now" — and how they function in logic and semantics, particularly in systems that try to formalize the concept of *belief* and *propositional attitudes*. The paradox emerges when we attempt to represent beliefs involving indexicals in a way that respects both the subjective perspective of the believer and the objective truth conditions of the proposition.

Kaplan's central insight is that indexicals carry essential contextual meaning, meaning that cannot be fully captured by traditional propositional content. The paradox reveals a conflict between the semantics of indexicals and the principles of belief attribution, particularly the idea that we can quantify over all possible beliefs or propositions an agent might hold.

Example

Imagine two people: Lois Lane and Superman. Lois Lane believes, "He is strong," pointing to Superman flying overhead. However, she does *not* believe, "Clark Kent is strong," even though Clark Kent is Superman. Now, imagine Superman himself thinks, "I am strong." This is a belief with an indexical — "I."

If we try to model this belief in a logical system that treats propositions as sets of possible worlds (as in standard modal logic), we encounter a problem: "I am strong" as uttered by Superman cannot be the same proposition as "Clark Kent is strong," even though in objective terms they refer to the same person. Kaplan's Paradox arises from trying to account for this mismatch between what the content of a belief seems to be and how it's modelled in formal semantics.

Why It Works
Kaplan's Paradox works because it targets the core of belief representation: how we model what someone believes when that belief is expressed with indexicals. Traditional propositional logic assumes that two statements expressing the same truth conditions are interchangeable. But in belief contexts, this isn't true. Someone can believe "I am hungry" without believing "David Kaplan is hungry," even if David Kaplan is the speaker.

This mismatch between *character* (the linguistic rule for using an indexical) and *content* (the proposition expressed in context) is the root of the paradox. Kaplan's framework aimed to handle this, but the paradox shows that if we treat all propositions as content alone, we lose important distinctions relevant to belief attribution.

How It Works
Kaplan distinguishes between *character* (context-sensitive meaning) and *content* (truth-conditional meaning). The paradox shows that belief cannot simply be about content, because indexical beliefs involve a subject's internal point of

view. When systems of belief representation try to formalize beliefs solely based on content — ignoring the character — they fail to capture critical distinctions, leading to errors or contradictions.

This reveals that the semantics of belief reports must include more than objective truth-conditions; they must also model the believer's subjective perspective, especially when indexicals are involved.

Application

Kaplan's Paradox has profound implications in linguistics, artificial intelligence, cognitive science, and philosophy of mind. In AI, for instance, modelling an agent's beliefs is central to decision-making systems. If agents use indexicals internally — e.g., "I am in danger" — then a failure to properly model these beliefs can result in incorrect predictions or flawed reasoning.

In natural language semantics, Kaplan's work underlies modern theories of context-sensitive expressions and supports the idea that meanings are not static but depend heavily on perspective and context.

Key Insights

1. **Indexicals Matter Deeply**: Words like "I" and "now" cannot be eliminated or reduced to fixed references in belief contexts.

2. **Belief Is Perspective-Based**: Formal models must account for the subjective stance of the believer.

3. **Content Is Not Enough**: Propositions alone can't capture everything about belief; character is crucial.

4. **Limits of Traditional Semantics**: Standard propositional logic oversimplifies belief by ignoring the agent's cognitive perspective.

5. **Refinement of Logic Needed**: Systems must evolve to represent self-locating beliefs and context-sensitive thinking accurately.

Kaplan's Paradox remains a compelling challenge to rigid, truth-conditional models of language and thought, urging more nuanced, context-aware approaches to meaning and belief.

13. Specker's Paradox

Specker's Paradox: A Breakdown

Theory

Specker's Paradox, formulated by the Swiss logician Ernst Specker in 1960, is a foundational paradox in logic and quantum theory. At its core, the paradox demonstrates the problem of assigning consistent truth values to propositions when decisions depend on each other, even if those decisions are only hypothetical. It's an early precursor to ideas later formalized in quantum mechanics and non-classical logics, showing that classical logic's assumptions about truth and decidability break down under certain conditions.

Specker's Paradox can be viewed as a logical version of the "Kochen–Specker theorem," which challenges the notion that all propositions (about a physical system or abstract situation) can have predetermined, context-independent truth values. It highlights the limitations of "global" truth assignments — where every possible proposition must already have a truth value, even if not yet known.

Example

Imagine a situation where you are presented with a set of boxes. Each box may or may not contain a gem, but you are told that:

- You may choose any two boxes to open.

- The gem distribution is such that **no matter which two boxes you open, at most one will contain a gem.**

Now suppose you try to reason about which boxes might have gems before opening any of them. You might think: "Box A has a gem." But then, logically, if A has a gem, neither B nor C can have one (otherwise, opening A and B or A and C would show two gems). But suppose you apply this reasoning to B and C as well. You'll find that you cannot consistently assign "has a gem" or "does not have a gem" to all three boxes without violating the condition. This creates a paradox: the conditions seem reasonable locally (two at a time), but globally they cannot be satisfied.

Why It Works
The paradox works by exposing a conflict between local consistency and global consistency. For any pair of boxes, you can apply the rule and get a valid result. But once you try to extend that reasoning to all possible combinations, you find that no consistent assignment of truth values works for the entire system.

This directly challenges classical logic's assumption that every proposition has a fixed truth value (true or false), independent of how or whether it's tested. In this paradox, what you *can* know seems to depend on *what you choose to observe*, which anticipates key features of quantum theory.

How It Works
Specker's Paradox constructs a finite set of propositions that are **pairwise decidable** — you can decide the truth of any

two at once — but not **jointly decidable** — you cannot assign truth values to all of them simultaneously without contradiction. This undermines classical assumptions about bivalence (every proposition is either true or false) and omniscience (that the truth values of all propositions are predetermined).

The paradox forces us to rethink whether truth is a static property of propositions, or if it's contextual and dependent on how information is accessed — a notion central to quantum logic.

Application

Specker's Paradox has profound implications in quantum mechanics and the foundations of physics. It is the conceptual seed for the **Kochen–Specker theorem**, which shows that hidden variable theories (theories assuming pre-determined outcomes for quantum measurements) cannot reproduce all the predictions of quantum mechanics. In essence, it proves that the values of quantum observables cannot all be pre-assigned in a way that is independent of measurement context.

It also has philosophical applications in decision theory and epistemology, especially in understanding the limits of knowledge, consistency, and rational belief.

Key Insights

1. **Local Consistency ≠ Global Consistency**: What works for individual parts may break down when applied to the whole system.

2. **Context Matters**: Truth may depend on how information is accessed or what's being measured — not just on intrinsic properties.

3. **Challenges Classical Logic**: Classical assumptions like bivalence and omniscience may not hold in complex systems.

4. **Foreshadows Quantum Logic**: Specker's ideas anticipated deep features of quantum mechanics where measurements affect outcomes.

5. **Limits of Hidden Variables**: Not all properties can have predetermined, observer-independent truth values.

Specker's Paradox remains a profound example of how logic, philosophy, and physics intersect — revealing the subtle boundaries between what can be known, said, or predicted in any system that tries to reason about itself.

14. Frege's Puzzle

Theory

Frege's Puzzle, first introduced by the German philosopher and logician Gottlob Frege in his seminal 1892 paper *"On Sense and Reference"*, concerns the nature of meaning in language—specifically, how two expressions can refer to the same object but convey different cognitive values. The puzzle centres on how identity statements like "a = a" and "a = b" can differ in meaning and informativeness even when "a" and "b" refer to the same entity.

Frege distinguished between **reference** (*Bedeutung*), the actual object a term refers to, and **sense** (*Sinn*), the way in which that object is presented. According to Frege, while two terms may have the same reference, they can differ in sense. The puzzle challenges the idea that meaning is reference alone and forces us to consider how language conveys knowledge and information beyond mere denotation.

Example

A classic example of Frege's Puzzle involves the names "Clark Kent" and "Superman." Both refer to the same individual. However, consider these two statements:

1. "Clark Kent is Clark Kent."

2. "Clark Kent is Superman."

The first is trivial, known a priori, and seemingly uninformative. The second, although referring to the same individual, is informative and may surprise someone who does not know that Clark Kent and Superman are the same person. If meaning were simply reference, both statements would express the same proposition. Yet clearly, they differ in cognitive significance.

This contradiction reveals that reference alone cannot account for the full meaning of a sentence.

Why It Works

Frege's Puzzle works because it highlights a gap in purely referential theories of meaning. If names are just tags pointing to objects, then substituting one for another should preserve the meaning of a sentence. But this fails in cases like "Clark Kent is Superman" or "The morning star is the evening star," where substitution seems to change what the statement conveys to a listener.

The puzzle shows that people can believe "a = a" without believing "a = b," even if a and b refer to the same thing. That challenges assumptions about logical equivalence and how belief reports function.

How It Works

Frege's solution was to introduce a two-level theory of meaning: **sense** and **reference**. The *reference* of a name is the object it denotes; the *sense* is the mode of presentation —

how the name picks out that object. "Clark Kent" and "Superman" have the same reference but different senses. This explains why the identity statement "Clark Kent is Superman" can be informative — it links two distinct senses referring to the same object.

Furthermore, in contexts like belief reports (e.g., "Lois believes that Superman can fly"), the substitution of coreferential names can change the truth-value of the sentence, suggesting that belief contexts are *opaque* — resistant to substitution — and thus demand a finer-grained semantic analysis.

Application
Frege's Puzzle plays a crucial role in the philosophy of language, semantics, cognitive science, and artificial intelligence. It influences how we model meaning in natural language processing, especially in tasks involving reference resolution, ambiguity, and belief representation. In AI, for instance, an intelligent agent must understand that two labels may refer to the same entity but be treated differently depending on the informational context.

In epistemology and logic, it reshapes how we think about identity, information content, and how knowledge is structured and conveyed.

Key Insights

1. **Meaning Is More Than Reference**: The sense of a term plays a crucial role in determining its meaning.

2. **Cognitive Significance Matters**: Statements can differ in informativeness even when their terms refer to the same thing.

3. **Opaque Contexts Complicate Logic**: Substituting coreferential terms in belief reports can change truth-values, challenging classical logic.

4. **Language Is Structured by Perspective**: Different names or descriptions encode different perspectives or information routes to the same object.

5. **Vital for Modelling Belief and Knowledge**: Frege's ideas underlie how we model propositional attitudes in philosophy, linguistics, and AI.

Frege's Puzzle remains a cornerstone of modern semantics and a key philosophical insight into how language, thought, and reference intertwine.

15. Knowability Paradox (Fitch's)

Theory

The Knowability Paradox, also known as *Fitch's Paradox*, is a powerful challenge in epistemic logic and philosophy, particularly concerning the relationship between truth and knowability. First formalized by philosopher Frederic Fitch in 1963, the paradox reveals a deep and unexpected tension between two plausible ideas:

1. **All truths are knowable** (i.e., every truth could, in principle, be known).

2. **Not all truths are known** (i.e., there are truths that no one currently knows).

Fitch's Paradox shows that if all truths are knowable, then *all truths must in fact be known* — a conclusion that seems implausible and contradicts the second assumption. This surprising result poses a serious problem for any epistemic system that tries to uphold the principle that truth implies possible knowledge while maintaining the existence of unknown truths.

Example

Let's suppose the following statement is true:

(P) "There is at least one truth that is not known."

This seems reasonable — surely, we haven't discovered *every* truth. Now, apply the principle that every truth is knowable. Then (P) must be *knowable*. That means there is a possible state where someone *knows* (P).

But if someone knows (P), then they know there is at least one truth that is not known — and now they *know* that it is not known, which is a contradiction. Because the moment a truth is known to be unknown, it becomes known. Thus, the statement that "some truths are not known" cannot be knowable without generating contradiction.

Why It Works

Fitch's Paradox works by formalizing a tension between **modal logic** (what is possible) and **epistemic logic** (what is known). The paradox exploits the logical properties of the knowledge operator (K), the truth predicate (T), and the knowability operator ($\Diamond K$).

It shows that if you accept:

- $T\phi \rightarrow \Diamond K\phi$ (if ϕ is true, then it is possibly known)

Then it logically follows that:

- $T\phi \rightarrow K\phi$ (if ϕ is true, then it is known)

This leap is troubling because it collapses the distinction between potential knowledge and actual knowledge — forcing an unwanted conclusion: **omniscience**.

How It Works

The logic behind the paradox involves a move called *Fitch's Lemma*. Let's assume a truth φ that is not known. If it's truly knowable, then the proposition "φ is true and unknown" should itself be knowable. But when someone knows that φ is unknown, they are in effect *knowing that it is not known*, which is contradictory. This leads to an explosion of inconsistency if one insists that all truths must be knowable yet some are not known.

To avoid the paradox, you must give up at least one assumption: that all truths are knowable, that some truths are unknown, or that knowledge obeys certain logical principles (like closure under known implication).

Application

Fitch's Paradox is central in epistemology, logic, and the philosophy of science. It has shaped debates around anti-realism (especially the Dummettian idea that truth is defined by knowability), as well as efforts to formalize human knowledge. In computer science, it affects how we think about the limits of computability and verification — such as whether all truths about programs are knowable or provable in principle.

In theological and metaphysical contexts, the paradox also plays a role in discussions about divine omniscience, epistemic humility, and the limits of human understanding.

Key Insights

1. **Knowability ≠ Knowledge**: Assuming all truths are knowable risks collapsing into omniscience.

2. **Epistemic Modality Is Tricky**: Mixing "possible to know" and "actually known" leads to subtle contradictions.

3. **Limits of Verificationism**: The paradox challenges views equating truth with potential verification.

4. **Formal Systems Have Boundaries**: Even minimal assumptions about truth and knowledge can create logical pitfalls.

5. **Paradox Reveals Fragility**: What seems intuitively plausible can be logically disastrous when formalized.

Fitch's Knowability Paradox remains a landmark challenge in understanding the nature of truth, knowledge, and the logical boundaries of human (or even divine) cognition.

16. Goodman's Grue Paradox

Theory

Goodman's Grue Paradox, introduced by philosopher Nelson Goodman in his 1955 book *Fact, Fiction, and Forecast*, challenges the foundations of inductive reasoning — the process by which we predict the future based on past observations. Goodman's aim was to highlight the problem of *projectability*: why certain predicates (like "green") seem naturally suited for induction, while others (like "grue") do not, even when both are equally supported by past evidence.

The paradox introduces the artificial predicate "grue," defined as follows: an object is *grue* if and only if it is observed before a specific future time t and is green, or if it is not observed before t and is blue. Thus, all emeralds observed before time t are both green and grue. The question arises: why do we predict that future emeralds will be green, rather than grue?

Example

Imagine that today is before time t, and you've observed thousands of emeralds. Every single one is green. This supports the inductive generalization: "All emeralds are green." But, based on the same data, you could just as easily have concluded: "All emeralds are grue," because all the emeralds you've seen are both green and grue.

Now suppose time *t* passes. A new emerald is discovered. Should you expect it to be green (as per usual inductive reasoning), or blue (because if it's to remain grue, and it's discovered after *t*, it must be blue)? The paradox lies in the fact that both predictions are supported by the same evidence, yet they conflict.

Why It Works

The Grue Paradox works because it exposes a hidden assumption in induction: that some predicates (like "green") are more *natural* or *projectible* than others (like "grue"). Yet there's no formal logical difference between the two. Both are defined precisely, both are supported by past data, and both make falsifiable predictions.

Goodman's point is that logic alone cannot distinguish between legitimate and illegitimate predicates. This challenges the very heart of induction, which relies on the idea that past observations can meaningfully predict future ones.

How It Works

The paradox arises by constructing a predicate that switches its meaning over time, but in a way that's completely hidden before a specific moment. "Grue" mimics the behaviour of "green" until a future cutoff point, making it indistinguishable by empirical evidence up to that time. Thus, any attempt to base predictive knowledge solely on past observations becomes ambiguous.

Goodman argued that the choice of projectible predicates depends not just on data but on entrenched linguistic and conceptual practices — what we consider "lawlike" or scientifically useful. This means that induction depends as much on our epistemic framework as it does on the raw evidence.

Application

Goodman's Grue Paradox has profound implications in epistemology, philosophy of science, and even machine learning. It challenges the assumption that patterns in data alone can justify predictions. In AI, for instance, the problem of choosing the right features or representations for learning models echoes Goodman's concern: the same data can support many, even contradictory, generalizations depending on how it's framed.

In scientific theory choice, it also raises questions about why we favour some hypotheses over others when multiple are consistent with the evidence. The answer often lies in pragmatic or theoretical virtues — simplicity, coherence, explanatory power — rather than pure logic.

Key Insights

1. **Induction Is Not Just About Data**: Background assumptions and language shape what predictions we make.

2. **Projectability Is Epistemically Loaded**: Some predicates "fit" better with our conceptual frameworks, but not due to logic alone.

3. **Grue Shows Limits of Empiricism**: Observation alone cannot determine which generalizations are valid.

4. **Predicate Choice Matters**: The way we define categories influences what we consider reasonable inference.

5. **Supports Theory-Ladenness of Observation**: What we observe is always filtered through prior conceptual lenses.

Goodman's Grue Paradox is not just a clever linguistic trick — it's a deep philosophical challenge that forces us to confront how and why we trust certain generalizations over others.

17. Lottery Insurer Paradox

Theory

The **Lottery Insurer Paradox** is a thought experiment that emerges at the intersection of epistemology, probability theory, and rational belief. It challenges our intuitions about reasonable belief in highly probable events, especially when they involve large-scale systems like lotteries. The paradox stems from the idea that it's rational to believe that *some event in a set will happen*, but irrational to believe *any individual instance of it will happen*, even though the event must occur. This creates tension between individual rational beliefs and collective certainty.

The paradox is often discussed in the context of knowledge and justification, particularly in critiques of the *lottery problem* in epistemology — the difficulty in justifying beliefs that are highly probable but not certain. The "insurer" twist adds a practical dimension: what would it mean to insure outcomes in such a high-probability, low-certainty context?

Example

Suppose there's a national lottery with 10 million tickets, and exactly one ticket will win. Now imagine a rational insurance company is deciding whether to insure the possibility that *a specific ticket* wins. If someone asks the insurer: "Will ticket

#1 win?" the rational response, based on probability, is "almost certainly not."

Now repeat this reasoning for every other ticket — each one individually is almost certain to lose. Therefore, it seems rational to believe of each ticket that it will not win. But we also *know* that one ticket *must* win. So if the insurer believed each individual ticket will not win, they would believe that *no* ticket will win — a contradiction.

This becomes a paradox for belief and rational decision-making: the insurer must reject each claim individually, yet collectively know that at least one of them is false.

Why It Works

The paradox works because it forces a clash between local rationality (what seems justified for each specific case) and global consistency (what we know must be true overall). It reveals that rational belief based on high probability does not always aggregate into a rational belief set.

In epistemology, this problem challenges the idea that knowledge or justified belief can be equated with high probability. If every individual belief ("Ticket #n will not win") is reasonable, but the conjunction of all such beliefs is necessarily false, something has gone wrong with our model of rational justification.

How It Works

The Lottery Insurer Paradox uses the logic of large numbers to stretch probabilistic reasoning to its limits. It assumes that rational agents avoid beliefs in outcomes with extremely low probability — yet if applied uniformly, this leads to an impossible belief set. The insurer, by refusing to back any ticket, is treating each as a sure loser — which violates the known outcome that one ticket must win.

This reveals a kind of epistemic inconsistency: what seems rational in isolation becomes irrational in aggregation. The paradox is an instance of *the lottery problem*, extended into real-world contexts like insurance, risk management, and knowledge attribution.

Application

The paradox is relevant in **legal reasoning**, **insurance**, **machine learning**, and **philosophical logic**. In law, juries might treat each piece of probabilistic evidence as insufficient to convict, even when the total evidence practically guarantees guilt — echoing the structure of the paradox. In AI, probabilistic classifiers might individually dismiss likely cases, while collectively failing to account for inevitability.

In epistemology, the paradox undermines probabilistic theories of knowledge, prompting alternative approaches like contextualism or pragmatic encroachment — which adjust standards for knowledge based on context or stakes.

Key Insights

1. **High Probability ≠ Knowledge**: Even highly probable beliefs can be unjustified if they aggregate into a contradiction.

2. **Local vs Global Rationality**: What's rational to believe in isolation can be irrational when considered as a set.

3. **Challenges Probabilistic Epistemology**: Belief can't always track probability without generating inconsistency.

4. **Real-World Relevance**: Insurance and risk-based decisions often mirror the structure of this paradox.

5. **Epistemic Humility Is Necessary**: Sometimes rational belief must acknowledge its own limitations in dealing with large-scale probability.

The Lottery Insurer Paradox vividly illustrates how probability, belief, and logic can come apart — showing that rational thinking must be sensitive not just to the parts, but to the whole.

18. Brandenburger–Keisler Paradox

Theory Overview

The **Brandenburger–Keisler Paradox** is a logical and epistemic paradox introduced by Adam Brandenburger and H. Jerome Keisler in 2006. It originates in the field of **epistemic game theory**, which studies how agents reason about each other's knowledge, beliefs, and strategies. This paradox extends the themes of **self-reference** and **diagonalization** (as seen in Gödel's and Russell's paradoxes) into a **multi-agent setting**, where beliefs about beliefs produce a contradiction.

The paradox reveals that it is logically impossible to create a complete model in which two rational agents can hold fully consistent second-order beliefs about each other—especially when those beliefs involve self-reference and negation. In simpler terms, if two agents try to fully model each other's beliefs (including beliefs about their own beliefs), the system breaks down into a contradiction.

Example

The paradox can be illustrated through a scenario involving two agents, **Ann** and **Bob**. Consider the following belief statement:

Ann believes that Bob assumes that Ann believes that Bob's assumption is wrong.

Now try to evaluate whether Ann's belief is true or false:

- If Bob's assumption **is wrong**, then **Ann believes it is wrong**, which means Bob's assumption **is correct**, contradicting the idea that it is wrong.

- If Bob's assumption **is correct**, then Ann **doesn't** believe it's wrong, which again contradicts the assumption that she does.

In both cases, a contradiction arises. This suggests that the original belief is **not logically coherent**, and no consistent assignment of belief states can make the system work.

This is akin to a multi-agent version of the **Liar Paradox**, extended into the domain of beliefs, assumptions, and modelling minds.

Why It Works

The Brandenburger–Keisler Paradox works because of its clever use of **nested beliefs** and **self-reference** in a multi-agent framework. Unlike traditional paradoxes which are confined to a single agent or system, this paradox arises when:

- Agent A tries to model what Agent B thinks.

- Agent B, in turn, models what Agent A believes about B's assumptions.

- The loop creates a **self-referential cycle** that leads to contradiction.

This logic system is formally modelled using **modal logic**, particularly systems that account for beliefs (*doxastic logic*). The paradox demonstrates that certain belief-attribution statements are **non-well-founded**, meaning they cannot be grounded in a consistent truth structure.

How It Works

Brandenburger and Keisler formalized the paradox using **Kripke-style models** in modal logic, where each agent's beliefs are represented in structured possible worlds. They proved that:

No belief model can simultaneously satisfy the statement "Ann believes that Bob assumes that Ann believes Bob's assumption is wrong" without contradiction.

The contradiction emerges from the **fixed-point construction**—a method used in logic to express self-referential truths. The paradox thus shows a deep flaw in **fully recursive belief modelling** in multi-agent systems.

Application

The paradox has significant implications in:

- **Epistemic game theory**: Modelling rational players and predicting behaviour in strategic settings.

- **Artificial intelligence**: Designing agents that reason about others' beliefs—particularly in negotiation or adversarial settings.

- **Philosophy of mind**: Understanding limits in how consciousness might model other conscious minds.

- **Computer science**: Multi-agent systems, distributed computing, and logical consistency in simulations.

It challenges the feasibility of complete mutual understanding between agents when self-referential beliefs are involved.

Key Insights

- Self-reference leads to contradiction even in multi-agent belief systems.

- There are **logical limits to modelling others' beliefs about one's own beliefs**.

- The paradox is not about faulty logic but about the **structure of belief hierarchies**.

- It connects epistemology, logic, game theory, and computer science in a deep and surprising way.

- It underscores the need for **bounded rationality**—limiting how deep agents go in modelling recursive beliefs.

19. Skolem's Paradox

Theory Overview

Skolem's Paradox is a foundational puzzle in mathematical logic and set theory that arises from the interplay between **first-order logic, model theory,** and **set-theoretical notions of size**. Named after Norwegian mathematician **Thoralf Skolem**, the paradox reveals a seeming contradiction: that a **countable model** of set theory can include sets that are **uncountable**, according to the model's internal logic.

The paradox does **not** point to a true contradiction in logic or mathematics, but it creates a **counterintuitive scenario** that forces us to rethink the meaning of size, countability, and the scope of mathematical models. It draws attention to the distinction between what is **true inside a model** and what is **true from an external (meta-theoretical) perspective**.

Example

According to **Zermelo–Fraenkel set theory (ZF)**, one can prove the existence of uncountable sets—most famously, the set of real numbers $\mathbb{R}$, which is larger than the set of natural numbers $\mathbb{N}$ in terms of cardinality.

However, by the **Löwenheim–Skolem Theorem**, any first-order theory that has an infinite model also has a **countable model**. This means there exists a **countable model of ZF set**

theory, called a **Skolem model**, in which all axioms of ZF hold—including the existence of uncountable sets.

So here's the paradox:

How can a countable model of set theory contain uncountable sets?

From the **external viewpoint**, the entire model is countable—we can enumerate all its elements. But from **within the model**, there exist sets (like $\mathbb{R}$) that satisfy all the properties of being uncountable. The model's internal logic cannot construct a bijection between these sets and the natural numbers, so they remain uncountable **within the model**, despite being part of a countable domain externally.

Why It Works

Skolem's Paradox works by highlighting a **clash of perspectives**:

- **Externally**, a logician can see that a model is countable.
- **Internally**, the model satisfies the axioms of ZF, which define uncountable sets.

The paradox hinges on the fact that **first-order logic cannot capture absolute cardinality**. First-order definitions can express properties like "there exists a bijection," but cannot quantify over **all** possible functions from $\mathbb{N}$ to another set in a way that captures true uncountability in an absolute sense.

Thus, the paradox arises from the **limitations of first-order logic** and how it models infinite sets.

How It Works

The steps are:

1. ZF set theory proves uncountable sets exist.
2. Löwenheim–Skolem Theorem guarantees the existence of a countable model of ZF.
3. Inside the model, all axioms hold—including the existence of uncountable sets.
4. From outside, we can enumerate all elements of the model—making it countable.
5. Inside, sets like $\mathbb{R}$ are still "uncountable" because **no function in the model** maps $\mathbb{N}$ onto them.

So "uncountable" is **model-relative**—a statement about the internal structure, not an absolute property.

Application

Skolem's Paradox plays a critical role in:

- **Model theory**: Demonstrating the limitations of first-order expressiveness.
- **Set theory foundations**: Emphasizing the relativity of mathematical concepts in different models.

- **Philosophy of mathematics**: Fuelling debates between **Platonism** and **formalism**—does uncountability "truly" exist, or is it a feature of the axioms?
- **Computational logic**: Understanding limits in modelling infinities in automated proof systems.

It also illustrates that truths in mathematics can be **contextual to the model** we're reasoning within.

Key Insights

- Countability and uncountability are **not absolute in first-order logic**.
- A countable model can internally contain "uncountable" sets—showing that size is **model-relative**.
- Skolem's Paradox reveals a gap between **mathematical intuition** and **formal expressiveness**.
- It does not refute set theory or uncountability but reveals limits in what first-order logic can capture.
- It underscores that **semantic content** (truth) and **syntactic form** (proof and structure) may diverge.

20. Infinite Monkey Theorem (in formal logic terms)

Theory
The **Infinite Monkey Theorem** is a thought experiment that originates in probability theory but has deep implications in formal logic, computability, and the philosophy of language. It states that given an infinite amount of time, a monkey hitting keys at random on a typewriter will almost surely type out any given text — such as the complete works of Shakespeare, or the *Principia Mathematica*. Formally, it shows that any finite sequence of characters will appear in an infinite sequence of random inputs with probability 1.

In logic, the theorem is used to illustrate the tension between **possibility**, **probability**, and **meaning**. It also demonstrates how randomness, given infinite resources, can simulate structured output — even though it lacks understanding or intention. Importantly, it draws attention to issues in formal systems regarding **recursion**, **enumerability**, and **decidability**.

Example
Suppose we have a monkey typing letters from a 26-letter alphabet. The probability that it types the exact sentence "THE LAW OF IDENTITY" in the correct order is extremely

small. But if the monkey types randomly *forever*, the probability that this sentence eventually appears is 1 — even though the monkey is not aiming to produce it.

Formally, let A be the set of all finite strings over some alphabet Σ. The infinite sequence generated by the monkey is an element of Σ^ω (an infinite string). For any string $s \in A$, the probability that s appears as a substring somewhere in that infinite sequence is 1. This is a direct consequence of the **Borel-Cantelli Lemma** in probability theory and underpins the theorem in mathematical logic.

Why It Works

The Infinite Monkey Theorem works by leveraging the properties of **infinite sequences** and **probabilistic certainty**. While the probability of typing a specific string in a single try is minuscule, the space of all infinite sequences ensures that every finite string will occur somewhere within it.

In logic, this mirrors the concept that any *finite* proof or derivation can, in theory, be stumbled upon by an infinitely running process — a key insight in the theory of **Turing machines**. A machine with unbounded time and tape could eventually enumerate all provable theorems of a system, even if blindly.

How It Works

In formal logic, especially in the context of computation, this is akin to a **brute-force enumeration** of all possible symbol strings. If we think of the monkey as a non-deterministic Turing machine outputting random symbols, then over infinite time, it will generate every possible finite string.

Thus, the theorem demonstrates the distinction between **effective computability** and **theoretical possibility**. It may be possible in principle for randomness to yield order, but it is not *feasible*, nor does it imply understanding, intention, or meaning.

Application

In computer science and logic, the Infinite Monkey Theorem relates to concepts such as **decidability**, **semi-decidability**, and **enumerability**. It suggests that if we allow infinite time, any theorem that can be proven in a formal system will eventually be found by a brute-force enumeration of all syntactically valid proofs.

It also appears in debates on **evolution**, **AI**, and **creativity** — where the question arises whether complex outputs (like a novel or a mathematical proof) imply intelligence or could arise from randomness over infinite iterations.

Key Insights

1. **Probability 1 ≠ Certainty**: Even though the chance of a specific string appearing is 1, this doesn't mean it *will* appear in practice.

2. **Infinite Time Breaks Intuition**: What seems impossible in finite terms becomes inevitable in the infinite case.

3. **Enumerability vs Computability**: Infinite processes can enumerate all possibilities, but that doesn't mean they compute or understand them.

4. **Order from Randomness**: Randomness can simulate structured output given infinite resources, challenging notions of intentional creation.

5. **Limits of Brute Force**: While brute-force search is theoretically exhaustive, it is not epistemically or practically useful for understanding.

The Infinite Monkey Theorem shows that infinite time and randomness can, in theory, generate structured complexity — but that logic, meaning, and comprehension require more than possibility; they require direction, structure, and interpretation.

21. Semantic Closure Paradox

Theory Overview

The **Semantic Closure Paradox** arises when a language attempts to **fully define its own semantics**, especially concepts like **truth, reference, or meaning**, within itself. The term "semantic closure" refers to a language that is **powerful enough to express statements about its own sentences**—such as "this sentence is true" or "this sentence is not provable."

This paradox is most famously tied to the **Liar Paradox** and is deeply entwined with **Tarski's Indefinability Theorem**, which states that **truth cannot be consistently defined within the same formal language it applies to**. Semantic closure leads to self-referential paradoxes because, once a language can talk about its own truth, it becomes susceptible to constructing **statements that undermine its own consistency**.

Example

Consider the statement in English:

"This sentence is false."

This is a classic **self-referential statement**. If the sentence is **true**, then it must be **false**, as it claims. But if it's **false**, then it must be **true**, since it states that it is false. This circular structure leads to contradiction and highlights the **instability** of allowing a language to declare the truth or falsity of its own sentences.

Now imagine a formal language (like arithmetic or set theory) that includes a truth predicate **T(x)**, where **x** is a sentence in that language. If the system allows you to construct a sentence that says:

"T('this sentence is not true')"

you've recreated the liar paradox **within the system itself**—which results in **logical inconsistency**.

Why It Works

The Semantic Closure Paradox works because it leverages **unrestricted self-reference** in languages that attempt to talk about their own properties. In a **semantically open** language, statements about truth are made in a separate, higher-level language called a **meta-language**. Problems only occur when a language **closes itself semantically**, i.e., when it allows for statements that make claims about their own truth value **within the same system**.

Tarski showed that **no language that is both expressive and semantically closed can consistently define its own truth predicate**. To avoid paradoxes, languages must either **limit self-reference** or **define semantic concepts externally**.

How It Works

Here's the logical breakdown:

1. Assume a language **L** is semantically closed.
2. Define a truth predicate **T(x)** inside L.
3. Construct a sentence **S** such that:

$$S \equiv \text{"}\neg T(\text{'}S\text{'})\text{"}$$ — i.e., "S is not true."

4. Evaluate S:
   - If **S is true**, then **T('S')** is true → contradiction, because S asserts it is **not** true.
   - If **S is false**, then **T('S')** is false, which means **S is true**.

This loop demonstrates that any such sentence destabilizes the truth predicate **T(x)**, making it impossible for the system to remain consistent while containing its own truth definitions.

Application

The Semantic Closure Paradox has broad implications:

- **Formal logic and set theory**: Drives the separation between **object language** and **meta-language**, and motivates hierarchical theories of truth.

- **Computer science**: Affects **programming languages** and **automated reasoning systems** that must be cautious about self-evaluation or reflective statements.

- **Linguistics and philosophy of language**: Informs debates on meaning, reference, and the limits of expressibility in natural language.

- **AI and epistemology**: Helps frame the boundaries of self-awareness and knowledge representation in intelligent systems.

Key Insights

- Languages that can express their own truth lead to paradox and inconsistency.

- Semantic closure must be handled carefully through **meta-linguistic layering** or **type restrictions**.

- The paradox underscores the limits of **self-reference** and the need for **hierarchies of language and logic**.

- Tarski's solution—separating the language that talks from the language that is talked about—remains foundational in logical theory.

- Ultimately, the Semantic Closure Paradox is a warning about the **fragility of systems that lack structural discipline** when defining their own semantics.

22. Turing's Halting Paradox (self-referential computational logic)

Theory

Turing's Halting Paradox is a foundational result in theoretical computer science and logic, formulated by Alan Turing in 1936. It reveals the inherent limitations of computation and formal systems by demonstrating that **no general algorithm** can decide whether an arbitrary computer program will halt (i.e., finish running) or continue to run forever.

This paradox, sometimes referred to as the **Halting Problem**, uses **self-referential computational logic** to prove that there can be no universal method for determining halting behaviour for all possible programs and inputs. The deeper implication is that there are true statements about computation that cannot be determined algorithmically — echoing Gödel's incompleteness theorems in arithmetic.

Example

Suppose we try to construct a program called HALT(P, x) that takes another program P and an input x, and determines whether P(x) halts. For simple programs, this might work. For example, a program that adds two numbers and stops clearly halts.

Now, consider a new program D(P) defined as follows:

- If HALT(P, P) says that P(P) halts, then D(P) runs forever.

- If HALT(P, P) says that P(P) runs forever, then D(P) halts.

Now ask: what happens when we run D(D)?

- If HALT(D, D) says that D(D) halts, then D(D) runs forever.
- If HALT(D, D) says that D(D) runs forever, then D(D) halts.

This contradiction shows that HALT cannot exist as a general-purpose solution. The paradox arises precisely from the **self-referential structure** of asking a program to analyse itself.

Why It Works

The Halting Paradox works because it exposes the **logical impossibility** of certain kinds of self-analysis in formal systems. By constructing a program that contradicts its own predicted behaviour, Turing showed that any supposed "universal halting-decider" would necessarily fail on some inputs — particularly when asked to evaluate its own behaviour.

This is a computational analogue to the **liar paradox**: "This sentence is false." The act of referencing oneself in a decision-making process leads to contradiction or undecidability.

How It Works

Formally, Turing's proof uses **diagonalization** — a technique also used by Cantor and Gödel — to construct a function that lies outside the set of computable functions. If all programs could be listed and their halting behaviour determined, one could construct a new program that behaves differently from each listed program at the corresponding step. This program cannot be in the list, contradicting the assumption of completeness.

In computational terms, Turing machines are formal models of algorithms. The Halting Problem shows that **no Turing machine** can decide the halting behaviour of all Turing machines — implying that some problems are inherently **undecidable**.

Application

The Halting Paradox has vast implications in **computer science**, **logic**, and **AI safety**. It shows that there are limits to program verification: no tool can guarantee that arbitrary software is free from infinite loops. In **cybersecurity**, it implies that detecting all malicious behaviour is impossible.

In **AI alignment**, it warns against building systems that must fully understand their own code or behaviour. In logic and mathematics, it reinforces the idea that not all truths can be mechanized or formalized.

Key Insights

1. **Limits of Computability**: Some questions, even simple ones, cannot be answered algorithmically.
2. **Self-Reference Leads to Undecidability**: Asking programs to decide about themselves causes logical contradictions.
3. **Diagonalization as a Tool**: The technique exposes gaps in supposedly complete systems.

4. **Program Verification Is Incomplete**: No system can guarantee correct behaviour for all possible code.

5. **Echoes Gödel's Incompleteness**: There are true computational facts that lie beyond algorithmic proof.

Turing's Halting Paradox remains one of the most profound results in logic, reminding us that computation, no matter how powerful, has fundamental boundaries — especially when it turns its analysis upon itself.

🕰 Temporal & Time Travel Paradoxes

Arising from contradictions in time travel or temporal logic.

23. Grandfather Paradox

Theory Overview

The **Grandfather Paradox** is one of the most well-known time travel paradoxes in philosophy and physics. It highlights the logical inconsistencies that arise when a time traveller goes back in time and takes an action that **prevents their own existence**. The paradox poses a fundamental challenge to our understanding of **causality, temporal logic, and determinism.**

It gets its name from a thought experiment:

What if you travelled back in time and killed your grandfather before he had children?
If you succeed, your parent would never be born—and neither would you. But if you were never born, how could you have travelled back in time to kill your grandfather in the first place?

This circular contradiction creates an impossible situation—a **causal loop with no consistent resolution**, often considered a strong argument against the possibility of backward time travel.

Example

Let's say a scientist invents a time machine and travels back 70 years to when his grandfather was a young man. Driven by some motive, he kills his grandfather before he meets his future wife.

As a result:

- His father is never born.
- The scientist is never born.
- Therefore, he never invents the time machine.
- Which means he couldn't have travelled back to kill his grandfather.

If he didn't go back, his grandfather lives, and the scientist is eventually born, which again enables the act of traveling back—creating a **contradictory loop**.

Why It Works

The Grandfather Paradox works because it exposes a **logical contradiction** in time travel to the past. The paradox hinges on **causal inconsistency**: the time traveller's actions affect the past in a way that invalidates the very conditions that made the time travel possible.

This tension violates the principle of **causal determinism**, which holds that causes precede effects and the same cause cannot lead to mutually exclusive outcomes.

How It Works

The paradox operates on the assumption of:

1. **Backward time travel** being physically possible.
2. The **ability to alter past events**.
3. Causal links being **linear and dependent**—your existence depends on your grandfather's survival.

It generates a **self-negating scenario** where an effect (your time travel) cancels its own cause (your existence), undermining the **temporal coherence** of the universe.

Application

While purely theoretical, the Grandfather Paradox is frequently used in:

- **Philosophy**: As a tool for analysing determinism, free will, and the metaphysics of time.
- **Physics**: In discussions about time travel under general relativity and quantum mechanics.
- **Science fiction**: Featured in countless films and novels (e.g., *Back to the Future*, *The Terminator*, *Looper*) as a narrative device exploring consequence and choice.
- **Temporal logic and computation**: Posing problems about the consistency of systems with feedback loops or recursive dependencies.

In theoretical physics, some models attempt to avoid the paradox via constraints such as:

- **Novikov's self-consistency principle**: Which suggests that time travel is only possible if it does not result in contradictions—meaning events in the past are fixed, and time travellers cannot change them.

- **Multiverse theories**: Where altering the past creates a new timeline or universe, thus avoiding the paradox in the original one.

Key Insights

- The Grandfather Paradox challenges the **coherence of time travel to the past**.

- It reveals how **causal loops** can create logical inconsistencies.

- The paradox forces a re-evaluation of the **relationship between time, cause, and identity**.

- Solutions often involve rethinking linear time, adopting multiverse interpretations, or asserting fixed timelines.

- It remains a central fixture in debates about **free will, determinism, and the nature of time**.

24. Chronology Protection Conjecture

Theory

The **Chronology Protection Conjecture** is a theoretical proposition introduced by physicist Stephen Hawking in 1992. It addresses the possibility of **closed timelike curves (CTCs)** — paths in spacetime that loop back on themselves, effectively allowing time travel into the past. The conjecture suggests that the laws of physics **prevent** the formation of such curves, thereby **protecting causality** and preventing paradoxes like the infamous grandfather paradox.

In essence, Hawking's conjecture proposes that while general relativity permits solutions (such as rotating black holes or wormholes) that could, in theory, allow time loops, **quantum effects or instabilities** at small scales will prevent their actual formation in any physically realistic scenario. This idea preserves the logical structure of cause preceding effect and maintains consistency in the timeline.

Example

One of the classic theoretical constructions for a time machine involves a traversable wormhole. Suppose you create a wormhole and then accelerate one end near the speed of light (due to time dilation, time slows down on that end). When the wormhole is brought back and connected to its original position, one end may be in the past relative to the other. This creates the potential for a closed timelike curve: an object could enter one end and emerge before it entered.

If this setup were stable and allowed time travel, it would raise paradoxes. For instance, a person could travel back and prevent the creation of the wormhole in the first place. Hawking's conjecture claims that **something in the laws of physics — likely quantum in nature — will always intervene** to stop this from happening.

Why It Works

The conjecture works because it aligns with both empirical observation (we've never seen a time traveller or time loop) and theoretical intuition. Hawking argued that quantum field theory in curved spacetime predicts that **vacuum fluctuations** near the formation of a CTC would become infinite — essentially generating a massive energy buildup that would destroy the wormhole or time loop before it could form.

This self-regulating mechanism implies that even if general relativity allows for solutions involving time loops, **the complete physical picture, including quantum mechanics, disallows them in practice**.

How It Works

Hawking's analysis relies on **semiclassical gravity**, where classical general relativity is combined with quantum field theory. In spacetimes that permit CTCs, the energy-momentum tensor — which describes the distribution of energy and momentum in space — becomes unbounded due to quantum effects. These instabilities would back-react on the spacetime geometry, preventing the CTCs from forming.

Thus, a feedback loop of quantum instability acts as a natural barrier — a "chronology protection agency" — preventing violations of causality and preserving the logical consistency of temporal order.

Application

The Chronology Protection Conjecture has major implications in **theoretical physics**, particularly in **cosmology**, **quantum gravity**, and **string theory**. It acts as a guiding principle when evaluating the plausibility of spacetime geometries in general relativity and helps constrain the kinds of exotic matter or topologies considered in theories of quantum gravity.

It also informs **science fiction**, grounding narratives of time travel in the limits imposed by actual physics, and serves as a philosophical touchstone for debates on determinism and the nature of time.

Key Insights

1. **Causality Is Likely Fundamental**: The conjecture implies that time travel into the past is not physically realizable.

2. **Quantum Effects Protect Time**: Quantum fluctuations act as safeguards against causality violations.

3. **General Relativity Isn't the Full Story**: Classical solutions may allow CTCs, but full quantum treatments appear to block them.
4. **Logical Consistency Is Preserved**: The paradoxes of time travel are avoided not by philosophy, but by physics itself.
5. **Framework for Quantum Gravity**: Any future theory uniting general relativity and quantum mechanics must account for chronology protection.

The Chronology Protection Conjecture is a compelling fusion of physics and philosophy, asserting that nature has built-in mechanisms to preserve the consistent flow of time — and to protect the universe from the paradoxes of temporal chaos.

25. Newcomb's Paradox

Theory Overview

Newcomb's Paradox is a thought experiment in **decision theory**, designed to test how we think about **rational choice, prediction, and free will**. Introduced by physicist **William Newcomb** and popularized by philosopher **Robert Nozick** in the 1960s, the paradox presents a conflict between two dominant approaches to rational decision-making: **expected utility theory** and **dominance reasoning**.

At its heart, the paradox questions whether one should base decisions on **causal control** (what your actions can influence) or on **predictive correlation** (what your actions reveal about likely outcomes).

Example

You are presented with two boxes:

- **Box A** contains **$1,000**.
- **Box B** contains **either $1,000,000 or nothing**.

You can choose either:

- **Only Box B**, or
- **Both Boxes A and B**.

Here's the twist: a **highly reliable predictor**, who has correctly predicted many such decisions in the past, has already filled the boxes:

- If they predicted you would take **only Box B**, they placed **$1,000,000 in Box B**.
- If they predicted you would take **both boxes**, they left **Box B empty**.

You don't know what the predictor decided—but the decision has already been made.

What do you choose?

Why It Works

The paradox creates a sharp conflict between **two styles of reasoning**:

1. **Dominance reasoning (Two-boxing)**: No matter what's in Box B, taking both boxes gives you **$1,000 more**. So, two-boxing seems better in every scenario.

2. **Expected utility reasoning (One-boxing)**: Since the predictor is nearly always right, if you one-box, you **probably get $1,000,000**, and if you two-box, you **probably get only $1,000**. So, one-boxing has a higher expected return.

This contradiction highlights a paradox of **evidential decision theory (EDT)** vs. **causal decision theory (CDT)**:

- **EDT** suggests you should choose the action that **correlates with the best outcomes**, even if you can't causally influence them.

- **CDT** suggests you should choose based only on the **direct consequences** of your actions, ignoring mere correlations.

How It Works

The tension arises from:

- **Predictive reliability**: The predictor's accuracy implies a **strong correlation** between your choice and what's in Box B.

- **Temporal direction**: The contents of the boxes are already set, so it feels like you **can't change** them.

- Yet, your choice **seems to reveal something** about the predictor's past decision—producing an eerie sense of **reverse causation**.

The paradox exploits our **intuition** that actions shouldn't affect past events, while simultaneously forcing us to acknowledge that **our decision is deeply entangled** with those past events via prediction.

Application

Newcomb's Paradox has relevance in:

- **Artificial intelligence**: Especially in designing agents that reason based on predictions and self-modelling.

- **Philosophy of free will**: It challenges how we think about choice in a deterministic or probabilistically predictable world.

- **Economics and strategy**: Decisions based on others' expectations, like stock markets or negotiations.

- **Behavioural psychology**: Reveals how framing and belief in prediction influence decisions.

It's also central to debates in **formal epistemology** and **decision-theoretic modelling**.

Key Insights

- Rationality is not a one-size-fits-all concept—different frameworks yield **opposite choices**.

- Your decision can be **predictive evidence**, not just a causal intervention.

- The paradox invites us to ask: **Should we act based on how things are, or how things are predicted to be?**

- It challenges the boundary between **free choice** and **predictive determinism**.

- In a world of predictive machines or AI, understanding this tension becomes **increasingly practical**, not just theoretical.

26. Prediction Paradox

Theory Overview

The **Prediction Paradox** refers to a class of logical and philosophical dilemmas where the act of predicting a future event seems to alter, undermine, or negate the accuracy or possibility of that very prediction. It often arises when a **prediction becomes self-defeating or self-fulfilling**, depending on how it's communicated or understood.

The paradox challenges our understanding of **knowledge, time, determinism, and agency**, especially in cases where awareness of a prediction changes the behaviour of those involved, thereby affecting the outcome. It is conceptually related to the **Unexpected Hanging Paradox, Newcomb's Problem**, and elements of **free will vs determinism** debates.

At its core, the paradox reveals a **tension between foreknowledge and autonomy**: If someone tells you what you will do in the future, can you still freely choose not to do it?

Example

Imagine a teacher tells a class:

"There will be a surprise quiz next week. You won't know the day of the quiz until it happens."

The students begin to reason:

- The quiz can't be on Friday, because if it hasn't occurred by Thursday, then Friday isn't a surprise.
- If Friday is ruled out, then Thursday isn't possible either—because by Wednesday night, they'll expect it on Thursday.
- This reasoning continues until all days are ruled out.

However, when the quiz is given on Wednesday, the class is **genuinely surprised**. Their reasoning failed to eliminate the possibility because their expectation depended on **not knowing** when the event would occur. Thus, the prediction (of a surprise) is paradoxically **validated by being violated** in logic but confirmed in practice.

This is a version of the Prediction Paradox: a prediction's validity depends on **being believed but not acted upon** in a way that undermines it.

Why It Works

The paradox works because it highlights how **knowledge of a future event can change behaviour**, especially when individuals attempt to **outsmart or negate** the prediction. Predictions are typically treated as neutral forecasts, but in cases involving **human agency**, foreknowledge becomes an **intervention**.

This creates a recursive loop:

- The prediction causes a change in behaviour.

- The changed behaviour invalidates or fulfils the prediction.
- The prediction's truth-value becomes entangled with the subject's awareness of it.

This feedback loop is what turns a straightforward forecast into a paradox.

How It Works

There are two key mechanisms at play:

1. **Self-reference**: The prediction refers to an outcome that is contingent upon the subject's awareness and reaction to the prediction.
2. **Logical paradox**: The act of making the prediction influences the conditions under which the prediction is evaluated, either causing it to come true or preventing it.

This creates an unstable situation in which the **truth of the prediction becomes causally dependent** on its reception and interpretation.

Application

The Prediction Paradox appears in:

- **Economics and finance**: If everyone believes a market will crash tomorrow, they might sell today—causing it to crash today instead.

- **Psychology**: Self-fulfilling and self-defeating prophecies, especially in behaviour and motivation.

- **Artificial intelligence**: Predictive systems influencing the behaviours they are meant to observe neutrally.

- **Strategic planning and politics**: Policy decisions based on forecasts can make the forecasts irrelevant or accurate.

Key Insights

- Prediction is not always passive; it can be **interventionist**.

- Foreknowledge can be paradoxical when it **alters the future it describes**.

- The paradox blurs the boundary between **causal determinism and free will**.

- Sometimes the **best way to fulfil a prediction** is to make sure people **don't believe or act on it**.

- Understanding prediction paradoxes is vital for systems where **agents adapt to expectations**, including markets, AI, and decision-making environments.

27. Temporal Causal Loop Paradox

Theory

The **Temporal Causal Loop Paradox**, also known as a *bootstrap paradox* or *ontological paradox*, occurs when an object, event, or piece of information is caught in a self-sustaining loop in time — with no clear point of origin. In such a loop, a cause leads to an effect which in turn becomes the original cause, forming a closed temporal cycle. This challenges traditional views of causality, where every effect must have a preceding, external cause.

The paradox arises in the context of **time travel**, particularly in theories that permit **closed timelike curves** (CTCs), where spacetime loops back on itself. It is not logically inconsistent in the way some time travel paradoxes are (like the grandfather paradox), but it is deeply counterintuitive. The issue is not about contradiction, but about **causal origin** and whether something can exist without ever being "created" in the usual sense.

Example

Imagine a scientist receives a blueprint for a time machine from their future self. They then use this blueprint to build the time machine and, later in life, travel back in time to give the blueprint to their younger self. In this loop, the time machine design has no original creator; it exists solely because it was passed from future to past in a continuous cycle.

Where did the blueprint *come from*? It was never invented, never derived from original thought — it simply exists in a loop, raising questions about how something can exist without an external cause.

Why It Works

The paradox works because it pushes our intuitive and philosophical assumptions about **causality** to the limit. Normally, causation implies a linear, forward-moving chain from cause to effect. But in a causal loop, this directionality is disrupted. Each part of the loop is both cause and effect — it causes itself to exist through time travel.

From a formal standpoint, this isn't a contradiction in logic. The events are consistent with each other — there's no point in the loop where an effect contradicts its cause. That's why causal loops are sometimes considered "paradox-free" within certain interpretations of physics (like general relativity). But they are troubling because they imply **acausal genesis** — creation without origination.

How It Works

Causal loops depend on the theoretical existence of **closed timelike curves**, which are allowed solutions to Einstein's field equations under general relativity (in exotic scenarios like rotating universes or wormholes). In these models, particles or information can follow a path through spacetime that returns to its own past.

If time is treated as a dimension similar to space, then looping through time becomes mathematically permissible — though still physically speculative. Within such a loop, every point is both earlier and later than others depending on the frame of reference, allowing events to perpetuate themselves in an eternal cycle.

Application

Causal loops appear frequently in **science fiction**, but they also have serious implications in **philosophy of time**, **metaphysics**, and **theoretical physics**. They challenge the **principle of sufficient reason** — the idea that everything must have an explanation. In quantum gravity and cosmology, some have speculated that the entire universe might be part of such a self-contained loop.

In **information theory**, they raise problems of origin and entropy: can information exist without ever being generated? In **computational models**, they provoke thought about recursive functions and circular definitions.

Key Insights

1. **Causal Loops Are Logically Coherent**: Though strange, they don't violate logical consistency.

2. **Originless Entities Are Possible**: The paradox suggests something could exist without an external cause.

3. **Time Travel Challenges Causality**: Traditional cause-effect relations break down in looped time.

4. **Raises Metaphysical Questions**: It confronts the very foundations of how we understand existence and creation.
5. **Physics Permits, But Doesn't Predict**: While allowed in theory, we lack empirical evidence for CTCs or loops.

The Temporal Causal Loop Paradox reveals that even in the absence of contradiction, our understanding of cause, creation, and the flow of time is deeply challenged by the implications of time travel and closed loops.

28. Omnipotence Paradox

Theory Overview

The **Paradox of Omnipotence** explores whether the concept of an all-powerful being (commonly referred to as God) is logically coherent. At its core, the paradox asks:

Can an omnipotent being create a stone so heavy that even it cannot lift it?

If the answer is **yes**, then there exists something the being cannot do (i.e., lift the stone), meaning it is *not* omnipotent. If the answer is **no**, then there is also something the being cannot do (i.e., create the stone). Either way, the being seems limited, contradicting the very definition of omnipotence.

The paradox challenges the idea of **absolute power** and whether it can exist without contradiction. It is both a logical and theological problem that has been debated for centuries in philosophy, particularly in the contexts of medieval scholasticism, modern theology, and metaphysics.

Example

Take the classic formulation:

Can God create a square circle?

If God is truly omnipotent, shouldn't He be able to do even logically impossible things? But if square circles are **nonsensical**

contradictions, then asking whether God can create one may not be a genuine limitation of His power—just a misuse of language.

This leads to the deeper issue: does omnipotence include the power to **violate logic**, or is omnipotence limited to doing only what is logically possible?

Why It Works

The Paradox of Omnipotence works because it **uses the idea of unlimited power against itself**. It forces a definition of omnipotence that leads to self-contradiction. The trick lies in framing a challenge that seems to both require and deny omnipotence at the same time.

The paradox hinges on **semantic precision**—how we define "power" and "possible." By constructing a scenario where omnipotence undermines itself, the paradox raises essential questions about whether such a concept is even logically coherent.

How It Works

There are several philosophical responses to this paradox:

1. **Logical Limitation View**: Omnipotence means the ability to do all things that are logically possible. Nonsensical or self-contradictory tasks (like creating a stone so heavy it cannot be lifted) are not "things" at all and thus don't fall within the scope of power.

2. **Paradox as Proof of Limits**: Others argue that the paradox shows the incoherence of omnipotence. If a concept leads to contradiction, it might be fundamentally flawed and not truly meaningful.

3. **Redefinition**: Some redefine omnipotence as the ability to do anything that aligns with the nature or will of the being. Thus, omnipotence is not about *doing the illogical*, but about having *unbounded capacity* within reason.

Application

The Paradox of Omnipotence is more than just a word game—it has serious implications for **theology, philosophy of religion**, and **ethics**. It shapes how people define divine attributes such as **perfection, free will**, and **moral responsibility**.

In religious contexts, how one resolves the paradox can influence views on prayer, miracles, divine justice, and the limits of human understanding. In **philosophical logic**, it's a critical case study in how language and abstract concepts can lead to self-undermining conclusions.

Key Insights

- The paradox exposes the **conceptual fragility** of absolute power.
- It reveals the importance of **logical consistency** in defining omnipotence.

- Not all "actions" are logically coherent—some are contradictions in disguise.
- Omnipotence may not mean "doing anything," but "doing anything logically possible."
- The paradox is a **lens** through which we question language, divinity, and the limits of thought.

29. Abilene Paradox (indirectly temporal)

Theory Overview

The **Abilene Paradox** is a concept in **group dynamics and organizational behaviour** that describes a situation in which a group of people collectively decides on a course of action that **none of them individually support**, simply because each assumes that everyone else wants it. Coined by management theorist **Jerry B. Harvey** in 1974, the paradox explores how **misperceived consensus** and a failure of honest communication can lead to decisions that contradict the preferences of all involved.

It is not a paradox in the strict logical sense but rather a **social and psychological contradiction**: people act in opposition to their own interests and desires, not because of coercion, but due to an **illusion of agreement**—a systemic miscommunication that emerges from the desire to avoid conflict or be agreeable.

Example

Harvey's original anecdote tells of a family in Texas sitting on a hot afternoon. Someone casually suggests a 50-mile drive to Abilene for dinner. One by one, everyone agrees, though none of them truly wants to go. After returning from an unpleasant meal, they realize **no one actually wanted to go to Abilene**, but each thought the others were enthusiastic and went along not to cause conflict.

The key insight: **every person privately opposed the trip, yet the group still made the trip**—a classic instance of the Abilene Paradox.

Why It Works

The paradox works because of **pluralistic ignorance**—a phenomenon in which individuals wrongly believe that their thoughts, feelings, or behaviours are different from those of the group. Each person assumes silence or passive agreement means endorsement, even though **everyone might be thinking the same private objection**.

This is reinforced by:

- **Social pressure** to conform or not "rock the boat."
- Fear of **rejection, embarrassment, or conflict**.
- A sense of **duty or politeness**, especially in hierarchical or tight-knit groups.

The irony is that **everyone is trying to accommodate others**, and in doing so, they create a result that **nobody actually wants**.

How It Works

The Abilene Paradox unfolds through these stages:

1. A suggestion or decision is made—often casually or without commitment.

2. Others, wanting to appear agreeable, **nod or agree**, believing others support it.

3. **No one voices dissent**, fearing conflict or being seen as difficult.

4. The group **follows through**, despite mutual private disagreement.

5. Afterward, it's revealed that **no one truly supported the decision**, leading to frustration or even resentment.

The paradox isn't about bad intentions, but rather about **a collective breakdown of honest communication**.

Application

The Abilene Paradox has broad applications:

- **Corporate environments**: Teams approve strategies or projects that none believe in, simply to avoid confrontation.

- **Politics and policy**: Lawmakers may pass or support legislation they internally oppose, assuming others endorse it.

- **Military and government**: Command decisions may reflect perceived consensus rather than real belief.

- **Family and social life**: People agree to events, plans, or actions they dislike to keep the peace.

To avoid it, organizations must cultivate **psychological safety**, where dissenting views are not only tolerated but encouraged.

Key Insights

- Consensus is **not always real**—it can be an illusion sustained by silence and politeness.

- **Lack of open communication** is more damaging than open disagreement.

- The paradox reveals the dangers of **conflict avoidance**, particularly in group settings.

- Encouraging **honest dialogue** and validating dissent can prevent self-defeating group decisions.

- The Abilene Paradox teaches us that **agreement should never be assumed without confirmation**—and that speaking up might actually reveal a shared truth.

30. Unexpected Hanging Paradox

Theory Overview

The **Unexpected Hanging Paradox** is a philosophical and logical puzzle that explores the limits of reasoning and self-reference. It presents a situation in which a person's **logical deduction** seemingly contradicts **what actually happens**, thereby revealing a paradox of expectation and prediction.

Also known as the **Surprise Execution Paradox**, the setup involves a **prisoner** who is told by a judge that he will be **hanged at noon on one weekday next week**—but the execution will be a **surprise**, meaning he won't know the day of the hanging until the executioner arrives.

At first glance, the condition seems straightforward, but when the prisoner starts **deducing the logic** of when the hanging can or cannot occur, he concludes that **it cannot happen at all**. Yet, when the hanging does happen—and surprises him—it turns out the paradox lies not in the logic itself, but in the **assumptions about knowledge and expectation**.

Example

A judge tells a prisoner on Sunday:

"You will be hanged at noon on one weekday next week, but the execution will be a surprise—you won't know the day of the hanging in advance."

The prisoner reasons:

1. **It can't be Friday**, because if he's not hanged by Thursday, it must be Friday—and he would expect it.
2. If Friday is ruled out, then **Thursday is also impossible**, because by Wednesday night, knowing Friday is excluded, he would then expect a Thursday hanging.
3. This backward logic continues through the week, eliminating every day.
4. He concludes, logically, **the hanging cannot happen** without violating the surprise condition.

However, on **Wednesday at noon**, he is hanged—**completely surprised**. His logical deduction was sound in form, but **failed in its outcome**.

Why It Works

The paradox works by exploiting a **self-referential loop of reasoning**, where the prisoner's attempt to predict the unpredictable collapses under its own logic. His deduction assumes that **expectation can be eliminated through backward reasoning**, but it **misapplies logical certainty to a condition based on psychological surprise**.

The prisoner's logic fails because he **confuses knowing the structure of the surprise** with actually **being able to anticipate it** in real-time. The surprise remains effective because his own deduction convinces him it won't happen at all, ironically setting him up for the very surprise promised.

How It Works

The mechanics of the paradox include:

1. **Backward induction**: The prisoner reasons from the end of the week toward the beginning, ruling out days recursively.

2. **Self-defeating logic**: The act of ruling out each day builds the prisoner's belief that the hanging won't occur—thus preserving the surprise.

3. **Mismatch between knowledge and belief**: Even if the hanging is logically possible, the prisoner's belief that it is impossible **restores the conditions** for surprise.

This paradox blurs the line between **logical deduction**, **expectation**, and **knowledge of future events**.

Application

The Unexpected Hanging Paradox is used in:

- **Epistemic logic**: Studying how knowledge, belief, and time interact.

- **Philosophy of language and paradoxes**: Related to the **Liar Paradox** and **Yablo's Paradox**, where self-reference leads to contradiction.

- **Legal and psychological analysis**: Understanding how information and expectation influence behaviour and perception.
- **Computer science and AI**: In planning and predictability in systems with conditional responses.

Key Insights

- **Knowing a condition logically** doesn't mean it can be applied predictively in real time.
- Paradoxes often arise from **recursive reasoning and self-reference**.
- The paradox highlights a gap between **deductive certainty** and **human psychology**.
- Sometimes, **belief in certainty can cause surprise**—a logical twist that undercuts prediction.
- The Unexpected Hanging shows that **truths about knowledge can behave differently** from truths about physical events.

Ethical & Decision Theory Paradoxes

Involve conflicting choices, utilities, and moral dilemmas.

31. Prisoner's Dilemma

Theory Overview

The **Prisoner's Dilemma** is a classic model in **game theory** that illustrates how two rational individuals might not cooperate—even if it's in their best collective interest—due to incentives that reward self-interest over mutual benefit. First formalized by **Merrill Flood and Melvin Dresher** in the 1950s and later popularized by **Albert W. Tucker**, it's widely used in economics, politics, psychology, and evolutionary biology to explain **conflict, cooperation, and strategic decision-making**.

The paradox lies in the tension between **individual rationality** and **collective rationality**: each person acts in their own self-interest, yet both would be better off if they cooperated.

Example

Two suspects are arrested for a crime and placed in separate interrogation rooms. Each is offered the same deal:

- If one **defects** (betrays the other) while the other **cooperates** (stays silent), the defector goes free and the cooperator gets 10 years in prison.

- If both **defect**, they each get 5 years.
- If both **cooperate**, they each get 1 year on a lesser charge.

The matrix of choices looks like this:

	Prisoner B: Cooperate	Prisoner B: Defect
Prisoner A: Cooperate	A: 1 yr, B: 1 yr	A: 10 yrs, B: free
Prisoner A: Defect	A: free, B: 10 yrs	A: 5 yrs, B: 5 yrs

Rational self-interest pushes both prisoners to defect—because no matter what the other does, defecting leads to a better or equal outcome individually. Yet if both defect, they each get 5 years, worse than the 1-year sentence they would have received through mutual cooperation.

Why It Works

The Prisoner's Dilemma works because it encapsulates **real-world strategic conflicts** where the optimal individual choice leads to **suboptimal group outcomes**. The paradox arises from a **lack of trust and communication**, as each player fears being exploited if they cooperate and the other defects.

It reveals how **rational strategies can lead to collectively irrational outcomes**, especially in **one-shot** scenarios (played only once). This insight applies to numerous domains where cooperation would benefit all, but individual incentives discourage it.

How It Works

At its core, the dilemma functions through:

1. **Dominant strategies**: Defecting is always better for each player, regardless of what the other does.
2. **Nash equilibrium**: Mutual defection is the stable outcome, even though it's not optimal.
3. **Temptation vs. trust**: Defecting offers the highest individual reward if the other cooperates—but at the risk of mutual punishment.
4. **Repeated interactions**: In *iterated* versions of the game, cooperation can emerge over time through strategies like **Tit-for-Tat**, which reward trust and punish betrayal.

This transforms the paradox into a broader framework for modelling **cooperation over time**.

Application

The Prisoner's Dilemma is applicable in:

- **International relations**: Arms races, climate change agreements, trade disputes.

- **Economics**: Price wars between firms, labour negotiations, antitrust behaviour.
- **Sociology and psychology**: Understanding trust, betrayal, and altruism in social groups.
- **Evolutionary biology**: Explaining cooperation among non-related individuals or species.

It's also foundational in the design of **algorithms and AI**, especially in environments where autonomous agents must interact.

Key Insights

- Rational agents may act against their own long-term interest if isolated and incentivized poorly.
- Cooperation can be fragile without **communication, trust, or shared enforcement mechanisms**.
- Repetition, reputation, and transparency foster **pro-social behaviour** even among self-interested agents.
- The dilemma reveals the importance of **system design**, not just individual ethics, in achieving good outcomes.
- It's a powerful model for **collective action problems**, like pollution, tax evasion, or digital misinformation.

32. Trolley Problem

Theory Overview

The **Trolley Problem** is one of the most famous thought experiments in **moral philosophy**, designed to test the boundaries between **consequentialist** and **deontological** ethics. First introduced by **Philippa Foot** in 1967 and later expanded by **Judith Jarvis Thomson**, the dilemma reveals deep tensions between **outcome-based reasoning** (utilitarianism) and **duty- or rights-based ethics** (deontology).

At its core, the Trolley Problem asks:

Is it morally permissible to **cause harm to one person** if it means **saving more lives overall**?

The scenario pits two ethical principles against each other:

1. The **utilitarian principle**, which aims to maximize overall well-being.

2. The **deontological principle**, which stresses that certain actions (like killing an innocent) are morally wrong, regardless of outcomes.

Example

In the basic version of the Trolley Problem:

A runaway trolley is heading toward **five people** tied to the tracks. You are standing next to a **lever** that can divert the trolley onto another track, where **one person** is tied down.

You have two options:

- **Do nothing**, and five people die.
- **Pull the lever**, redirecting the trolley and killing one person, but saving five.

From a **utilitarian** standpoint, pulling the lever is the moral choice: one death is better than five. From a **deontological** perspective, pulling the lever means **actively causing harm to an innocent person**, which may be morally unacceptable, even if it leads to a better outcome.

Why It Works

The Trolley Problem works because it **exposes the conflict** between our moral instincts and moral theories. Most people feel a strong emotional aversion to intentionally harming others, yet also recognize that minimizing harm is generally a good thing.

It challenges the **consistency of our moral intuitions** and asks whether the **means used to achieve an end matter as much**

as the end itself. When extended into different variations (e.g., the Fat Man or Loop scenarios), it becomes even more psychologically complex, revealing how **small changes in framing can drastically affect moral judgment**.

How It Works

The structure of the problem involves:

1. A **forced choice** between two harmful outcomes.
2. A **moral agent** (you) with the ability to intervene.
3. A question of whether taking action that **kills one** to **save more lives** is ethically justified.
4. A contrast between **passive inaction** (letting five die) and **active intervention** (causing one death).

This simplicity makes it an ideal tool for examining how people reason through **ethical trade-offs**, particularly when consequences and moral duties collide.

Application

The Trolley Problem is widely applied in:

- **Ethics education**: Teaching foundational concepts in moral philosophy.

- **Artificial intelligence**: Programming ethical decisions into autonomous vehicles, such as how self-driving cars should react in no-win situations.

- **Medical ethics**: Triage and organ transplant decisions, where doctors must allocate scarce resources.

- **Military and policy ethics**: Just war theory, drone strikes, and collateral damage evaluations.

By forcing clear choices under ethical pressure, it helps **clarify the values** that guide action in complex systems.

Key Insights

- Moral reasoning often involves **competing frameworks**, not one universal rule.

- People's intuitions may support **contradictory principles** depending on context.

- The problem reveals the ethical tension between **doing harm and allowing harm**.

- It highlights the **limits of both utilitarianism and deontology** in real-world dilemmas.

- The simplicity of the Trolley Problem makes it a powerful lens through which to examine complex moral decisions in modern technology and governance.

33. Fat Man Variation

Theory Overview

The **Fat Man Variation** is a provocative ethical thought experiment in **moral philosophy** and **utilitarian ethics**, often used to explore the tensions between **deontological** and **consequentialist** reasoning. It is a variant of the classic **Trolley Problem**, which asks whether it's morally permissible to divert a runaway trolley to kill one person in order to save five others.

In the **Fat Man** version, the situation changes slightly:

A trolley is headed toward five unsuspecting people tied to the tracks. You are standing on a footbridge above, next to a **large man**. If you push him onto the tracks, his body will stop the trolley, killing him but saving the five. Do you push him?

Unlike the original trolley scenario—where you pull a switch and passively divert harm—the Fat Man Variation involves **actively and physically causing the death** of an individual to save others. This shift in framing introduces significant psychological, ethical, and philosophical complications.

Example

You are on a bridge over trolley tracks. A trolley is out of control and heading toward five people. Standing beside you is a man large enough that, if pushed, he would fall onto the tracks and stop the trolley due to his mass. You could save five lives—**but only by pushing this man to his death**.

- **Option A**: Do nothing, and the trolley kills five.
- **Option B**: Push the man, saving five but killing one.

From a **utilitarian** perspective, pushing the man is morally justified: it minimizes total harm (1 death vs. 5). However, **deontologists** (like Kant) argue that using a person **as a means to an end** is inherently immoral, regardless of the outcome.

Why It Works

This variation works because it **triggers a deeper emotional and ethical conflict** than the switch-pulling scenario. People who are comfortable pulling a lever to divert the trolley often hesitate—or outright refuse—to push the fat man.

The reason lies in:

- **Direct physical involvement**: Pushing someone to their death feels more personal and morally weighty.
- **Intentionality**: You are not just allowing harm to happen, but **intending to cause harm.**
- **Moral intuition vs. moral logic**: Our gut feelings and moral instincts often clash with cold utilitarian calculations.

The paradox reveals that people often **reject consistent moral principles** when the form of action changes, even if the **outcome remains identical**.

How It Works

The Fat Man scenario amplifies moral tension through:

1. **Active harm vs. passive harm**: Shifting responsibility from omission to commission.

2. **Proximity and agency**: You must physically engage with the victim, making the decision more psychologically visceral.

3. **The moral weight of means vs. ends**: You're not just causing harm for the greater good—you're using someone **as the instrument** of that good.

This change in framing forces a deeper examination of what makes an action moral: **consequences** or **principles**?

Application

This paradox is widely applied in:

- **Moral philosophy**: As a case study in debates between **utilitarianism** and **deontology**.

- **AI and autonomous systems**: Programming moral decisions in self-driving cars or medical triage algorithms.

- **Military ethics**: Questions about collateral damage and the intentional killing of few to save many.
- **Bioethics and medicine**: Life-and-death resource allocation decisions, such as organ distribution or emergency triage.

Key Insights

- Morality is not just about outcomes, but **intent, action, and agency**.
- People's moral intuitions are **context-sensitive**, often inconsistent across similar outcomes.
- Ethical theories offer **different frameworks**—no single theory satisfies all intuitions in complex scenarios.
- The Fat Man scenario reveals the difficulty of aligning **theoretical ethics** with **emotional and cultural norms**.
- It's a powerful reminder that **moral dilemmas often involve trade-offs between deeply held values**, not clear-cut answers.

34. Mere Addition Paradox (Population Ethics)

Theory

The **Mere Addition Paradox**, introduced by philosopher Derek Parfit in his 1984 book *Reasons and Persons*, is a central problem in **population ethics**—the field of moral philosophy that deals with the ethical implications of decisions affecting the size and quality of future populations. The paradox highlights a tension between intuitively plausible moral judgments and the conclusions reached when we try to apply them systematically to population outcomes.

The paradox arises when we consider whether simply adding people with good—but lower-than-average—lives to a population can make the world worse, better, or ethically neutral. Parfit shows that intuitively acceptable premises about well-being and aggregation lead to a conclusion that many find ethically disturbing: namely, the so-called **Repugnant Conclusion**—that a very large population with lives barely worth living could be better than a smaller population with very high quality of life.

Example

Imagine the following scenario:

- **Population A**: 100 million people living very high-quality lives (deep relationships, creativity, fulfilment).

- **Population B**: 100 million of the same people from A, and 100 million additional people living good, but slightly less excellent lives.

Most people would say that Population B is **not worse** than A—it contains everyone from A, and the newcomers have good lives. This is the "mere addition" step: we added more people whose lives are worth living without making anyone worse off.

Now repeat this process multiple times: each time, add more people whose lives are still worth living but slightly less satisfying than those already alive. Eventually, you reach:

- **Population Z**: a massive number of people living lives barely worth living—perhaps no suffering, but also little pleasure, meaning, or richness.

Despite each step seeming ethically acceptable, the final result seems unappealing: we are now saying that this massive, low-quality population is **better than** the small, high-quality one. That's the paradox.

Why It Works

The paradox works because it exposes a deep conflict between three moral intuitions:

1. **Non-Antiegalitarianism**: Adding people with positive lives doesn't make a situation worse.
2. **Transitivity of "better than"**: If B is better than A, and C is better than B, then C is better than A.

3. **Repugnance Avoidance**: A world full of lives barely worth living should not be considered the best outcome.

Parfit shows that these three principles, while individually appealing, lead to the **Repugnant Conclusion** when combined. This reveals a structural tension in our moral reasoning about populations.

How It Works
Parfit uses a **series of small, intuitively acceptable steps** to show how seemingly benign choices (adding people with decent lives) can lead to a counterintuitive and disturbing overall conclusion. This method mirrors the **sorites paradox** (the paradox of the heap), where adding one grain of sand never seems to create a heap, but enough additions eventually do.

Each step respects ethical intuitions about improving total well-being. But when transitivity and aggregation are applied rigorously, we are forced to accept an outcome that seems morally troubling.

Application
The Mere Addition Paradox is foundational in **population ethics**, influencing discussions about climate policy, reproductive ethics, resource distribution, and long-term human survival. It is especially relevant to debates over **effective altruism** and **longtermism**, which aim to improve the lives of future generations.

In practical ethics, the paradox challenges policymakers: Should they aim to maximize total happiness, average well-being, or something else? The paradox shows that no approach is free from counterintuitive implications.

Key Insights

1. **Ethical Reasoning Is Fragile**: Even widely accepted principles can lead to troubling conclusions when combined.

2. **Transitivity Isn't Always Safe**: Moral judgments may not behave like simple mathematical relations.

3. **Quantity vs. Quality Tension**: Bigger populations with lower quality of life may outscore smaller, happier ones under total utilitarianism.

4. **Frameworks Matter**: Choosing between total, average, or critical-level utilitarianism radically affects outcomes.

5. **Ethical Theories Need Limits**: The paradox shows the need for nuanced theories that can resist repugnant conclusions without rejecting important moral intuitions.

The Mere Addition Paradox remains a powerful challenge to utilitarian ethics and a guiding problem for those thinking seriously about humanity's future.

35. Tragedy of the Commons

Theory Overview

The **Paradox of Omnipotence**—also known as the **Omnipotence Paradox**—challenges the coherence of the concept of an **all-powerful being**. At its core, the paradox asks whether **omnipotence is logically self-consistent**, or whether the very definition contains contradictions that render the concept incoherent.

A classic formulation of the paradox is the question:

"Can an omnipotent being create a stone so heavy that even they cannot lift it?"

If the answer is **yes**, then the being **cannot lift it**, implying a **limit** to their power. If the answer is **no**, then the being **cannot create it**, which is also a limit. Either way, the being fails to meet the standard of omnipotence.

The paradox is not just a theological puzzle but a **philosophical and logical one**, probing the boundaries of power, self-reference, and logical possibility.

Example

Suppose a deity claims to be omnipotent. A sceptic challenges this by asking:

"Can you create a rock so massive that you can't lift it?"

- If the deity **can create** such a rock, then **lifting it becomes impossible**—indicating a **lack of power**.
- If the deity **cannot create** such a rock, then there exists **something the deity cannot do**—again, a **limit** on power.

Thus, in either case, the notion of **unlimited power leads to a contradiction**.

Other variations of the paradox include:

- Can an omnipotent being **destroy itself**?
- Can it create **rules it cannot break**?
- Can it make **2 + 2 = 5**?

Each version reveals a fundamental tension between **logical consistency and boundless capability**.

Why It Works

The paradox works because it **exploits self-referential logic** and our intuitive discomfort with limits. It forces us to confront whether "all-powerful" should mean **"can do the logically impossible"**, or if omnipotence must still **respect the bounds of logic**.

Most responses to the paradox involve clarifying or redefining the scope of omnipotence. If omnipotence includes the power to do the **logically impossible**, then it becomes **meaningless**, as any contradiction could be true.

But if it excludes contradictions, then **omnipotence has limits**—albeit rational ones.

How It Works

The structure of the paradox follows this sequence:

1. Define omnipotence as the ability to do **anything**.
2. Pose a self-referential challenge that traps the definition in **mutual contradiction**.
3. Conclude that either outcome results in a **failure of omnipotence**, implying that such a being **cannot exist logically**—or that omnipotence **requires a different understanding**.

Many philosophers, including Thomas Aquinas, argue that **omnipotence excludes logical contradictions**. In this view, **nonsensical tasks** like creating a square circle or a stone too heavy to lift are **not "things" at all**, but **ill-formed ideas**. Thus, **failing to do the logically impossible is not a failure of power**.

Application

The paradox is relevant in:

- **Theology**: For refining the nature of divine attributes and addressing criticisms of classical theism.

- **Philosophy of language and logic**: Exploring the limits of definition, coherence, and self-reference.

- **Metaphysics**: For understanding concepts of infinity, necessity, and possibility.

- **Ethics and moral theology**: For examining whether omnipotence extends to moral contradictions or "evil acts."

Key Insights

- Omnipotence may require **logical coherence**, not the ability to perform contradictions.

- The paradox reveals the importance of **precise definitions** when discussing ultimate concepts.

- **Not all "actions" are logically possible**, even in theory—language can frame nonsense as a question.

- The debate helps distinguish between **absolute power** and **logically structured power**.

- Resolving the paradox often involves redefining omnipotence as the **ability to do all things that are logically possible**.

36. Catch-22

Theory Overview

The **Catch-22 Paradox** is a form of **circular logic** that creates a no-win situation—where the conditions for escape or success are inherently contradictory, making resolution impossible. The term originates from **Joseph Heller's 1961 novel *Catch-22***, which satirizes the absurdities of bureaucratic systems, particularly in military contexts.

A **"Catch-22"** is a situation where you're **trapped by contradictory rules or logic**, such that fulfilling one condition makes it impossible to fulfil the other, and vice versa. It has since become a widely used cultural and philosophical metaphor for **self-defeating systems** and **illogical constraints** that block rational action.

Example

In *Catch-22*, a U.S. Army Air Force pilot named **Yossarian** wants to be declared insane so he can be grounded and avoid flying dangerous bombing missions. According to army regulations:

- Any pilot who continues to fly dangerous combat missions is obviously **insane**.

- But if a pilot **requests to be grounded** for insanity, this demonstrates **rational concern for one's safety**, and is thus evidence of **sanity**.

This is the paradox:

If you're sane enough to recognize the danger and ask to be removed from duty, you're too sane to be considered insane and therefore must continue flying.

The rule, "Catch-22," is written in such a way that no matter what a person does, they are trapped. It ensures **no escape**, as every possible route to freedom invalidates itself.

Why It Works

The paradox is effective because it **mimics the irrational structures** found in bureaucracy, legal loopholes, and rigid systems of authority. It captures the **existential frustration** of being caught in a loop where **all options cancel each other out**.

What makes Catch-22 compelling—and infuriating—is that the logic **appears valid within the system**, even though it **defies basic fairness and reason**. It's a powerful commentary on how institutions can become **self-protective**, enforcing rules that **sustain their power while undermining individual agency**.

Catch-22s often emerge in **real life** where rules are opaque, self-referential, or designed to prevent accountability.

How It Works

A typical Catch-22 involves:

1. **Two interdependent conditions** that must be met.
2. Each condition **logically or practically negates** the possibility of fulfilling the other.
3. **The individual is locked** in a self-cancelling loop, unable to proceed or exit.
4. The system remains **immune to contradiction**, because its rules reinforce themselves.

This feedback loop creates a **closed, circular system** where logic is subverted in service of control, satire, or absurdity.

Application

Catch-22 logic is often seen in:

- **Bureaucracy**: "You need experience to get a job, but need a job to get experience."
- **Healthcare**: "You need insurance to get treatment, but you need a diagnosis to get insurance."
- **Legal systems**: "You must appeal within 30 days, but you can't appeal until the court provides a ruling—which takes more than 30 days."

- **Surveillance and dissent**: "Only guilty people refuse to be monitored, so your desire for privacy makes you suspicious."

In psychology, it also manifests in **double binds**, where every action or choice leads to a negative consequence.

Key Insights

- **Catch-22s expose the absurdity of rigid systems** that prioritize rules over reason.
- They reflect how **logic can be weaponized** to entrap, rather than enlighten.
- The paradox captures a deep **existential frustration** with institutions that defy fairness or escape.
- It shows how **language and policy** can be manipulated to enforce compliance while denying accountability.
- Catch-22 remains a powerful metaphor for **modern bureaucratic, legal, and political dilemmas**, where seemingly rational systems can lead to irrational outcomes.

37. Voting Paradox (Condorcet)

Theory

The **Voting Paradox**, also known as the **Condorcet Paradox**, is a foundational concept in **social choice theory** and **political philosophy**. Named after the 18th-century French mathematician and philosopher **Marquis de Condorcet**, the paradox reveals that collective preferences can be **cyclic** and thus **irrational**, even if individual preferences are rational. It challenges the idea that majority voting will always yield a clear, consistent outcome that reflects the will of the people.

The core of the paradox is that **majority rule**, when applied to more than two alternatives, can lead to a situation where preferences "loop" in a cycle: A is preferred over B, B over C, and yet C over A. This is a violation of **transitivity**, a key principle of rational choice — and it shows that democracy, even when perfectly fair and logical at the individual level, can produce unstable or contradictory collective outcomes.

Example

Consider three voters choosing among three candidates: **A**, **B**, and **C**.

- Voter 1 prefers: A > B > C
- Voter 2 prefers: B > C > A
- Voter 3 prefers: C > A > B

Now examine the pairwise majority votes:

- **A vs B**: Voters 1 and 3 prefer A over B → A wins
- **B vs C**: Voters 1 and 2 prefer B over C → B wins
- **C vs A**: Voters 2 and 3 prefer C over A → C wins

This results in a cycle: A > B > C > A. Each option is both defeated and victorious in different pairings, so **there is no clear winner** under majority rule. The group's preference is **intransitive**.

Why It Works

The paradox works by revealing the limitations of **aggregating individual preferences** into a coherent group decision. While each voter's preferences are perfectly rational and transitive, the collective preference relation derived from pairwise majority voting can be **non-transitive**, meaning the group preference cannot be represented by any consistent ranking.

This undermines the assumption that democratic decisions necessarily reflect a "rational will of the people." Even when everyone votes honestly and the process is fair, the outcome can be **logically inconsistent**.

How It Works

The paradox arises because majority voting is based on **pairwise comparisons**, rather than global rankings. It also assumes that the majority preference in each comparison should determine the outcome. However, when voters' preferences are distributed in certain ways (as in the example above), this method fails to produce a transitive overall ranking.

Mathematically, this paradox is tied to **Arrow's Impossibility Theorem**, which generalizes the idea: any voting system that satisfies a few basic fairness conditions cannot guarantee a consistent (transitive) group preference when there are three or more choices.

Application

The Voting Paradox has practical implications in **elections**, **committee decisions**, **multi-agent systems**, and **collective bargaining**. It shows that voting systems must be carefully designed to mitigate cyclical majorities. Systems like **ranked-choice voting, Borda count,** or **Condorcet methods** attempt to avoid or reduce the problem, though each introduces its own trade-offs.

In political science and game theory, the paradox is used to illustrate strategic voting, agenda manipulation, and the importance of voting rules in shaping outcomes.

Key Insights

1. **Majority Rule Isn't Always Rational**: Collective decisions can be inconsistent, even if all individual voters are rational.

2. **Democracy Has Structural Flaws**: Fair procedures don't always produce fair or coherent results.

3. **Preference Cycles Are Real**: Intransitive group preferences can and do occur in real-world voting scenarios.

4. **Voting Systems Must Be Designed Carefully**: No system is perfect, but some handle preference aggregation better than others.

5. **Arrow and Condorcet Are Linked**: The paradox is part of a broader set of impossibility results in social choice theory.

The Condorcet Voting Paradox is a compelling demonstration that the mechanics of collective decision-making are far from straightforward, and it serves as a crucial insight for anyone seeking to understand the complexities of democratic systems.

38. Doestoevsky's Paradox

Theory Overview

Dostoevsky's Paradox refers to the philosophical tension between **absolute freedom** and **the human need for moral boundaries, structure, or meaning.** This paradox is drawn from the works and themes of **Fyodor Dostoevsky**, the 19th-century Russian novelist and thinker, whose novels grapple with existentialism, free will, suffering, and the consequences of rejecting God or objective morality.

The paradox can be distilled from a line in *The Brothers Karamazov*—arguably one of Dostoevsky's most famous works—where one character claims:

"If God does not exist, everything is permitted."

This statement reflects the heart of the paradox: **If there is no divine authority, no objective morality, and humans are free to choose their values—can meaning, virtue, or society endure?** Dostoevsky explores whether humans can **bear the burden of total moral freedom**, or whether it leads to chaos, nihilism, and despair.

Example

In *Crime and Punishment*, the protagonist **Raskolnikov** commits murder under the belief that **he is above conventional morality**—that some individuals, like Napoleon, are justified in stepping outside moral norms for the sake of higher goals. He believes that without divine or objective moral laws, **power and intellect define morality**.

But after the act, Raskolnikov is consumed by guilt, paranoia, and existential suffering. Despite his rational justification, his **inner conscience** and sense of **moral reality** torment him. Dostoevsky uses Raskolnikov to show that **freedom from morality does not result in liberation, but in psychological and spiritual collapse**.

Why It Works

The paradox works because it pits two deep human drives against one another:

1. The desire for **freedom, autonomy, and rebellion** against imposed systems—be they religious, moral, or political.

2. The need for **structure, meaning, and moral certainty** to live cooperatively and meaningfully.

Dostoevsky's characters often explore this boundary. When people are told they can do whatever they want, some are crushed by the **weight of moral responsibility**; others descend into **nihilism or cruelty**. Thus, the paradox questions whether **freedom without limits** is sustainable—or even desirable.

How It Works

The core mechanics involve:

- **Removing external moral authority** (e.g., God, religion, societal codes).

- Giving individuals **absolute moral autonomy**.

- Observing the consequences: either the creation of a new, internalized moral system—or descent into **disorientation, guilt, or immorality**.

Dostoevsky suggests that humans crave **moral anchoring**, even when they intellectually reject traditional frameworks. His paradox doesn't argue for blind faith, but rather that the **absence of any shared moral centre** is deeply destabilizing.

Application

Dostoevsky's Paradox is relevant in:

- **Existential philosophy**: Especially in the works of Camus, Sartre, and Kierkegaard, who grapple with meaning, choice, and absurdity in a godless universe.

- **Modern ethics**: Raises questions about relativism, secular morality, and whether society can sustain moral norms without metaphysical grounding.

- **Psychology**: Seen in the effects of moral dislocation, guilt, and the need for purpose in identity formation.

- **Political theory**: Explores how ideologies that reject traditional values must construct new forms of collective meaning—or risk collapse.

Key Insights

- Absolute freedom, while attractive, may become a **burden too heavy** for the human psyche.
- Without shared moral grounding, individuals may struggle to find **meaningful purpose** or act ethically.
- Dostoevsky warns that rejecting traditional morality doesn't erase its emotional or existential consequences.
- His work suggests that **moral structure is not only social but deeply personal and psychological**.
- The paradox reflects the timeless struggle between **freedom and responsibility**, and the dangers of mistaking liberation for meaninglessness.

39. McNamara Fallacy

Theory Overview

The **McNamara Fallacy**, also known as the **Quantitative Fallacy**, refers to the error of relying exclusively on **quantitative metrics** while ignoring or dismissing important **qualitative factors** that are harder to measure. The term originates from **Robert McNamara**, the U.S. Secretary of Defence during the Vietnam War, whose management style emphasized data-driven decision-making. McNamara famously relied on **body counts and statistical indicators** to evaluate success in Vietnam, despite growing qualitative evidence—such as morale, political instability, and local sentiment—that the war effort was failing.

The fallacy illustrates a broader and persistent problem in many domains:

"If it can't be measured, it doesn't count."

This mentality leads to **oversimplified models of reality**, where important but unquantifiable elements (e.g., human experience, culture, ethics) are ignored, leading to poor or even disastrous decisions.

Example

In Vietnam, military success was increasingly assessed by the number of **enemy combatants killed**—a seemingly objective and trackable figure. But this metric failed to account for:

- The **resilience and morale** of the Viet Cong.
- The **political objectives** of the war.
- The **hearts and minds** of the Vietnamese population.
- The **strategic context**, including regional and global repercussions.

While body counts rose, support for the war eroded at home and abroad, and the U.S. eventually withdrew—making clear that **quantitative success did not equal strategic victory**.

Modern examples abound. A business might judge employee performance solely by sales figures, ignoring teamwork, innovation, or ethical behaviour. A school system might measure quality by test scores, ignoring creativity, well-being, or critical thinking. In each case, **metrics overshadow meaning**.

Why It Works

The fallacy is compelling because **numbers feel authoritative**. Quantitative data appears neutral, objective, and easier to compare. Leaders and analysts often find comfort in **data-**

driven dashboards, mistaking precision for completeness. In complex systems, however, this **false sense of control** can lead to misinformed policies and distorted priorities.

The fallacy also persists because **qualitative insights**—like culture, emotion, context—are harder to capture, validate, or summarize. They resist simplification, making them seem subjective or anecdotal, even when they carry immense weight.

How It Works

The McNamara Fallacy typically unfolds in four stages:

1. **Measure what can be easily measured** (e.g., test scores, revenue, body counts).
2. **Disregard what can't be measured easily** (e.g., morale, satisfaction, justice).
3. **Assume what can't be measured isn't important**.
4. **Conclude that only what's measurable matters**.

This progression results in **data reductionism**: reducing reality to a narrow set of metrics, leading to **policy blindness**.

Application

The McNamara Fallacy has wide relevance in:

- **Military strategy**: Overreliance on kill ratios or drone strikes to measure effectiveness.
- **Education**: Standardized testing as a proxy for learning or teaching quality.

- **Business management**: KPIs (key performance indicators) overshadowing innovation, ethics, or employee well-being.
- **Healthcare**: Focusing on treatment numbers rather than patient experience or holistic outcomes.
- **AI and algorithmic systems**: Models optimizing for narrow metrics while ignoring ethical, social, or emotional impact.

Key Insights

- **Not everything important is measurable**, and not everything measurable is important.
- Overreliance on numbers can **obscure complex realities** and **dehumanize decision-making**.
- Effective leadership requires **judgment, context, and narrative**, not just data.
- The fallacy warns against **mistaking data for wisdom**—especially in morally or socially complex domains.
- Qualitative insights must be **valued and integrated**, even when messy or subjective.

40. Bootstrap Paradox

Theory Overview

The **Bootstrap Paradox** is a time travel paradox where an object, piece of information, or person is sent back in time and becomes trapped in an infinite causal loop—having no clear point of origin. The name comes from the phrase "pulling oneself up by one's bootstraps," an impossible task, just like an object existing without a clear cause.

The paradox challenges our understanding of **causality**, the idea that every effect must have a cause. In a bootstrap scenario, the cause and effect form a closed loop, undermining the linear chain we typically expect in time-bound systems. The paradox doesn't involve a logical contradiction, like some other paradoxes, but it introduces a **philosophical and metaphysical puzzle**: can something exist without being created?

Example

A classic example involves a time traveller who finds a copy of Shakespeare's *Hamlet* in the future and brings it back to Elizabethan England. He gives it to a young William Shakespeare, who publishes it under his own name. Centuries later, the same time traveller finds it again and repeats the process.

In this scenario, *Hamlet* was never truly **written**—it exists in a loop, passed between past and future with no origin. The book is its own cause and effect. Who actually wrote *Hamlet*? No one—it just "exists."

Another popular version features a scientist receiving blueprints for a time machine from her future self, building it, and eventually traveling back in time to deliver those same blueprints to her younger self. The plans were never **invented**, only passed in a loop.

Why It Works

The Bootstrap Paradox "works" in the sense that it's logically consistent within the framework of certain interpretations of time travel—particularly those allowing for **closed timelike curves**, as described in solutions to Einstein's equations of General Relativity.

In physics, if time is treated as a dimension like space, and if the universe permits loops in time, then such causally closed loops might be possible—though incredibly difficult to reconcile with our intuitive sense of cause and effect.

What makes the paradox so striking is that it seems **self-sustaining**, yet defies explanation. It challenges the **Principle of Sufficient Reason**, which states that everything must have a cause or explanation.

How It Works

Bootstrap paradoxes typically involve:

1. **Time travel** to the past.
2. An **object or information** being introduced into the timeline.
3. That object eventually becoming the very cause of itself—without any external origin.

The timeline remains consistent—there's no contradiction—but there's a profound lack of **explanatory grounding**. This contrasts with paradoxes like the **Grandfather Paradox**, which cause logical inconsistency by breaking causality outright.

Some interpretations of time (like the **block universe theory**) accept all moments as equally real, which can accommodate bootstrap loops. Others, like dynamic presentism, struggle to justify such loops.

Application

While speculative, the Bootstrap Paradox has applications in:

- **Philosophy of time**, where it challenges assumptions about causation, identity, and determinism.
- **Quantum physics**, especially discussions of retrocausality and information conservation.
- **Science fiction**, where it's a popular storytelling tool (seen in *Doctor Who*, *Predestination*, *Tenet*, and others).

- **Artificial intelligence and knowledge systems**, where recursive, self-originating information may metaphorically resemble bootstrap logic.

Key Insights

- The paradox exposes a flaw in our assumption that everything must have an origin.
- It presents a consistent—but deeply puzzling—model of time travel without contradiction.
- It reveals a philosophical tension between **consistency** and **causal completeness**.
- The paradox doesn't "break" physics, but it stretches our notions of how time and causality can work.
- It reminds us that some mysteries may be structurally closed, not logically broken.

41. Utility Monster Paradox

Theory

The **Utility Monster Paradox** is a provocative thought experiment introduced by philosopher **Robert Nozick** in his 1974 book *Anarchy, State, and Utopia*. It challenges the foundations of **utilitarianism**, particularly **classical utilitarianism**, which aims to maximize total or average happiness (utility) across individuals. The paradox shows that if we accept the idea that the morally best action is the one that increases overall utility the most, we may be forced into disturbing or unjust conclusions.

The paradox envisions a hypothetical being — the **Utility Monster** — who gains vastly more utility from a given resource or action than anyone else. According to utilitarian logic, all resources, pleasures, or benefits should therefore be given to this being, even if it causes suffering or deprivation to everyone else. This highlights a troubling implication of utilitarianism: it may justify extreme inequality as long as the total utility is higher.

Example
Suppose a society has 1,000 people, each of whom would gain 10 units of happiness from receiving a cookie. Now imagine there is a being — the Utility Monster — who gains **10,000 units of happiness** from the same cookie.

Under utilitarianism, giving the cookie to the Utility Monster is the right choice because it maximizes total happiness. But if the monster always gains more from any good, then all resources — food, money, attention — should be given to the monster. The rest of the population would live in deprivation, yet the outcome would be "morally optimal" under classical utilitarianism.

This feels **morally repugnant**, despite being logically consistent within utilitarianism. That is the core of the paradox.

Why It Works
The paradox works by **amplifying** utilitarian principles to an extreme and intuitively implausible scenario. It exposes how utilitarianism, though appealing in everyday contexts, might collapse into **moral absurdity** when taken to its logical endpoint. The key feature is the **asymmetry of utility gain** — the idea that one being's pleasure can outweigh the aggregated well-being of many others.

It exploits utilitarianism's **impartiality** and **aggregationism**: the view that only the total amount of happiness matters, not how it's distributed.

How It Works
The paradox assumes that utility is **quantifiable and comparable** across individuals, and that the only relevant factor in moral decision-making is the **sum total** of that utility. If one being's capacity for joy or satisfaction is arbitrarily high, utilitarianism is committed to privileging that

being over all others — regardless of fairness, equality, or rights.

This scenario doesn't rely on any contradiction within utilitarianism — rather, it **reveals a counterintuitive implication**. It functions similarly to a *reductio ad absurdum*: it accepts the utilitarian logic and follows it to an uncomfortable conclusion, suggesting a flaw in the initial premise.

Application

The Utility Monster Paradox plays a major role in **moral philosophy**, especially critiques of consequentialist theories. It has implications for **AI ethics**, **animal welfare**, and **public policy**, where aggregating utility often guides decisions. For instance, if future artificial intelligences could experience vastly more utility than humans, utilitarianism might prioritize their interests to the exclusion of our own.

It also raises questions about **distributive justice**, compelling ethicists to consider not just total utility, but *how* it is distributed — a concern more aligned with **egalitarian** or **deontological** ethics.

Key Insights

1. **Total Utility Isn't Everything**: Maximizing happiness can lead to morally objectionable outcomes.

2. **Equality Matters**: The paradox highlights the need for fairness, not just efficiency.

3. **Utilitarianism Ignores Moral Intuition**: The theory may justify exploitation if it increases aggregate utility.

4. **Quantification of Utility Is Problematic**: Assuming infinite utility for one being undermines moral balance.

5. **Paradox as Critique**: Nozick's argument is less about monsters and more about pushing utilitarianism to its limits.

The Utility Monster Paradox serves as a powerful philosophical tool to test the robustness of utilitarian ethics, reminding us that moral reasoning must account not just for outcomes, but for principles of fairness, dignity, and rights.

🧠 Epistemological & Information Paradoxes

Relate to knowledge, belief, or the nature of truth.

42. Paradox of the Court

Theory Overview

The **Paradox of the Court**, also known as the **Paradox of Protagoras**, is an ancient legal and philosophical dilemma that exposes the **conflict between legal logic and contractual reasoning**. It centres on a real or apocryphal story involving **Protagoras**, a famous sophist and teacher in ancient Greece, and his student **Euathlus**. The paradox reveals how **circular logic** can lead to a situation where **both parties can seemingly prove they should win a legal case**, but no resolution satisfies both arguments without contradiction.

This paradox is one of the earliest examples of **self-referential legal reasoning**, and it raises timeless questions about **conditions, obligations, and interpretive consistency**.

Example

Here is the story:

- Protagoras agrees to teach Euathlus law. The payment arrangement is unusual: Euathlus will **only pay Protagoras** once he wins his **first case in court**.

- After completing his studies, Euathlus **delays practicing law** and does not take on any court cases.

- Frustrated, Protagoras **sues Euathlus** to recover his fee.

This sets up a paradox:

- **Protagoras argues**: "If I win this case, then the court has ruled Euathlus owes me money. If I lose, then Euathlus has won his first case—so by our contract, he owes me money either way."

- **Euathlus counters**: "If I win the case, then the court says I don't have to pay. If I lose, then I haven't yet won a case, so according to our contract, I still don't have to pay."

In both cases, each party claims that **regardless of the court's decision**, **they win**—leading to a loop of contradictory outcomes.

Why It Works

The paradox works by exploiting **conditional obligations** and **recursive logic**. Each party builds a case based not solely on the court's judgment, but on what that judgment **implies about their prior agreement**. This creates a circular situation: the verdict determines the condition, but the condition itself reinterprets the verdict.

It also shows how **contracts and outcomes can interact in ways that defy resolution**. The paradox hinges on interpreting the **condition for payment**: Is it satisfied by winning this specific lawsuit, or only by winning a case unrelated to the teacher-student agreement?

How It Works

The logical structure of the paradox involves:

1. A **contractual clause** based on a **future event** (winning a case).

2. The attempt to **force or preempt that condition** through a court case directly tied to it.

3. A **feedback loop**, where each outcome redefines the meaning of the agreement:
    - Winning enforces the contract, but fulfilling the contract invalidates the obligation.
    - Losing invalidates the contract, but also fulfils its condition.

This recursive structure creates **no stable conclusion** without negating part of the original logic.

Application

While primarily a philosophical puzzle, the paradox has implications in:

- **Legal reasoning**: Highlighting problems with **conditional contracts, self-referential clauses**, and ambiguous contingencies.

- **Logic and semantics**: Offering early insights into **conditional paradoxes**, later explored in programming, law, and artificial intelligence.

- **Education and rhetoric**: As a case study in **argumentation, reasoning, and logic puzzles**.

It also serves as a cautionary tale in **contract law**, reminding legal drafters to avoid terms that can be triggered or invalidated **within the context of their own enforcement**.

Key Insights

- Self-referential logic creates **paradoxes with no stable resolution**.

- **Contracts based on future actions** can collapse when entangled with **retroactive legal outcomes**.

- Legal systems must address not just **truth**, but also **interpretive coherence**.

- The paradox challenges notions of **justice, fairness, and enforceability**, especially when all outcomes appear contradictory.

- It invites deeper reflection on the **boundaries of logic and law**, showing how even clear agreements can generate complex disputes.

43. Surprise Examination Paradox

Theory

The **Surprise Examination Paradox**, also known as the **Unexpected Hanging Paradox**, is a logical and epistemic puzzle that explores the tension between prediction, knowledge, and self-reference. First formulated in the mid-20th century, it challenges our understanding of how future events and knowledge about them interact. The paradox typically involves a teacher announcing a surprise test, or a judge declaring a surprise execution, and the reasoning process that follows leads to a seemingly unavoidable contradiction.

The paradox arises when a person is told that a future event will occur as a surprise — meaning it will happen, but they will not expect it. As they try to reason through when the event might occur, they eliminate each possible day, concluding it can't happen. Yet when it does happen, it is, in fact, a surprise — despite the earlier conclusion that it couldn't.

Example

A teacher tells their students:

"There will be a surprise exam next week, on one of the weekdays (Monday to Friday). But you will not know the day of the exam until it happens."

The students reason as follows:

- It can't be on **Friday**, because if the exam hasn't occurred by Thursday night, they'll know it must be on Friday — so it wouldn't be a surprise.

- If Friday is ruled out, then it can't be on **Thursday** either — because if the exam hasn't happened by Wednesday night, and they've ruled out Friday, then it must be on Thursday, making that not a surprise either.

- They apply this logic backward and eliminate all days. Conclusion: the exam can't happen.

Yet, when the teacher gives the test on, say, **Wednesday**, the students are genuinely surprised — the paradox lies in the contradiction between their logical deduction and their actual experience.

Why It Works
The paradox works because it exploits the **self-referential nature** of the statement "you won't expect it." The students' reasoning seems airtight, but it collapses when they fail to anticipate that their own logic might mislead them. The paradox reveals the difficulty in reasoning about future knowledge — and particularly in reasoning about what one *will not* know.

It's a paradox of **epistemic logic**: reasoning about knowledge itself. It shows that certain predictions involving surprise or self-reference can short-circuit logical deduction by creating feedback loops between what is expected and what actually occurs.

How It Works
At its core, the paradox involves a **fixed-point problem** in epistemology. The students try to anticipate an event that is defined partly by their inability to anticipate it. Their backward reasoning — eliminating days from Friday to Monday — is valid within their framework, but it collapses because the act of ruling out possibilities reintroduces the element of surprise.

In more formal treatments, the paradox is modelled using **modal logic** (particularly logics of knowledge and belief) to show that certain statements about future knowledge can create contradictions when agents try to fully deduce them.

Application
The Surprise Examination Paradox has applications in **epistemology, philosophy of logic, game theory**, and **computer science** (particularly in systems involving prediction and information asymmetry). It challenges the idea that agents can always reason accurately about their future beliefs, which has implications for modelling rational behaviour in uncertain environments.

In **legal and military strategy**, the paradox is analogous to cases where unpredictability is essential — such as surprise raids or unannounced audits. It also plays a role in **artificial intelligence**, where agents must make decisions based on uncertain or incomplete knowledge about the future.

Key Insights

1. **Self-Reference Creates Instability**: Statements about future surprise can loop back and contradict themselves.

2. **Epistemic Reasoning Has Limits**: Trying to predict what one won't expect leads to paradox.

3. **Expectation ≠ Prediction**: Knowing all logical possibilities doesn't guarantee accurate future knowledge.

4. **Uncertainty Can Be Rational**: Even perfect logic can lead to flawed conclusions about unpredictable events.

5. **Paradox Reveals the Limits of Deduction**: Not all truths about the future are logically knowable in advance.

The Surprise Examination Paradox remains a fascinating puzzle, showing how human (and artificial) reasoning can be disrupted when logic is applied to knowledge about itself.

44. Meno's Paradox

Theory

Meno's Paradox, sometimes called the **Paradox of Inquiry**, originates from Plato's dialogue *Meno*, in which Socrates and Meno discuss the nature of virtue. The paradox raises a fundamental epistemological problem: **how is it possible to learn something genuinely new?** If you already know something, then you don't need to learn it. But if you don't know it, how would you even recognize it if you stumbled upon it? The paradox challenges the very possibility of inquiry and learning.

Plato has Socrates express the paradox this way:

"A man cannot inquire either about what he knows or about what he does not know. He cannot inquire about what he knows, because he knows it, and in that case, there is no need for inquiry. Nor can he inquire about what he does not know, for he does not know what to look for."

In other words, inquiry seems either unnecessary or impossible. This leads to a sceptical conclusion: **learning is impossible** because you must already know what you're looking for in order to find it.

Example

Imagine you're trying to find out what a "quark" is, but you have no idea what it is — not even that it's a particle or something from physics. According to Meno's Paradox, you wouldn't even know where to begin or how to recognize a correct answer, since you have no prior knowledge to guide you. Conversely, if you *did* know what a quark is, you wouldn't need to inquire.

So: if you don't know, you can't search effectively. If you do know, there's no need to search. Where does that leave genuine learning?

Why It Works

The paradox works by presenting a dilemma that collapses the logical space for inquiry. It assumes a strict binary: either you *completely know* something, or you *completely do not*. This leaves no room for partial understanding, guesses, or gradual discovery. Since real-life inquiry often depends on partial information and exploratory thinking, Meno's Paradox feels both deeply troubling and oddly detached from actual learning processes — and yet it highlights real epistemic concerns.

The paradox is compelling because it challenges the assumption that knowledge can be acquired from a state of total ignorance, casting doubt on the very mechanisms by which learning and discovery occur.

How It Works

Meno's Paradox operates through a **semantic and epistemological trap**. It assumes that for inquiry to succeed, the inquirer must already have a precise conceptual target. Without that, inquiry is like shooting in the dark. But this ignores how most learning actually unfolds: through hypothesis, testing, observation, approximation, and correction.

Plato's proposed solution comes in the form of **anamnesis** — the theory of recollection. He suggests that the soul is immortal and has known all truths in a prior existence. What we call "learning" is actually remembering. While metaphorical, this answer sidesteps the paradox by claiming we *already know* at some level — we just have to retrieve it.

Application
Meno's Paradox has major implications in **epistemology**, **education theory**, and **cognitive science**. It raises questions about how knowledge is structured, how inquiry begins, and how concepts form. In **AI and machine learning**, the paradox mirrors challenges in training models without predefined structures or labels. It also influences debates around **constructivist learning**, where learners build new knowledge based on prior understanding.

In philosophy, it serves as a starting point for discussions about **concept acquisition**, **a priori knowledge**, and the distinction between **knowing-that** and **knowing-how**.

Key Insights

1. **Inquiry Requires a Middle Ground**: Total ignorance and total knowledge are extremes; learning often happens in-between.

2. **Learning Is Gradual and Iterative**: Discovery can begin from partial knowledge or even mistaken beliefs.

3. **Epistemology Must Account for Discovery**: A robust theory of knowledge must explain how new understanding emerges.

4. **Challenges Static Views of Knowledge**: The paradox reveals the limitations of viewing knowledge as a fixed set of facts.

5. **Philosophy as Self-Correcting Inquiry**: The paradox reminds us that questioning itself is a key mode of discovery.

Meno's Paradox remains a foundational puzzle in the philosophy of learning — raising essential questions about how we come to know anything at all.

45. Information Bottleneck Paradox

Theory

The **Information Bottleneck Paradox** arises in the context of **information theory, machine learning**, and **cognitive science**, particularly in how systems process, compress, and preserve meaningful information. At its core, the paradox highlights a tension between **compression and relevance**: how can a system reduce the amount of data it retains while still keeping the information that matters most?

The paradox emerges from the **Information Bottleneck Method** (developed by Tishby, Pereira, and Bialek in 1999), which proposes that the goal of learning is not to memorize raw data but to extract **the minimal sufficient representation** — that is, to compress the input data in such a way that the **output** (or relevant variable) can still be predicted effectively. The paradoxical element arises when systems **retain less data** yet **improve or preserve performance**, suggesting that *less is more* in terms of meaningful representation. This seemingly contradicts the intuition that more data or information should lead to better understanding or prediction.

Example

Imagine a machine learning model trained to identify handwritten digits. The input is a complex, high-dimensional image, and the output is a single digit (0–9). Using the Information Bottleneck principle, the system learns to compress the image into a much smaller internal representation — say, a vector of a few features — that still allows it to accurately classify the digit.

Now here's the paradox: **even though the internal representation contains far less information than the original image**, the model may perform *better* because the representation filters out noise and irrelevant variation (like handwriting style or background patterns). It seems counterintuitive that throwing away data can **enhance** understanding — hence the paradox.

Why It Works
The paradox works by challenging our assumptions about **information richness and utility**. We tend to equate high data volume with more insight, but the bottleneck principle shows that only **relevant** information matters. In fact, retaining too much irrelevant information can overwhelm a system, leading to overfitting, noise sensitivity, and poor generalization.

This is especially true in learning systems where the goal is not to reproduce inputs but to **predict or infer outcomes**. By aggressively compressing inputs and keeping only what helps predict the output, the system optimizes its internal representation — revealing that **efficiency can lead to better intelligence**.

How It Works
Formally, the Information Bottleneck framework balances two goals:

1. **Minimize I(X;T)**: Compress the input variable XX into a representation TT, reducing mutual information between them.

2. **Maximize I(T;Y)**: Ensure that the representation TT retains as much information as possible about the target output YY.

The paradox lies in the trade-off: as the model compresses XX (losing data), it may **increase** its ability to predict YY, because it filters out irrelevant details and focuses on structure that truly matters.

This principle has analogues in neuroscience, where the brain filters massive sensory input to extract minimal but actionable representations for decision-making.

Application

The Information Bottleneck Paradox has broad applications in **deep learning**, especially in understanding **generalization** in neural networks. It also informs **natural language processing**, **cognitive modelling**, and **neuroscience**, offering insights into how intelligent systems — artificial or biological — prioritize relevant over raw data.

It also affects **data compression**, **feature selection**, and **privacy-preserving machine learning**, where minimal representations are needed to balance performance and confidentiality.

Key Insights

1. **More Data Isn't Always Better**: Effective learning often requires removing irrelevant or noisy information.

2. **Compression Enhances Generalization**: Simpler internal models can lead to more robust and accurate predictions.

3. **Information ≠ Meaning**: Systems must distinguish between quantity of information and its relevance to a task.

4. **Paradox of Less Leading to More**: Minimal representations can yield maximal understanding — flipping intuition on its head.

5. **Learning Is About Relevance**: Intelligent systems thrive not on memorization, but on isolating what matters most.

The Information Bottleneck Paradox reframes how we think about learning and cognition: not as a process of collecting *all* information, but of refining the *right* information.

46. Anthropic Principle Paradox

Theory Overview

The **Anthropic Principle Paradox** arises from attempts to explain why the universe appears finely tuned for life, especially intelligent observers like us. At its core, the **anthropic principle** is not a paradox itself but a **philosophical reasoning tool**. The paradox emerges when this principle is used to **explain seemingly improbable conditions** by asserting:

"Of course the universe permits life—if it didn't, we wouldn't be here to notice it."

This leads to an uncomfortable and sometimes **circular line of reasoning**: the universe must appear the way it does **because we are here to observe it**, not necessarily because it's fundamentally special or designed that way. While seemingly logical, this explanation can feel **tautological**, and it raises challenges in interpreting probability, causation, and explanation.

There are two main forms:

1. **Weak Anthropic Principle (WAP)**: The conditions we observe in the universe must allow for our existence, or else we wouldn't be here to observe them.

2. **Strong Anthropic Principle (SAP)**: The universe **must** have properties that allow life to develop, often interpreted as implying **purpose or design**.

Example

Imagine someone asks:

"Why does Earth orbit the Sun at a distance just right for liquid water and life?"

The anthropic answer is:

"Because if it didn't, no one would be around to ask the question."

This seems to **dodge the need for a deeper explanation**. Instead of addressing *why* Earth is in the habitable zone, it shifts focus to the **observer's perspective**, which introduces the paradox: **does this reasoning explain anything, or does it just assert a tautology?**

This becomes more pronounced in cosmology. For instance, certain constants—like the strength of gravity or the cosmological constant—must lie within incredibly narrow ranges for life to exist. The anthropic principle suggests that these values are **not surprising**, since only a universe with such values would produce observers.

But that line of reasoning risks **circular logic**:

- We exist → The universe must permit existence → Therefore, the universe's fine-tuned properties are unsurprising.

Why It Works

The paradox "works" because it offers a kind of explanation that **doesn't truly explain**, at least not in the traditional causal or mechanistic sense. It provides **observational selection effects**—we can only observe universes in which observers can exist—but leaves open whether that observation carries any **predictive or explanatory power**.

This leads to a **philosophical tension**: is the anthropic principle a useful guide for interpreting cosmological data, or merely a statement of logical necessity?

How It Works

The paradox often appears in multiverse theories:

- If there are **many universes** with varying physical constants, then **some** will support life.
- We find ourselves in **one of those rare life-supporting universes**—not because it's probable, but because it's **the only kind we could observe.**

This line of reasoning **blunts the shock of fine-tuning**, but without independent evidence of a multiverse, it can feel speculative or even metaphysical.

Application

The anthropic principle is used in:

- **Cosmology**: To explain fine-tuning of constants and parameters in the universe.

- **Astrobiology**: In understanding why Earth-like planets are rare but not surprising.

- **Philosophy of science**: To debate what counts as a valid explanation.

- **Probability theory**: In selection bias, where observations are filtered through the conditions necessary for their existence.

Key Insights

- The anthropic principle highlights **selection bias** in cosmological observation.

- It raises deep questions about **causation vs. correlation** in explanations.

- It is both **undeniably true** and **philosophically unsatisfying**, making it paradoxical.

- In multiverse frameworks, it provides a mechanism for **predicting likelihoods**—but without empirical access to other universes, it remains controversial.
- Ultimately, the paradox teaches us that **not all explanations are satisfying**, even if logically coherent.

47. Russell's Paradox

Theory Overview

Russell's Paradox is one of the most significant discoveries in the history of logic and mathematics. It was introduced by **Bertrand Russell** in 1901 and exposed a fundamental flaw in **naive set theory**, where any definable collection is assumed to form a set. The paradox arises when considering sets that **may or may not contain themselves**, leading to a contradiction that undermines the consistency of the foundational system.

Before Russell's insight, set theory—especially as conceived by **Georg Cantor**—allowed for **unrestricted comprehension**, the idea that for any property, there exists a set of all things satisfying that property. Russell showed that this assumption leads directly to a **logical contradiction**, necessitating major revisions in the foundations of mathematics.

Example

Let's define a set **R** as follows:

R = the set of all sets that **do not contain themselves**.

Now we ask: **Does R contain itself?**

There are two possibilities:

1. **Suppose R ∈ R** (i.e., R contains itself).
   By definition, R only contains sets that **do not** contain themselves, so this leads to a contradiction: R cannot contain itself if it contains itself.

2. **Suppose R ∉ R** (i.e., R does not contain itself).
   But then, according to the definition, R must contain itself—because it's a set that does not contain itself.

In either case, whether R contains itself or not, a contradiction arises. This is the core of **Russell's Paradox**.

Why It Works

The paradox works because it reveals a **fundamental inconsistency** in naive set theory. It relies on **self-reference** and the unrestricted use of set definitions. When a definition allows a set to refer to itself in its membership conditions, it opens the door to **circular reasoning** that can't be logically resolved.

The problem is not the concept of sets, but the **unrestricted comprehension axiom**—the idea that any definable collection is automatically a valid set. Russell showed that this assumption must be abandoned or modified to avoid paradox.

How It Works

Russell's Paradox follows this structure:

1. Let **S = {x | x ∉ x}**, the set of all sets that are not members of themselves.

2. Ask whether **S ∈ S**.

3. Both assumptions (S ∈ S and S ∉ S) lead to contradictions.

Thus, naive set theory is **inconsistent**. To resolve the paradox, **more sophisticated frameworks** were introduced, such as:

- **Zermelo–Fraenkel Set Theory (ZF or ZFC)**, which restricts set formation through axioms.

- **Type theory**, developed by Russell himself, where sets are organized into a hierarchy that prevents self-reference.

Application

Russell's Paradox has had profound implications in:

- **Mathematics**: It led to the development of formal axiomatic systems that are still in use today.

- **Computer science**: Influencing **type systems, formal languages**, and programming logic to prevent self-referential errors.

- **Philosophy of logic**: Raising fundamental questions about **truth, language, and reference**.

- **Artificial intelligence and databases**: Informing rule-based systems that must avoid self-inclusion loops.

Key Insights

- **Unrestricted self-reference** in logical systems can produce contradictions.

- The paradox shows that **not every definable collection can be a set**.

- Russell's discovery catalysed a reformation of the foundations of mathematics, especially in formal logic and set theory.

- To maintain consistency, systems must use **axioms that restrict set formation**, such as in ZFC.

- Russell's Paradox illustrates that **philosophical insights into language and logic** can have sweeping implications for mathematics and computation.

48. Two-Child Paradox

Theory Overview

The **Two-Child Paradox** (also known as the **Boy or Girl Paradox**) is a classic problem in probability theory that reveals how **conditional information** dramatically changes our understanding of likelihood. It illustrates the subtle, often counterintuitive ways that **how we learn something** affects what we should believe, particularly when reasoning under uncertainty.

The paradox asks:

"A family has two children. What is the probability that both children are boys, given some piece of information?"

The answer depends heavily on **what exactly you know and how you learned it**—a nuance that leads to different intuitive (but incorrect) answers, making it a rich and educational puzzle in probability.

Example

Let's consider two versions of the problem.

Version 1:

A family has two children. One of them is a boy. What is the probability that both children are boys?

Most people intuitively say **1/2**, assuming that once we know one child is a boy, the other has a 50/50 chance of being either gender.

However, the correct answer is **1/3**. Here's why:

There are **four equally likely combinations** of children's genders:

1. Boy – Boy
2. Boy – Girl
3. Girl – Boy
4. Girl – Girl

If we're told **at least one is a boy**, we eliminate the Girl–Girl case, leaving three possibilities:

1. Boy – Boy
2. Boy – Girl
3. Girl – Boy

Only one of these has **two boys**, so the probability is **1 out of 3**.

Version 2:

A man says, "I have two children, and one is a boy born on a Tuesday." What is the probability that both children are boys?

This twist—called the **Tuesday Boy variant**—introduces extra information that paradoxically **increases** the probability to **about 13/27**, depending on how you interpret the conditions. The paradox deepens because **additional but seemingly irrelevant information** (like the day of the week) alters the probability outcome when conditioned correctly.

Why It Works

The paradox works because it exposes how easily our intuitions about probability are misled by **ambiguity in conditioning**. We often fail to account for **how the information was obtained**. Did someone say "one is a boy" because they randomly chose one child to describe, or because that was the only child of interest?

The distinction between:

- "At least one is a boy"
- "This specific child is a boy"

...leads to different **reference classes** and changes the sample space we're reasoning from.

How It Works

The paradox plays out through:

1. **Enumerating all possible outcomes** (e.g., BB, BG, GB, GG).

2. **Applying conditional probability**: eliminating outcomes that contradict the given information.

3. **Misjudging symmetry**: assuming equiprobable outcomes without adjusting for filtering conditions.

The Tuesday variant demonstrates how **filtering by rare conditions** (e.g., birthday or other descriptors) shrinks the sample space and shifts probability—**not because of the birthday**, but because of how the filter changes the dataset.

Application

The Two-Child Paradox has implications in:

- **Statistics and Bayesian reasoning**: Emphasizes correct use of conditional probability.

- **AI and machine learning**: Reinforces the need to understand the structure and source of data.

- **Psychology and cognitive science**: Demonstrates how easily humans are misled by intuitive heuristics.

- **Law and medical diagnostics**: Relevant in interpreting evidence or test results when conditional contexts are unclear.

Key Insights

- **Context matters**: How you learn something changes what it tells you.

- **Intuition is often unreliable** in conditional probability problems.
- **Enumerating the full sample space** with care is critical.
- The paradox teaches a **Bayesian mindset**: always consider the filter through which information is presented.
- Seemingly irrelevant details (like birthdays) can matter—not because they're meaningful, but because they **affect how information is selected**.

49. Cheating Husband Paradox

Theory Overview

The **Cheating Husband Paradox (or Muddy Children Paradox)** is a classic logic puzzle in **epistemic logic**—the logic of knowledge and belief. It explores how **common knowledge** and **public announcements** can lead to surprising chains of reasoning and behaviour, even when no new factual information is introduced.

At its core, the paradox shows how individuals can deduce something about their situation **not because they are directly told**, but because they observe others not acting, and **know that everyone knows that everyone knows**, and so on. This recursive structure of knowledge is what makes the paradox both elegant and profound.

Example

Here is the common formulation using the "cheating husband" version:

In a village, wives are told by a visiting queen that **at least one husband is cheating**. Every wife knows whether other men are cheating but **does not know about her own husband**. If a wife ever finds out her husband is cheating, she must **publicly declare it the next day**.

Suppose there are **three cheating husbands**. Each of their wives sees the other two cheating but is unsure about her own. Since no one announces anything on the first day, each of the three wives reasons:

"If my husband is not cheating, then there are only two cheaters. The two wives of those men will each see only one cheater, and should announce their discoveries on the second day."

When **no one announces anything on the second day**, each of the three wives realizes there must be **a third cheater**—her own husband. So, on the **third day**, all three wives simultaneously declare their husbands are cheating.

Why It Works

The paradox works because of **common knowledge**—not just what each person knows, but what each person knows that others know, and so on. The queen's announcement that "at least one is cheating" doesn't provide **new specific information**; everyone already knew of at least one cheater. But making this fact **publicly known** initiates a logical countdown.

Each wife's reasoning depends not only on what she sees but on what she knows the others are thinking. This creates a **cascading logical inference**, where the lack of declarations on previous days serves as information.

How It Works

The reasoning is recursive:

1. **1 cheater** → his wife sees no cheaters → she declares it **on day 1**.

2. **2 cheaters** → each wife sees one cheater, expects day 1 declaration → silence on day 1 → declare **on day 2**.

3. **3 cheaters** → each sees two cheaters, waits to see if those declare on day 2 → silence again → deduce all three → declare **on day 3**.

The paradox generalizes: with n cheaters, the wives declare **on day n**, using the **non-actions** of others as stepping stones for logical deduction.

Application

The paradox is relevant in:

- **Epistemic logic and computer science**: In distributed systems, understanding what agents know and when they act based on it is critical.

- **Game theory**: Models how rational players make decisions based on nested beliefs.

- **Philosophy**: Explores the nature of knowledge, belief, and information flow.

- **Social dynamics**: Highlights how consensus and mutual awareness can drive action, even without new facts.

Key Insights

- **Knowledge about knowledge** (meta-knowledge) is crucial in group reasoning.
- **Public announcements** can cause action **without new data**, simply by aligning assumptions.
- Delayed actions in groups can signal deep underlying **inference chains**.
- The paradox demonstrates how **inaction can be informative**.
- It underscores the difference between **private knowledge**, **shared knowledge**, and **common knowledge**.

50. Sayre's Law

Theory Overview

Sayre's Law is a satirical but sharp observation about human behaviour, particularly within organizations and academia. It states:

"In any dispute, the intensity of feeling is inversely proportional to the value of the issues at stake."

Often paraphrased as:

"Academic politics are so vicious precisely because the stakes are so small."

Attributed to **Wallace Stanley Sayre**, a political scientist and professor at Columbia University, the law isn't a formal paradox in logic or mathematics but rather a **sociological insight** that becomes paradoxical when compared to expected rational behaviour. The underlying irony is that **the less consequential an issue**, the **more heated** and **personal** the conflicts over it can become.

This is counterintuitive because one might expect that **higher stakes would produce more intensity**. Yet in many settings—particularly in academic departments, local government, or niche communities—debates over trivial matters can provoke disproportionately strong reactions.

Example

Imagine a university department debating whether to **rename a course** or **change the font on official documents**.

While these issues have little to no impact on the broader world, or even on students' educational outcomes, the discussion can become remarkably passionate—complete with arguments, alliances, and long-winded emails.

In contrast, when more pressing matters arise—such as budget cuts or institutional reform—responses may be **more restrained, procedural, or abstract**. Ironically, people may be less emotionally engaged about issues that **truly matter** because they feel powerless, or because the complexity diffuses responsibility.

Why It Works

Sayre's Law works because it captures the **psychological and social dynamics** that arise in low-stakes environments:

1. **Control and ego**: People are more likely to assert themselves where they feel they can exert influence. Small issues are manageable, and thus become battlefields for asserting identity, authority, or intellect.

2. **Symbolic investment**: Minor issues often become **proxies for deeper conflicts**—personal rivalries, status competitions, or ideological divisions.

3. **Emotional safety**: Ironically, people may feel **safer** expressing passion over trivial matters. In high-stakes situations, they may retreat to avoid blame, uncertainty, or confrontation.

4. **Limited external consequences**: Since the outcomes of low-stakes arguments rarely matter outside the group, individuals may indulge more in combative or performative behaviour.

Thus, the paradox lies in how **irrational and disproportionate energy** can be directed toward **insignificant outcomes**, while **rational apathy** greets issues of actual importance.

How It Works

The dynamics of Sayre's Law emerge most vividly in:

- **Closed systems**: Small departments, committees, clubs, or online communities where everyone knows everyone else.
- **Low accountability environments**: When outcomes don't affect careers or reputations outside the immediate circle.
- **Egalitarian power structures**: When individuals have equal say but limited scope, leading to power struggles over symbolic issues.

These structures promote a **micro-political ecosystem** where **perceived status and control** matter more than the issue itself.

Application

Sayre's Law has relevance in:

- **Organizational behaviour**: Helping leaders understand and manage internal conflict.

- **Academic and bureaucratic institutions**: Explaining inefficiencies and friction over policy minutiae.

- **Team dynamics and workplace culture**: Identifying when interpersonal tensions are masked as procedural disputes.

- **Online forums and social media**: Where intense debates rage over trivial topics, while substantive issues receive less traction.

Key Insights

- Passionate disputes often signal **personal or symbolic investment**, not practical stakes.

- **Smaller problems are more accessible**, making them emotionally easier to fight about.

- The law reminds us to **examine the real source of conflict**: it's often not the issue, but the relationships or roles behind it.

- Effective leadership involves recognizing when to **de-escalate minor conflicts** and **focus attention on real priorities**.

- Sayre's Law is a mirror for any group prone to **internal politics, status jockeying, or insularity**.

51. Paradox of Inquiry

Theory

The **Paradox of Inquiry**, also known as **Meno's Paradox**, is a foundational problem in **epistemology** — the study of knowledge — famously presented by Plato in his dialogue *Meno*. The paradox questions how learning or inquiry is possible, particularly when the subject matter is something unknown. If you already know what you're looking for, inquiry is unnecessary. If you don't know what you're looking for, then how will you recognize it when you find it? This dilemma appears to undermine the very possibility of learning.

Socrates, speaking to Meno, frames the paradox like this:

"How will you search for something, Socrates, when you don't know at all what it is? How will you know when you've found it?"

In short: **If you know what you're looking for, you don't need to inquire. If you don't know what you're looking for, inquiry seems impossible.** Either way, inquiry appears pointless — hence the paradox.

Example

Imagine someone has never seen or heard of a pangolin. They're told to go find one, but they don't know what it looks like, sounds like, or where it might be found. According to the paradox, their search would be impossible: without any knowledge, they wouldn't even recognize a pangolin if they stumbled upon it.

On the other hand, if they had a clear idea of what a pangolin was, then their search wouldn't be a discovery — it would be confirmation. Thus, genuine learning seems caught in a trap between total ignorance and total knowledge.

Why It Works

The paradox is effective because it challenges a basic assumption of intellectual progress: that knowledge can be acquired from a state of ignorance. It exposes a hidden tension in how we conceive of inquiry. The dilemma arises from assuming that knowledge must be either **fully present** or **completely absent**, leaving no room for partial understanding or discovery through process.

This binary view overlooks the reality that much of human learning is **gradual, iterative, and guided by curiosity**, not a sudden leap from total ignorance to complete knowledge.

How It Works

The paradox operates by turning **epistemic logic** against itself. It asks: how can an unknown thing be the object of a directed search? It suggests that in order to inquire about something, one must already have some knowledge of it — but if that's true, then inquiry is redundant.

Plato addresses this issue through his theory of **anamnesis** (recollection). He argues that the soul is immortal and has already encountered all truths in a previous existence. Learning, then, is a form of remembering. This metaphysical solution sidesteps the paradox by proposing that inquiry is successful because the knowledge is latent within us, not generated from nothing.

Modern responses reject the metaphysics but resolve the paradox by recognizing the role of **hypothesis**, **approximation**, and **exploration**. Inquiry is possible because we often start with partial or vague concepts and refine them as we go.

Application

The Paradox of Inquiry continues to influence **educational theory**, **cognitive science**, and **AI research**. In teaching, it underlines the importance of scaffolding — providing learners with just enough information to guide discovery. In AI, it mirrors challenges in unsupervised learning, where machines must find patterns without being explicitly told what to look for.

It also informs philosophical discussions about **concept formation**, **curiosity**, and how minds engage with the unknown.

Key Insights

1. **Learning Emerges from Partial Knowledge**: We rarely begin inquiry from total ignorance.
2. **Inquiry Is Dynamic**: It evolves through stages of guessing, testing, and refining.

3. **Knowledge Is Recognized, Not Always Defined**: We can often recognize truth without being able to define it in advance.

4. **Refutes the Binary of Knowing vs. Not Knowing**: Inquiry operates in the gray areas.

5. **Supports Constructivist Theories**: Knowledge is built over time, not simply acquired in a single moment.

The Paradox of Inquiry remains a timeless reflection on the nature of learning, reminding us that the pursuit of knowledge is not only possible — it's often driven by the very uncertainties that seem to threaten it.

52. Löb's Paradox

Theory
Löb's Paradox arises from formal logic, specifically **provability logic**, and is based on **Löb's Theorem**, formulated by Martin Hugo Löb in 1955. The paradox reveals a subtle and surprising issue in formal systems capable of self-reference, such as Peano Arithmetic. Löb's Theorem states:

If a formal system can prove that "if a statement is provable, then it is true," then it can also prove the statement itself.

Formally, if a system proves **"□P → P"**, then it can prove **P**, where "□P" means "P is provable." While this might seem harmless at first glance, it leads to a paradox when applied to certain types of self-referential statements — especially those similar to the Liar Paradox or Gödel's incompleteness constructions.

The paradox emerges when one tries to reason about a sentence that says of itself: **"If I am provable, then I am true."** Löb's theorem implies that such a sentence, under certain conditions, must then be provable — even if it says something suspicious or counterintuitive.

Example
Suppose in a formal system, we have a sentence **L** that says:

"If L is provable, then I am Santa Claus."

At first, this seems like a meaningless or whimsical statement. But Löb's Theorem implies that if the system can prove "If L is provable, then I am Santa Claus," then it must also be able to prove "I am Santa Claus" — even though "I am Santa Claus" is clearly false (assuming we're not Santa Claus).

This becomes troubling when the system's ability to reflect on its own proofs leads it to endorse falsehoods, based solely on structural reasoning — not on the actual content or truth of the statements.

Why It Works
Löb's Paradox works by exploiting **self-reference** and the formal properties of provability in logical systems. It rests on three key ideas:

1. **Self-referential statements can be constructed** within the system (similar to Gödel numbering).

2. The system can prove meta-statements about its own proofs.

3. Logical inference rules like modus ponens allow implications to be chained.

When these elements come together, the system is forced into affirming statements not on the basis of their content, but because of how they are phrased in relation to provability — leading to paradoxical outcomes.

How It Works
Löb's Theorem is proven using **diagonalization**, a method for constructing self-referential sentences. The paradox arises

when a statement effectively says, "If I am provable, then something surprising (or false) must be true." The formal system, following Löb's reasoning, then ends up proving the surprising thing — not because it's true, but because of how the logic treats provability.

This undermines the idea that provability guarantees truth and reveals a dangerous gap between **syntactic provability** (what can be derived using formal rules) and **semantic truth** (what is actually true in the model).

Application

Löb's Paradox has critical implications in **mathematical logic**, **proof theory**, and **artificial intelligence**. It plays a role in the design of systems that reason about their own reasoning — such as reflective AI agents or automated theorem provers. It also contributes to foundational questions about **formal consistency**, **self-reference**, and the limits of **formal epistemology**.

In **Gödel-Löb provability logic**, the paradox forms part of the basis for understanding the relationship between proof, truth, and fixed-point constructions.

Key Insights

1. **Provability ≠ Truth**: Formal systems can prove things for structural reasons that aren't semantically valid.

2. **Self-Reference Is Dangerous**: When systems refer to their own proofs, contradictions and paradoxes can emerge.

3. **Limits of Formal Systems**: There are boundaries to what logical systems can reliably express about themselves.

4. **Gödel and Löb Are Connected**: Löb's theorem extends Gödel's insight about self-referential statements and incompleteness.

5. **Reflection Requires Caution**: Systems that reason about their own reasoning (like AI or proof assistants) must be carefully constrained.

Löb's Paradox is a powerful illustration of how formal logic, though seemingly precise, can unravel when faced with self-reference — reminding us that even in the most rigorous systems, paradox lies just beneath the surface.

Probability & Statistical Paradoxes

Statistical reasoning leads to counterintuitive outcomes.

53. Simpson's Paradox

Theory Overview

Simpson's Paradox is a phenomenon in **statistics and probability theory** where a trend present in several different groups of data **reverses or disappears** when the groups are combined. Also known as the **Yule–Simpson effect**, the paradox illustrates how **aggregated data can mislead**, especially when underlying subgroups differ significantly in size or composition.

First formally described by statistician **Edward H. Simpson** in 1951 (though earlier versions appeared from Karl Pearson and George Udny Yule), the paradox demonstrates that **correlations and comparisons can be completely reversed** when data is grouped differently. This has profound implications in **data science, medical studies, social sciences, and public policy**.

Example

Consider a university evaluating gender bias in admissions. Suppose:

- In **Department A**, 80% of women are accepted, 60% of men are.

- In **Department B**, 30% of women are accepted, 20% of men are.

So, within each department, **women have a higher acceptance rate**. However, when the data is combined:

- **Women** applied mostly to the highly competitive Department B.
- **Men** applied mostly to the less competitive Department A.

As a result, **overall acceptance rate** for women appears lower than for men—creating the illusion of gender bias **against women**, even though each department favoured them.

This reversal—where **aggregated data suggests one conclusion**, but **disaggregated data reveals the opposite**—is the hallmark of Simpson's Paradox.

Why It Works

The paradox works because it reveals the **confounding effect of lurking variables**, especially when group sizes differ. In the example, **department choice** is the hidden variable. Ignoring it leads to incorrect interpretations.

Humans naturally trust summary statistics. We assume that combining data gives us a clearer picture, but **aggregation can obscure essential context**. When confounding variables influence both the independent and dependent variables, conclusions from the aggregated data can be not just misleading, but **entirely wrong**.

How It Works

Simpson's Paradox is a result of:

1. **Weighted averages**: Combining percentages from different groups with different sizes distorts the overall rate.
2. **Confounding variables**: A third variable affects both the category being studied and the outcome.
3. **Data stratification**: Subgroup trends can conflict with the overall trend due to imbalanced distribution.

Mathematically, if:

- Group A has a high success rate but small sample size,
- Group B has a low success rate but large sample size,

Then the **group with more data** disproportionately influences the combined outcome—even if it had worse performance.

Application

Simpson's Paradox is critical in:

- **Epidemiology and medicine**: Drug effectiveness can appear reversed when not accounting for age or health condition.

- **Public policy**: Arrest or sentencing rates may show racial disparity unless properly stratified.

- **Sports statistics**: A player's performance might seem worse when combining years or conditions without context.

- **Machine learning**: Algorithms must avoid drawing false correlations from unadjusted data.

It's a key reminder that **data interpretation requires more than just numbers—it demands context and structure**.

Key Insights

- **Aggregation can mislead**: Trends in combined data may contradict subgroup trends.

- Always check for **confounding variables** or **uneven group sizes**.

- Statistical reasoning must be **sensitive to context**, not just raw output.

- Simpson's Paradox teaches caution: **summary statistics aren't always summary truths**.

- It highlights the need for **careful data segmentation**, especially in high-stakes decisions.

54. Two Envelopes Paradox

Theory Overview

The **Two Envelopes Paradox** is a classic problem in probability and decision theory that exposes the limitations of **expected value reasoning** and the misapplication of probabilistic logic. At its core, the paradox suggests that no matter which envelope you choose, you should always switch—leading to an infinite loop of second-guessing.

The setup involves two envelopes, each containing a **positive sum of money**. One envelope contains **twice as much as the other**, but you don't know which is which. You are allowed to choose one and, before opening it, are given the opportunity to **switch**. The paradox arises when a seemingly logical calculation implies that switching always yields a higher expected value—**no matter which envelope you initially picked**.

Example

Suppose you pick Envelope A. You don't know what's inside, but for argument's sake, let's say it contains **$100**.

Since one envelope has double the other, the other envelope (Envelope B) must contain **either $50 or $200**. Assuming a 50/50 chance of either:

- Expected value of switching =

    (½ × $50) + (½ × $200) = $25 + $100 = **$125**

This suggests switching gives you a higher expected value than sticking with your current envelope. But if this logic holds no matter what amount is in your envelope, it means **you should always switch**—even after switching—leading to an **infinite loop of irrational choice**.

Why It Works

The paradox works because it **misleads through expectation calculation** that doesn't correctly account for the **underlying distribution** of values. The key mistake is in assuming a 50/50 chance that the other envelope contains half or double **the amount you currently see**, without considering whether that amount could even appear in such a distribution.

For instance, if the envelope you open contains $100, it's only reasonable to consider the chances that the total money involved would permit such amounts. But if there's no clear upper bound, or if all amounts are equally likely, then the expectation calculation becomes ill-defined.

This paradox highlights the difference between **conditional and unconditional probabilities**, and the importance of knowing the **prior distribution** of amounts used in setting up the envelopes.

How It Works

The paradox involves:

1. **Symmetric reasoning**: Each envelope is equally likely to be the higher one.

2. **Faulty expected value logic**: Assuming that switching always leads to a higher expectation.

3. **Ignoring priors**: No information about how the envelope amounts were chosen, making the expectation calculation **invalid or undefined**.

A more rigorous approach would specify how the money amounts were chosen (e.g., from a finite set or a particular probability distribution), which would break the symmetry and clarify the rational choice.

Application

The Two Envelopes Paradox is influential in:

- **Decision theory**: Highlighting the limits of naive expected value calculations.

- **Economics**: Modelling choices under uncertainty.

- **Philosophy of probability**: Illustrating the difference between **epistemic probabilities** (what we believe) and **frequentist probabilities** (based on real frequencies).

- **Game theory and AI**: Designing agents that can make stable decisions under asymmetric or unclear information.

Key Insights

- **Naive expectation calculations** can lead to irrational infinite loops.

- **Context and information about distributions** matter in probabilistic decision-making.

- The paradox illustrates that **expectation alone isn't always a good guide** when information is incomplete.

- Real-world decision-making requires **constraints, priors, or utility functions** to avoid paradoxical reasoning.

- The problem is not with probability itself, but with the **improper framing and assumptions** of the scenario.

55. Raven Paradox (Hempel's)

Theory Overview

The **Raven Paradox** (also called **Hempel's Paradox**) is a thought experiment in the philosophy of science and logic, introduced by **Carl Gustav Hempel** in the 1940s. It explores the **problem of confirmation** in inductive reasoning, specifically how evidence supports universal generalizations. The paradox exposes a deep tension between **logical equivalence** and **intuitive relevance** in what counts as evidence for a hypothesis.

The paradox stems from considering how we confirm statements like:

"All ravens are black."

According to classical logic, the **contrapositive** of this statement is:

"All non-black things are not ravens."

Since the two statements are logically equivalent, any observation confirming the second should also confirm the first. This leads to a counterintuitive consequence: **observing a green apple (a non-black non-raven)** supports the claim that all ravens are black.

Example

Let's unpack the paradox with a real-world analogy:

Suppose you want to confirm the hypothesis "All ravens are black." You go out and observe a thousand black ravens. Each black raven seemingly strengthens your hypothesis.

But now, according to logical equivalence, any observation of a **non-black object that is not a raven** also supports your hypothesis—since it affirms that non-black things are indeed not ravens.

So, by this logic, **seeing a red book or a green apple** would also be evidence that all ravens are black.

This conclusion feels absurd. How can a green apple have anything meaningful to say about the colour of ravens?

Why It Works

The paradox works because it lays bare a conflict between **formal logic** and **our intuitive notions of relevance and empirical support**. In propositional logic, statements and their contrapositives are equivalent—what confirms one should confirm the other. But in practical scientific reasoning, we judge evidence not just by logical structure, but also by **causal or observational relevance**.

The paradox forces us to question **what it means for evidence to be confirmatory**, and whether all logical consequences are epistemically equal. It also highlights the challenge of **inductive logic**, where universal generalizations are formed from finite observations.

How It Works

The Raven Paradox hinges on:

1. **Universal generalization**: "All ravens are black."
2. **Contrapositive equivalence**: "All non-black things are not ravens."
3. **Confirmation theory**: Any instance confirming the contrapositive should, in principle, confirm the original statement.

Observing a black raven clearly supports the original statement. But by logical equivalence, so does observing a white shoe or a blue chair—since they are **non-black non-ravens**, which conform to the contrapositive.

The problem is that the number of non-black non-ravens is **vast**, so the **incremental confirmation** provided by any one such observation is negligible. Still, **formally**, it counts as support.

Application

The paradox is influential in:

- **Philosophy of science**: In debates on confirmation theory, falsifiability, and evidence relevance.

- **Bayesian epistemology**: Where degrees of belief and probabilistic confirmation modify how evidence is weighed.

- **Artificial intelligence and machine learning**: In logic-based inference engines and systems that assess evidential support.

- **Cognitive psychology**: Studies how people actually reason about generalizations and bias in evidence gathering.

Key Insights

- **Logical equivalence doesn't imply evidential equivalence**—relevance matters.

- The paradox reveals limits in **purely formal approaches to scientific reasoning**.

- Confirmation depends not just on structure, but on **context, background knowledge, and probabilities**.

- It challenges us to refine our understanding of **what counts as good evidence**.

- The paradox has pushed developments in **Bayesian confirmation theory** and alternative models of inductive logic.

56. Ross–Littlewood Paradox

Theory Overview

The **Ross–Littlewood Paradox**, also known as the **infinite balls and vase paradox**, is a mathematical thought experiment that explores the **counterintuitive nature of infinite processes**, particularly those involving **limits** and **infinite sequences of actions**. First introduced by **Shelby Ross** and **J.E. Littlewood**, the paradox demonstrates how applying infinite steps over a finite time can yield **unexpected or seemingly contradictory outcomes**—especially depending on *how* those steps are defined.

At its core, the paradox shows that depending on the **removal and addition process**, you can end up with a **vase that is full, empty, or any arbitrary configuration**—even when the steps are all "finite" at each stage. This is not due to faulty logic, but rather the **subtleties of infinity**, especially how limits and sequences converge.

Example

Here is the classic formulation:

You have an **empty vase** and an **infinite supply of numbered balls**: Ball 1, Ball 2, Ball 3, and so on.

At **1 minute before midnight**, you:

- Put balls 1 through 10 into the vase.
- Remove ball 1.

At **30 seconds before midnight**, you:

- Put in balls 11 through 20.
- Remove ball 2.

At **15 seconds before midnight**, you:

- Add balls 21 through 30.
- Remove ball 3.

And so on, halving the time between steps and always removing the lowest-numbered remaining ball. This process continues infinitely, ending exactly at midnight.

Question: How many balls are in the vase at midnight?

Answer (surprisingly): **Zero**.

Even though you're adding infinitely many balls, each ball **eventually gets removed**. Ball 1 is removed in the first step, ball 2 in the second, ball 3 in the third, and so on. Therefore, by midnight, **no ball remains**.

Why It Works

This paradox works because it challenges our intuition about **accumulation over time**. We usually think that if we keep adding objects faster and faster, the total should grow. However, because **each specific ball has a defined time of removal**, *no ball survives* the infinite process.

The paradox reveals the distinction between an **infinite number of operations** and the **limit** of what remains. Infinity is not just "a lot"—it's a fundamentally different type of quantity, governed by set theory, ordinal limits, and convergence behaviour.

How It Works

The core mechanics involve:

1. A **countably infinite** number of operations.
2. Each operation consisting of **finite addition and removal**.
3. **Diminishing time intervals**, summing to a finite endpoint (midnight).
4. A removal sequence that ensures **each ball has a known exit point**.

Mathematically, it's about how the **limit of a sequence** can yield results that defy step-by-step expectations. If the rules changed—for example, if you didn't remove any balls or removed a random selection—you could end with **infinitely many balls**, or a completely different result.

Application

This paradox has deep implications in:

- **Mathematical analysis**: Particularly in understanding **limits, convergence,** and **infinite series**.

- **Set theory and logic**: Illustrates properties of **ordinal numbers** and **countable infinities**.

- **Philosophy of mathematics**: Challenges assumptions about infinity and determinism in completed processes.

- **Computer science**: Influences thinking about iterative loops, convergence in algorithms, and resource modelling.

It also plays a role in discussions about **Zeno's paradoxes, supertasks**, and whether an infinite number of actions can be completed in finite time.

Key Insights

- Infinite processes can produce **non-intuitive outcomes** based on how they're structured.

- The **order and method** of infinite actions matter more than the sheer quantity.

- The concept of a **completed infinity** is logically consistent but philosophically rich.

- The paradox underscores that **limits** don't always reflect **cumulative behaviour**.

- It's a vivid example of how **mathematical infinity diverges sharply from physical intuition**.

57. Birthday Paradox

Theory Overview

The **Birthday Paradox** is a famous problem in probability theory that reveals a **counterintuitive truth** about how likely it is for two people in a group to share the same birthday. Despite being called a paradox, it's not a logical contradiction—it's a **surprising statistical result** that defies our intuitions about probability.

The paradox states that in a group of just **23 people**, there's over a **50% chance** that **at least two people share the same birthday**. That's far lower than most people would guess. Intuitively, we often compare individuals to a fixed date (e.g., "What are the odds someone has *my* birthday?"), rather than considering **all possible pairwise comparisons** within the group.

Example

Imagine a classroom with 23 students. Most people would think the chance of a birthday match is relatively low. After all, there are 365 days in a year, so it feels like the odds should be small.

But the math tells a different story.

Instead of calculating the probability that **someone shares a birthday**, we calculate the probability that **no one shares a birthday**, and subtract that from 1.

- For the first person, any birthday is fine: **365/365**.
- For the second person, to avoid a match: **364/365**.
- For the third: **363/365**, and so on.

Multiplying these probabilities for all 23 people:

$$P(nomatch) \approx 365/365 \times 364/365 \times 363/365 \times \ldots \times 343/365 \approx 0.4927$$

Therefore, the probability of **at least one match** is:

$$1 - 0.4927 \approx 0.5073$$

(or 50.73%)

This is the heart of the paradox: **just 23 people** suffice to make a birthday match **more likely than not**.

Why It Works

The paradox works by exploiting the **combinatorial explosion of pairings**. In a group of n people, there are $n(n-1)/2$ unique pairs. So even though each individual has a low chance of sharing a birthday with someone else, the number of comparisons **grows rapidly** with each additional person.

This means the total chance of any match increases much faster than intuition expects. Our brains are not naturally wired to handle exponential combinations or probability over large event spaces, which is why this result feels paradoxical.

How It Works

The paradox is best understood through **complementary probability**:

1. Calculate the probability that all birthdays are different (no matches).
2. Subtract that from 1 to find the probability of **at least one match**.

This method uses basic multiplication and fractional reduction. The paradox becomes stronger with more people:

- 30 people → 70.6% chance of a match
- 50 people → 97% chance
- 70 people → 99.9% chance

The increase is **nonlinear**, which surprises most people.

Application

The Birthday Paradox has practical use in:

- **Cryptography**: Particularly in **hash functions**, where it informs the design of algorithms to resist "birthday attacks," a method of exploiting hash collisions.

- **Computer science**: Used in randomized algorithms, hashing, and load balancing.

- **Probability education**: A go-to example for teaching how human intuition can misjudge statistical phenomena.

- **Simulation and data testing**: Helps anticipate collisions in randomly generated identifiers or dates.

Key Insights

- **Probability can defy intuition**, especially with combinations and large sample spaces.

- The paradox reveals how **group dynamics amplify probabilities**.

- Understanding complementary probability is key to grasping the concept.

- It shows how **multiple small probabilities** can add up to a **significant overall risk**.

- The Birthday Paradox is a prime example of how **statistical literacy** can clarify misleading assumptions.

58. Newcomb-like Variants

Theory Overview

Newcomb-like Variants are philosophical and decision-theoretic puzzles inspired by the original **Newcomb's Paradox**, a thought experiment introduced by physicist **William Newcomb** and made famous by philosopher **Robert Nozick**. These variants explore tensions between two fundamental principles in decision theory:

1. **Expected Utility Maximization** (associated with **Causal Decision Theory** or CDT), and
2. **Dominance Reasoning** (associated with **Evidential Decision Theory** or EDT).

Newcomb's Paradox and its variants involve scenarios where **prediction, causality, and rational choice** come into apparent conflict. The central question is: **Should we act based on how our choices causally affect the future, or based on what our choices indicate about the world?**

Variants of Newcomb's Paradox tweak assumptions about **predictive power, information asymmetry**, or **game structure**, creating new dilemmas that test our intuitions about rationality, free will, and knowledge.

Example (Standard Newcomb Scenario)

A superintelligent predictor places two boxes before you:

- **Box A** contains $1,000.
- **Box B** contains either $1 million or nothing.

You can either:

- Take **both boxes (A + B)**, or
- Take **only Box B**.

The predictor has already made a prediction about your choice. If it predicted you'd take only Box B, it **put $1 million in it**. If it predicted you'd take both boxes, it **left Box B empty**. The predictor is almost always right.

Evidential Decision Theory (EDT) suggests you should take only Box B: your action is strong evidence that the predictor filled it.

Causal Decision Theory (CDT) says you should take both: your current choice can't change what's already in Box B.

Newcomb-like Variants

Several variants introduce new twists:

1. **Retro-Newcomb**: A predictor makes its choice *after* you act but is still nearly always correct. This tests **retrocausality** and rational expectations.

2. **Transparent Newcomb**: Both boxes are see-through. If you see $1 million in Box B, do you still take both? Now the puzzle becomes one of **precommitment and trust**.

3. **Twin Prisoner Variant**: You're paired with an identical mind-twin who makes the same choice. What you choose becomes *probabilistic evidence* of their action, altering expected outcomes.

4. **Smoking Lesion**: A gene causes both smoking and cancer. Does choosing not to smoke reduce your chance of cancer? This pushes on **statistical correlation vs. causation**.

Each variant forces a re-evaluation of what "rational" really means under uncertainty.

Why It Works

Newcomb-like variants are paradoxical because they put two core intuitions at odds:

- **The dominance principle**: More is better, so take both boxes.

- **Predictive consistency**: If the predictor is nearly perfect, your one-boxing is evidence the money is there.

The paradox emerges when agents must decide **not only what action to take**, but **what kind of decision-maker to be**. These variants challenge how we think about **agency**, **evidence**, and **control** over outcomes.

How It Works

The key mechanics in Newcomb-like variants involve:

- **Highly accurate prediction** or symmetry (across time or agents).
- **Conflicts between causal and evidential reasoning**.
- **Temporal asymmetry**, where predictions influence or correlate with decisions.
- **Counterfactual dependence**, where what *could* have been matters more than what *is*.

Some theories—like **Functional Decision Theory (FDT)**—have been developed to resolve these conflicts, arguing agents should act based on the **logical structure** of decision-making, not mere causal or evidential consequences.

Application

These paradoxes are highly relevant in:

- **Artificial intelligence and game theory**: Informing how autonomous agents interact in strategic environments.
- **Ethics and rationality**: Challenging how we justify actions when reasoning under uncertainty.
- **Philosophy of mind**: Exploring how prediction, identity, and rational self-modelling influence action.

- **Economics and policy modelling**: Clarifying assumptions in behavioural incentives and game outcomes.

Key Insights

- Rationality depends not just on outcomes, but on **how decisions reflect and influence beliefs**.
- Predictions, even if passive, **reshape incentives**.
- Newcomb-like variants push us to rethink **causation vs. correlation** in real decisions.
- The choice you make can be evidence **about you**, not just **for you**.
- These scenarios suggest that rational agents may need to **commit to non-dominant actions** in order to win.

59. Zeigarnik Effect

Theory Overview

The **Zeigarnik Effect** is a psychological phenomenon that refers to the **tendency of people to remember incomplete or interrupted tasks better than completed ones**. Named after Soviet psychologist **Bluma Zeigarnik**, who discovered it in the 1920s, the effect highlights how our cognitive processes attach greater mental weight to tasks that remain unresolved.

Zeigarnik's insight originated from observing that waiters seemed to recall unpaid orders more vividly than paid ones. Once a bill was settled, the details faded. This led her to experimentally test the idea that **unfinished tasks create a kind of mental tension or cognitive dissonance**, which persists until the task is complete.

This tension acts as a **motivational force**, keeping the task active in working memory. The moment the task is completed, the tension—and the need to remember—dissipates.

Example

Imagine you're writing an email, but you're interrupted by a phone call halfway through. For the rest of the day, the incomplete email may keep popping into your mind. You may even recall its wording more vividly than the other emails you finished. Once you return to complete and send it, that mental "open loop" closes, and you likely stop thinking about it.

Another example is binge-watching a TV series that ends every episode on a cliffhanger. The unresolved tension **keeps your attention hooked**, making it hard to stop mid-series. This is a real-world application of the Zeigarnik Effect in media and design.

Why It Works

The Zeigarnik Effect works due to how human cognition manages memory, motivation, and task completion. Incomplete tasks create **internal cognitive tension** that prompts the brain to **keep the task active in working memory**. This tension isn't necessarily conscious, but it drives recall and focus.

It also connects to **goal-setting theory**: when a goal is defined but unfulfilled, the brain remains engaged until closure is achieved. Completion provides a sense of resolution, allowing memory traces to be safely discarded or moved to long-term storage.

How It Works

Zeigarnik's original experiments involved giving participants a series of tasks (puzzles, arithmetic, etc.), interrupting half before completion. Later, when participants were asked to recall the tasks, they remembered the interrupted ones **twice as often** as the completed ones.

Cognitively, the effect is supported by:

- **Working memory persistence**: The brain prioritizes active goals.
- **Tension-based memory encoding**: Incomplete tasks cause mild stress, which enhances memory encoding.
- **Goal non-completion**: The mind seeks closure and holds onto unresolved intentions (known as "open loops").

Neuroscientific research suggests that **dopamine systems** may play a role, as anticipation and tension keep the reward system activated, increasing attention and recall.

Application

The Zeigarnik Effect has wide-ranging implications:

- **Education**: Strategically pausing lessons or questions can enhance memory retention.
- **Productivity**: Awareness of open tasks can improve to-do list design and task management.
- **Marketing**: Advertisers use it by creating open loops—unanswered questions or stories that compel continued engagement.

- **User experience (UX)**: Progress bars, achievement tracking, or unfinished forms create motivational tension to complete interactions.

- **Psychotherapy**: In cognitive-behavioural therapy, unfinished emotional or cognitive loops may be identified and resolved.

Key Insights

- Incomplete tasks **occupy mental space**, increasing attention and recall.

- The human brain is naturally driven to **seek closure** and resolve tension.

- Awareness of this effect can improve **task management, memory, and motivation**.

- It's a double-edged sword: open loops can **drive focus** or cause **stress and mental clutter**.

- The effect underscores how **memory and motivation are not purely logical**—they're emotionally and cognitively intertwined.

60. Law of Small Numbers Paradox

Law of Small Numbers Paradox: A Breakdown

Theory
The **Law of Small Numbers Paradox** is a cognitive and statistical paradox that emerges from our tendency to expect **small samples** to reflect the **statistical properties of larger populations**. The paradox lies in the **misapplication of the Law of Large Numbers**, which states that, as sample size increases, the sample mean will converge to the population mean. The error occurs when people assume this principle applies **even to small samples**, expecting them to behave "fairly" and reflect overall probabilities — when in fact, small samples are prone to **extreme variation**.

This mistaken belief leads to flawed judgments in fields like psychology, economics, education, and medicine. The term was famously used by psychologists **Amos Tversky and Daniel Kahneman**, who demonstrated that humans consistently **overgeneralize from small samples**, leading to systemic biases and irrational conclusions.

Example
Imagine you flip a fair coin six times. You get: **Heads, Tails, Heads, Heads, Heads, Heads**. Many people would be surprised and suspect the coin is biased, because this outcome seems "unbalanced." However, statistically, this result is just as likely as any other combination of six flips.

People erroneously expect **"HTHTHT"** or similarly alternating patterns to be more common — as if randomness must look evenly mixed, even in tiny samples.

Similarly, if two hospitals record the number of days with more than 60% male births, the smaller hospital is more likely to show extreme values (very high or low percentages), yet people often think both hospitals should show the same rate. This misjudgement is a key illustration of the paradox.

Why It Works

The paradox works because it plays on our **intuitive misunderstanding of probability** and **pattern recognition**. The human brain is wired to see patterns and assume that randomness means balance or uniformity. We expect even short sequences to reflect underlying distributions (like a 50/50 coin flip), and we grow suspicious when they don't.

This is compounded by the **representativeness heuristic** — a cognitive bias where people judge probabilities based on how closely one thing resembles another. If a sample "doesn't look" like the population, people assume something must be wrong, when actually, that's normal for small datasets.

How It Works

The Law of Large Numbers guarantees long-term convergence to expected values, but in small samples, **statistical variance is large**. The paradox emerges when we **ignore variance** and assume small samples are just as reliable as large ones.

The error can be formalized through statistical simulations showing that small samples produce more extreme and volatile results. Yet, paradoxically, people **trust small samples too much**, assuming they tell the whole story. This is particularly dangerous in decision-making where limited data is treated as conclusive.

Application

The Law of Small Numbers Paradox has wide-reaching implications:

- In **medical trials**, early results from small studies may look promising but fail to replicate.

- In **finance**, investors may misjudge trends based on a few data points, leading to flawed forecasts.

- In **education**, identifying the "best" or "worst" schools from small populations can be misleading.

- In **machine learning**, overfitting occurs when models learn from insufficient or noisy data — essentially trusting small samples too much.

Tversky and Kahneman's research emphasized the need for **statistical literacy**, especially in fields where probabilistic reasoning affects real-world outcomes.

Key Insights

1. **Small Samples Are Misleading**: They tend to show more extreme outcomes and are poor representations of populations.

2. **People Overgeneralize Quickly**: We often form broad conclusions from limited evidence.

3. **Randomness Isn't Always Balanced**: Short-term irregularities are normal and shouldn't be mistaken for patterns.

4. **Cognitive Bias Drives the Paradox**: The representativeness heuristic skews our perception of randomness.

5. **Larger Samples Reduce Error**: Reliable inference requires adequate data size and statistical awareness.

The Law of Small Numbers Paradox reminds us that **more data isn't just better — it's essential**. Until then, our intuitions about randomness and probability may lead us consistently astray.

61. Parrondo's Paradox

Theory
Parrondo's Paradox is a counterintuitive result in **game theory** and **probability theory**, discovered by physicist Juan Parrondo in the late 1990s. It shows that two **losing strategies**, when combined in a specific way, can paradoxically result in a **winning outcome**. This challenges the intuition that combining two unfavourable situations should logically make things worse, not better.

Originally inspired by physical systems in **statistical mechanics** (like Brownian ratchets), the paradox has since been applied to economics, evolutionary biology, and artificial intelligence. At its core, it demonstrates that in **nonlinear, probabilistic systems**, the interaction between components can produce emergent behaviour that defies the behaviour of the parts taken individually.

Example
Imagine two simple games, **Game A** and **Game B**, both of which are losing games when played on their own.

- **Game A**: You flip a biased coin that wins you $1 with a 49% chance and loses you $1 with a 51% chance. Over time, you lose money.
- **Game B**: More complex. If your current capital is a multiple of 3, you use a very bad coin (9% chance to win). If not, you use a better coin (74% chance to win). Despite

the occasional good outcome, this game also causes a net loss over time.

Now, here's the twist: if you **alternate** between Game A and Game B — say, randomly or in a fixed pattern — the combined result can be a **winning game**, where your capital increases over time. This is Parrondo's Paradox in action.

Why It Works
The paradox works because it exploits **context-dependent outcomes** and **nonlinear feedback** in probabilistic systems. Each game alone sets up a losing condition, but they interact in a way that breaks the internal negative feedback loops of each other. Game A injects randomness into Game B's periodic structure, preventing Game B from exploiting its own worst-case scenarios.

This interplay leads to constructive interference — a kind of beneficial chaos — that, over time, yields a positive expected gain. It's not that randomness "cancels out" loss, but rather that **alternating between the two games disrupts the systemic losses built into each**, allowing room for growth.

How It Works
Mathematically, Parrondo's Paradox is explained through **Markov chains**, **stochastic processes**, and **state-dependent transitions**. Game B's structure depends on the player's capital, and alternating between the two games alters the transition probabilities between states in a way that makes favourable states more likely in the long run.

It's an instance of **nonlinear dynamics**, where the system's outcome isn't simply the sum of its parts. The paradox reveals how **temporal or structural interactions** can reverse expected outcomes in surprising ways.

Application

Parrondo's Paradox has applications in diverse fields:

- In **finance**, alternating investment strategies (even suboptimal ones) can outperform a single consistent strategy under certain market conditions.

- In **evolutionary biology**, alternating environmental pressures (each detrimental alone) may promote genetic diversity or resilience.

- In **computational algorithms**, random noise or switching between heuristics can help escape local optima and improve overall performance.

- In **game design and decision theory**, it shows how complex strategy cycles can yield better results than static ones.

Key Insights

1. **Interactions Matter More Than Parts**: The system's behaviour isn't just a sum of its components — the sequence and structure matter.

2. **Losing + Losing ≠ Losing**: In complex systems, two bad strategies can combine to yield good results.

3. **Randomness Can Be Constructive**: Strategic randomness can destabilize loss-making patterns and create opportunity.

4. **State Dependence Is Crucial**: Context (like capital mod 3 in Game B) determines outcomes more than static probabilities.

5. **Challenges Linear Thinking**: Parrondo's Paradox reveals the power of **nonlinearity**, randomness, and time-based interactions in shaping outcomes.

In essence, Parrondo's Paradox offers a profound insight: in the right structure, **failure itself can be a building block of success.**

62. Sleeping Beauty Paradox

Theory Overview

The **Sleeping Beauty Paradox** is a thought experiment in **probability theory and philosophy of belief**, particularly concerning **self-locating uncertainty**—that is, uncertainty about one's own place in time. Introduced by **Arnold Zuboff** and popularized by **Adam Elga** in the early 2000s, it presents a puzzle about how to update beliefs when learning information about subjective experience rather than objective facts.

The paradox questions how an agent should update their belief about the outcome of a random event after undergoing memory erasure and repeated awakening. It has sparked intense debate between two camps: the **"thirder"** position and the **"halfer"** position, which differ in how they interpret the probabilities involved.

Example

Here's the standard scenario:

1. **Sleeping Beauty** volunteers for a study.
2. On **Sunday**, she is put to sleep.
3. A fair coin is flipped:
    - If **Heads**, she is awakened once on **Monday**.

- If **Tails**, she is awakened **on Monday and again on Tuesday**, but her memory of Monday is erased before Tuesday, so both awakenings are subjectively indistinguishable.

4. After each awakening, she is asked:

"What is your degree of belief that the coin landed Heads?"

What should she say?

- **"Halfers"** argue her belief should be **1/2**, since the coin is fair and no new relevant information has been gained.

- **"Thirders"** argue it should be **1/3**, because in the long run, only 1 in 3 awakenings happens in the Heads scenario.

Why It Works

The paradox works because it separates **objective probability** (the coin toss) from **subjective experience** (her awakening). The coin is flipped once, but her memory is tampered with, so she cannot distinguish one awakening from another. This creates a **measure problem**: how do we count experiences or instances when updating beliefs?

The **thirder view** uses a frequentist logic: if this experiment were run many times, out of every three awakenings, only one corresponds to Heads. The **halfer view** appeals to a Bayesian update rule: since Beauty gains no new factual information about the coin toss, she should retain her prior belief of 1/2.

How It Works

The paradox hinges on different interpretations of probability:

- **Thirders** use **Bayesian reasoning** where the number of indistinguishable observer-moments (two for Tails, one for Heads) matters. Each awakening is treated as a random sample from a larger pool.

- **Halfers** treat the coin flip as an isolated event, and see no justification to revise the initial belief based on subjective experience alone.

Mathematically:

- Let **P(H)** = probability coin landed Heads.
- In the long run:
    - 1 Heads awakening : 2 Tails awakenings
    - So, **P(H | awakening)** = 1/3

However, without a third-person perspective on the frequency of awakenings, some argue this is not a proper Bayesian update.

Application

The Sleeping Beauty Paradox is relevant to:

- **Epistemology**: Examines belief updating and rational credence under uncertainty.

- **Decision theory**: Affects how agents should reason when duplicated or memory-altered.

- **Philosophy of time and identity**: Touches on how individuals understand self-locating beliefs.

- **Anthropic reasoning**: Influences arguments about observer selection in cosmology and AI alignment.

Key Insights

- **Self-locating uncertainty** complicates standard Bayesian reasoning.

- The paradox shows how identical subjective experiences can lead to **divergent rational beliefs**.

- The debate reflects deeper questions about **reference class selection**—what you consider as the "sample" for your reasoning.

- The "thirders vs. halfers" split illustrates how different assumptions about **what counts as evidence** can radically alter probability assessments.

- It's a vivid example of how **formal probability clashes with intuitive judgment**, even among experts.

63. Base Rate Fallacy Paradox

Theory

The **Base Rate Fallacy Paradox** is a cognitive and statistical error where people tend to **ignore general statistical information (base rates)** in favour of **specific information**, especially vivid or recent details. This fallacy becomes paradoxical when our intuitive judgments about probability lead to highly unreliable or even logically flawed conclusions — despite being based on seemingly sound reasoning.

The paradox arises in **Bayesian reasoning**, where rational inference depends on the proper weighting of **prior probabilities (base rates)** and **conditional evidence**. Ignoring base rates — or underweighting them — leads to dramatic misjudgements, especially in fields like medicine, law, finance, and social perception.

Example

A classic illustration:

Suppose 1% of people in a population have a rare disease. A test for the disease is 99% accurate — meaning it correctly identifies those with the disease 99% of the time and gives false positives only 1% of the time.

Now, if someone tests positive, what is the probability they actually have the disease?

Intuitively, many people say **"99%"** — after all, the test is highly accurate. But this ignores the **base rate** (only 1% of people have the disease). When we apply **Bayes' Theorem**, the actual probability is much lower.

Let's break it down:

- Out of 10,000 people:
    - 100 will have the disease (1%) → about 99 will test positive.
    - 9,900 do not have the disease → about 99 will falsely test positive.

So, for 198 total positive results, only **99 are true positives**. That means the chance of actually having the disease given a positive test is **about 50%**, not 99%.

This mismatch between statistical reality and human intuition is the base rate fallacy in action.

Why It Works

The paradox works because it leverages our natural tendency to overvalue **representative or specific evidence** and undervalue **background frequencies**. Psychologically, we find detailed or personal information more persuasive than abstract statistics. This is known as the **representativeness heuristic**, identified by Tversky and Kahneman.

Our brains are wired for **pattern recognition and narratives**, not statistical reasoning. The base rate fallacy is not just a math mistake — it's a deep cognitive bias that systematically distorts probabilistic thinking.

How It Works

The paradox can be formally modelled using **Bayes' Theorem**:

$$P(A|B) = \frac{P(B|A) \cdot P(A)}{P(B)}$$

Where:

- $P(A)$ is the base rate (prior probability),
- $P(B|A)$ is the likelihood of the evidence given A,
- $P(B)$ is the total probability of the evidence.

The fallacy occurs when we focus almost entirely on

$P(B|A)$,

the test's accuracy, and ignore

$P(A)$,

the base rate. This leads to overconfident or skewed interpretations of evidence.

Application

The Base Rate Fallacy Paradox has real-world consequences:

- In **medicine**, overdiagnosis based on test results without context can lead to unnecessary treatments.
- In **criminal justice**, juries may misinterpret DNA or eyewitness evidence if not guided by statistical literacy.

- In **finance**, investors may overreact to recent trends and ignore broader economic indicators.

- In **machine learning**, improper handling of class imbalance (ignoring base rates of different labels) leads to biased models.

Combating the fallacy requires deliberate education in **Bayesian reasoning, probabilistic thinking,** and **data literacy.**

Key Insights

1. **Specific Evidence Isn't Everything**: Context and prior probabilities matter.

2. **Human Intuition Is Statistically Flawed**: We systematically misjudge likelihoods.

3. **Bayesian Thinking Counters the Bias**: Proper inference depends on integrating both base rates and new data.

4. **Fallacy Fuels Misinformation**: Misleading statistics thrive on ignored base rates.

5. **Critical in High-Stakes Fields**: Law, healthcare, and policy must account for this bias to avoid serious errors.

The Base Rate Fallacy Paradox reminds us that **statistical truth often defies intuition** — and that accurate judgment depends on looking beyond the obvious to see the whole probabilistic picture.

Mathematical & Set-Theoretical Paradoxes

Formal reasoning in math leads to surprising conclusions.

63. Burali-Forti Paradox

Theory Overview

The **Burali-Forti Paradox** is a foundational paradox in set theory and logic, discovered by **Cesare Burali-Forti** in 1897. It arises from attempting to apply naive set theory to **ordinal numbers**, which are numbers used to describe the **order type of well-ordered sets**. The paradox reveals a contradiction when one tries to define **the set of all ordinal numbers**—a set that, by its very nature, cannot exist without causing inconsistency.

The key insight is this: if we assume the collection of all ordinals forms a set, we run into the problem that this "largest" ordinal must itself be an ordinal, and therefore must be **less than itself**, which is logically impossible.

This paradox, like Russell's Paradox, exposed fundamental flaws in naive set theory and motivated the development of **axiomatic systems** that carefully restrict how sets can be formed.

Example

Let's start by understanding what ordinal numbers are. In set theory, ordinal numbers extend the natural numbers to account for "orderings" of infinite sets. For example:

- 0, 1, 2, 3, ... are finite ordinals.
- ω (omega) is the first infinite ordinal—the order type of all natural numbers.
- ω+1, ω+2, ... are ordinals beyond the first infinity.
- You can keep going, defining ever-larger ordinals.

Now, suppose we try to define a set Ω = { all ordinal numbers }.

Since Ω includes all ordinals, it must itself be well-ordered and hence have an order type, meaning **Ω is itself an ordinal**. But if Ω is an ordinal, then it must be **included in the set of all ordinals**, and therefore **less than itself**, because by definition, an ordinal is less than any ordinal that follows it.

This leads to a contradiction: Ω < Ω, which is logically impossible.

Why It Works

The Burali-Forti Paradox works because it confronts us with a **self-referential inconsistency**. The assumption that **the collection of all ordinals forms a set** leads to a situation where an ordinal must be smaller than itself.

The paradox demonstrates that **some collections are too large to be sets**. In particular, the "set of all ordinals" is not a set in a properly constructed system—it is instead a **proper class**, a collection too large to be a set under standard axioms.

How It Works

The paradox operates through the following steps:

1. **Define the set of all ordinals** as Ω.

2. Since ordinals are well-ordered, Ω must have an order type and therefore be an ordinal.

3. But as an ordinal, Ω must be a member of itself ($\Omega \in \Omega$).

4. Yet by the definition of ordinals, **no ordinal can be a member of itself**.

5. This creates the contradiction: $\Omega < \Omega$.

The solution in modern set theory (e.g., Zermelo–Fraenkel Set Theory) is to **prohibit the formation of such "unbounded" sets**, designating them instead as **proper classes**, which are not allowed to behave like sets.

Application

The Burali-Forti Paradox is crucial in:

- **Set theory foundations**: It directly influenced the development of **axiomatic systems** that avoid such contradictions.

- **Ordinal theory**: Helped clarify the distinction between **sets** and **classes**.

- **Mathematical logic**: Informs consistency proofs and highlights limits of formal systems.

- **Philosophy of mathematics**: Raises questions about the **nature of mathematical infinity** and definability.

Key Insights

- Not all collections can be treated as sets—some are too large and become **proper classes**.

- **Self-reference** and **comprehension** must be restricted to avoid logical collapse.

- The paradox demonstrates the **limits of naive approaches to infinity and hierarchy**.

- It helped shape **modern axiomatic set theory**, especially distinctions like **class vs. set**.

- Like Russell's Paradox, it's foundational in understanding the **architecture of mathematical logic**.

64. Diagonalization Paradox

Theory Overview

The **Diagonalization Paradox** refers to a family of arguments and paradoxes that arise from **diagonal reasoning**, a method introduced by **Georg Cantor** in the late 19th century. The paradox primarily exposes the **limits of listing or enumerating infinite sets**, especially when dealing with different sizes (cardinalities) of infinity.

Cantor originally used diagonalization to prove that **the real numbers are uncountable**, showing that there are more real numbers than natural numbers, even though both sets are infinite. This result shattered the assumption that all infinities are equal, revealing a **hierarchy of infinities**. The method has since been used in various paradoxes and proofs—some leading to contradictions or surprising results in logic, computation, and set theory.

The paradoxical nature of diagonalization emerges when we attempt to build something that supposedly fits into a list, only to find, by construction, that **it cannot possibly be included in the list**, despite our efforts.

Example

Let's explore **Cantor's original diagonal argument**:

Suppose someone claims they have a complete list of all real numbers between 0 and 1, expressed in decimal form:

1. 0.123456...

2. 0.987654...

3. 0.314159...

4. 0.271828...

5. ...

Now construct a new number by taking the **diagonal digits**—the first digit from the first number, the second from the second, the third from the third, etc.—and modifying each digit (e.g., add 1 modulo 10, or just switch 1↔2).

From the example, the diagonal digits might be 1, 8, 4, 8... Changing each gives us 2, 9, 5, 9...

So we get a new number: 0.2959...

This new number **differs from every number on the list** in at least one digit—specifically, the nth digit of this new number differs from the nth digit of the nth number. Therefore, it **cannot** be on the list.

This leads to the paradoxical realization: **even if you attempt to list all the real numbers, there will always be at least one missing**. Hence, **the reals are uncountable**, and not all infinities are created equal.

Why It Works

The diagonalization method works because it guarantees **systematic divergence**. By altering each diagonal entry of a list, the constructed object **differs from every entry** in a precise and deliberate way.

The paradox lies in the clash between **assumed completeness** (that a list contains all elements) and **constructed incompleteness** (a new element that must exist outside the list). It shows that **infinity can be strictly larger than infinity**, at least in terms of set size.

How It Works

The core elements of diagonalization:

1. **Assume a complete list** of elements (like real numbers or Turing machines).

2. **Construct a new item** using a diagonal rule that differs from each list item at a corresponding point.

3. **Demonstrate** that the new item cannot be in the original list, thus contradicting the assumption.

This technique is also used in:

- **Gödel's Incompleteness Theorems**: By encoding statements that reference their own unprovability.

- **Turing's Halting Problem**: Showing there's no universal program that can decide whether all programs halt.

- **Russell's Paradox**: Creating sets that do not fit neatly within a list of all sets.

Application

Diagonalization is foundational in:

- **Mathematical logic**: Proving incompleteness and undecidability.
- **Set theory**: Differentiating between **countable and uncountable infinities**.
- **Theoretical computer science**: Establishing **limits of computation** and algorithmic solvability.
- **Information theory**: Demonstrating the uncompressibility of certain strings or sequences.

Key Insights

- Not all infinities are equal—**some are strictly larger** than others.
- Diagonalization creates paradoxes by **exposing limits of representation** and enumeration.
- The method shows how **self-reference and construction** can break assumed completeness.
- It's a powerful tool for **disproving total systems**, such as universal deciders or complete logics.
- The paradox deepens our understanding of **infinity, logic, computation, and truth**.

65. Hilbert's Hotel

Theory Overview

Hilbert's Hotel is a famous thought experiment conceived by German mathematician **David Hilbert** to illustrate the **strange and counterintuitive properties of infinite sets**—specifically, **countably infinite sets**. The paradox describes a hotel with an infinite number of rooms, all of which are occupied, and yet it can **still accommodate more guests**.

The paradox is not a contradiction but a demonstration of how **infinity defies ordinary arithmetic and logic**. While in real life a full hotel cannot take in new guests, an *infinite* hotel can—because infinity behaves in ways that challenge our finite intuitions.

Example

Imagine **Hilbert's Hotel** has rooms numbered 1, 2, 3, 4, and so on, continuing forever. Every room is occupied—there's a guest in each one.

Now, suppose a new guest arrives. You might think there's no room—but the hotel manager has a solution:

He asks **every guest in room n to move to room n+1**. Guest in Room 1 moves to Room 2, Guest in Room 2 moves to Room 3, and so on.

This process opens up **Room 1**, making space for the new guest. No one is kicked out, and yet an additional guest is accommodated in a hotel that was already "full."

Now suppose **an infinite number of new guests arrive**. Can the hotel still make room? Amazingly, yes. The manager can ask each current guest in Room *n* to move to **Room 2n**—doubling their room number. This move leaves all the **odd-numbered rooms** (1, 3, 5, 7...) open for the infinite new guests.

Why It Works

The paradox works because of how **countable infinity** functions in mathematics. The set of natural numbers {1, 2, 3, 4, ...} is **infinite but countable**, meaning there's a one-to-one correspondence with any other countable infinite set.

This property allows the hotel to rearrange its guests to make space—even infinitely many times. It's a striking example of how **set theory** and **infinite cardinality** diverge from our everyday experience.

How It Works

The paradox relies on the principles of **transfinite arithmetic**, particularly **aleph-null ($\aleph_0$)**, which denotes the cardinality (size) of the set of natural numbers.

- The hotel starts with $\aleph_0$ rooms, all filled.

- Adding one or even $\aleph_0$ more guests still yields a total of $\aleph_0$ guests.

- The key is that infinite sets can be **reordered or mapped** in ways that are impossible with finite sets.

This shows that in infinity math, $\infty + 1 = \infty$ and even $\infty + \infty = \infty$ (under countable cardinality).

Application

Hilbert's Hotel has powerful implications in:

- **Set theory**: It illustrates fundamental ideas about **infinite cardinality**.

- **Mathematics education**: Helps teach the **difference between finite and infinite logic**.

- **Philosophy**: Raises questions about the **concept of actual infinity**—whether such an infinity can exist in reality or only as an abstraction.

- **Cosmology**: Influences discussions about the size of the universe, infinite time, and multiverse theories.

- **Computer science**: Informs models of infinite loops, memory allocation, and theoretical machine states.

Key Insights

- Infinity **does not behave** like large finite numbers.
- **Countable infinities** can accommodate addition without increasing in size.
- Rearrangement is a powerful tool in **infinite systems**, but doesn't apply intuitively.
- The paradox reveals the **philosophical tension** between mathematical abstraction and physical possibility.
- Hilbert's Hotel challenges how we think about **space, time, capacity, and logic**—forcing a re-evaluation of what "full" and "more" mean when infinity is involved.

66. Banach–Tarski Paradox

Theory Overview

The **Banach–Tarski Paradox** is a result in set-theoretic geometry that appears mathematically sound yet wildly counterintuitive. Formulated by **Stefan Banach** and **Alfred Tarski** in 1924, the paradox states that:

A solid ball in 3-dimensional space can be divided into a finite number of non-overlapping pieces, which can be reassembled—using only rotations and translations—into two identical copies of the original ball.

In essence, **you can duplicate a ball using nothing but geometry**. This defies physical intuition and conservation principles like volume and mass. However, it's mathematically valid—**not because mass is being created**, but because the pieces involved are so "strange" that they defy classical measurement.

The paradox depends heavily on the **Axiom of Choice**, a controversial yet accepted principle in modern set theory, which allows for the selection of elements from infinite sets even without a specific rule.

Example

Suppose you have a ball with radius 1. According to Banach and Tarski's theorem, you can cut this ball into **five distinct**

pieces, and by moving (rotating and translating) these pieces—without stretching, scaling, or altering them—you can reconstruct **two balls of radius 1**, identical to the original.

This seems to imply that you've **doubled the volume** out of nowhere, violating physical laws. But the catch is that the pieces are **non-measurable sets**—they are so fragmented and mathematically "wild" that the concept of volume does not apply to them. In the real world, such a construction would be impossible due to atomic structure, quantum mechanics, and physical constraints.

Why It Works

The paradox works because it exploits the **weirdness of infinity** and the **Axiom of Choice**, which permits the creation of highly non-constructive and non-intuitive sets.

Specifically:

1. The **sphere** is divided using intricate geometric constructions involving **free groups** and rotations.
2. The resulting sets are **non-measurable**, meaning they lack a well-defined volume.
3. Since volume isn't preserved across these parts, there's **no contradiction** in recombining them into something larger.

This is valid within **pure mathematics**, where space can be dissected down to infinitesimally precise abstractions, unconstrained by physical reality.

How It Works

The proof involves several complex ideas:

- **Group theory**, specifically the concept of **free groups** (sets with operations that are not constrained by relations).
- **Equidecomposability**, where two objects are considered equivalent if they can be broken into parts and rearranged into each other.
- The use of the **Axiom of Choice** to select points in a way that's impossible to describe explicitly.

The pieces created are not like chunks of a puzzle—they are **infinitely scattered sets of points** that cannot be measured or constructed in any real-world sense.

Application

Though it has **no practical application in physics**, the Banach–Tarski Paradox has deep implications in:

- **Set theory** and the foundations of mathematics: It illustrates the **power and controversy** of the Axiom of Choice.

- **Mathematical logic**: Demonstrates that mathematical truth can be **radically divorced from physical intuition**.
- **Measure theory**: Informs us about the **limits of standard concepts like volume, area, and length**.
- **Philosophy of mathematics**: Sparks debate about **constructivism vs. non-constructivism** and the nature of mathematical existence.

Key Insights

- Not all mathematically valid operations **make physical sense**.
- The **Axiom of Choice** allows powerful but counterintuitive results.
- Some mathematical "objects" are so abstract they **cannot be visualized** or measured.
- Infinity, when combined with certain assumptions, can **break classical intuition**.
- The paradox challenges our understanding of **identity, duplication, and conservation**.

67. Peano's Arrow Paradox

Theory Overview

Peano's Arrow Paradox is a lesser-known but conceptually rich thought experiment, associated with Italian mathematician **Giuseppe Peano**, who contributed significantly to the formal foundations of mathematics. This paradox deals with **indeterminacy and infinite regression** in the context of **decision-making, motion, or action**. It's often framed in terms of **temporal hesitation**—where a theoretically simple action cannot begin because the conditions for initiating it are never fully satisfied.

Although not as commonly cited as Zeno's paradoxes, Peano's Arrow shares a similar structure: a task seems logically possible, even necessary, but **becomes impossible due to infinite hesitation or decision conflict**. The paradox illustrates how **over-analysis or strict preconditions for action** can paradoxically lead to **complete inaction**.

Example

The paradox can be described through a thought experiment like the following:

A person is standing at the starting point of a straight path, intending to shoot an arrow at a target downrange. They've decided that **before they release the arrow**, they must be certain of the *precise* right moment to do so—maximizing accuracy or effect. But at every instant, they ask themselves: *Is this the right moment?*

To be logically consistent and optimize timing, they must rule out all earlier and later possibilities. However, **no moment is ever definitively the "right" one**—there's always an infinitesimal earlier moment or better condition. So the decision process **never terminates**, and the arrow is **never released**.

This captures the essence of the paradox: **infinite logical scrutiny** prevents a finite action.

Why It Works

Peano's Arrow Paradox works because it reveals a deep flaw in **over-rationalized decision-making**. It shows that if action is dependent on a perfect decision point or optimal criteria that are **never fully resolvable**, the action is **infinitely postponed**.

It reflects a clash between **idealized reasoning and real-world practicality**. In logic or mathematics, one might strive for perfect precision, but in dynamic systems—like shooting an arrow, making a decision, or initiating motion—**some level of uncertainty or arbitrariness is necessary** for progress.

The paradox also illustrates how a system governed by strict **conditional logic** may become **paralyzed by its own rules**.

How It Works

The core mechanics of the paradox are:

1. **An action requires a specific condition to be met** (e.g., the perfect time).

2. **Each potential condition can be questioned or improved upon**, creating an infinite regress.

3. **No unique "best" condition emerges**, so the action is never initiated.

In formal terms, it touches on issues in **decision theory**, **logic**, and **temporal modelling**. It is similar to **Buridan's Ass**, another paradox in which a donkey starves between two equally distant haystacks, unable to choose due to perfect symmetry.

Application

Peano's Arrow Paradox has implications in:

- **Artificial intelligence and robotics**: Systems requiring certainty before acting can become stuck in loops of indecision.

- **Philosophy of action and free will**: Questions when and how action emerges from deliberation.

- **Cognitive science**: Models decision paralysis and analysis paralysis in human behaviour.

- **Ethics and moral reasoning**: Over-deliberation about the "right" thing may result in inaction, itself ethically problematic.
- **Economics and planning**: Emphasizes the cost of indecision and the need for bounded rationality in strategy.

Key Insights

- Absolute certainty is often **incompatible with action**.
- **Rational deliberation must be bounded** to avoid paralysis.
- Time-sensitive decisions cannot depend on **infinitely deferred analysis**.
- Real-world systems require **heuristics and thresholds**, not perfect conditions.
- The paradox highlights how **formal logic may fail in dynamic or practical domains**.

68. Paradox of Cheap Trick

Theory Overview

The **Paradox of Cheap Trick** refers to the **counterintuitive consumer tendency to devalue a product, service, or experience simply because it is inexpensive**, even when the quality remains high. In other words, when something is "too cheap," people may assume it's **inferior**, even when the low cost is intentional (e.g., a promotion, surplus, or market strategy).

This contradicts the rational economic assumption that **value is utility per unit cost**—that is, a good deal should increase a product's attractiveness. Instead, psychological and social factors intervene: price becomes a **signal of quality**, not just a measure of cost.

Hence the paradox: **lowering the price to increase access or demand may actually reduce perceived value**, leading to lower sales or satisfaction.

Example

Imagine a new high-quality concert experience offered at $15. Despite excellent reviews and production, it's poorly attended. Why? Many consumers see the low price and subconsciously infer: *"It must not be that good if it's this cheap."*

Contrast that with a similar event priced at $80. Even if the product is nearly identical, the higher price may **create an impression of exclusivity and quality**, increasing demand or engagement—despite the worse deal in economic terms.

This phenomenon is also well-documented in **wine studies**: participants often rate **identical wines more highly** when told they are expensive, and less favourably when told they are cheap.

Why It Works

The paradox works because of how consumers **associate price with value**, especially in markets where quality is hard to assess directly (experience goods, luxury items, art). In such cases, price becomes a **proxy signal** for quality, status, or craftsmanship.

Cognitive biases like **anchoring**, **status signalling**, and the **price-quality heuristic** influence decision-making. People aren't just buying products—they're buying **perceptions**, **narratives**, and **identities**.

In addition, the psychological principle of **effort justification** plays a role: if something costs more, we're more likely to justify it as better. Conversely, low cost creates **suspicion or undervaluation**.

How It Works

The paradox involves several behavioural mechanisms:

1. **Price as signal**: In absence of full information, price is taken as an indicator of quality.

2. **Social signalling**: Expensive goods communicate status; cheap ones may imply "low value" or mass-market appeal.

3. **Cognitive dissonance**: Consumers resolve the tension of high prices by upgrading perceived quality; cheap items don't offer that justification.

4. **Expectation shaping**: Lower price sets lower expectations, which affects how the experience is internally rated, regardless of objective quality.

Application

The Paradox of Cheap Trick is crucial in:

- **Marketing and pricing strategy**: Helps firms avoid devaluing their brand by under-pricing.

- **Cultural economics**: Explains why free or cheap access to high art (e.g., symphonies, galleries) doesn't always democratize audiences—it may alienate or confuse them.

- **Public policy**: Underscores challenges in promoting subsidized healthcare, education, or sustainable goods; "cheap" is not always seen as "good."

- **UX design and freemium models**: Helps explain drop-off in engagement when products are offered for free without clear value framing.

Key Insights

- Price is not just economic—it's **psychological and symbolic**.
- Lower cost doesn't always increase perceived value; it may **undermine it**.
- Consumers interpret price through **heuristics**, not pure logic.
- Strategic under-pricing can backfire if **brand perception** suffers.
- The paradox emphasizes the importance of **perceived value, framing, and market positioning** over raw utility.

69. Paradox of Value (Diamond–Water)

Theory Overview

The **Paradox of Value**, famously explored by **Adam Smith** in *The Wealth of Nations* (1776), raises a fundamental question in economics:

Why do essential goods like water typically have a low price, while non-essential goods like diamonds have high prices?

This observation seems paradoxical because water is vital for survival, while diamonds are primarily decorative. The contradiction lies between **use value** (how useful something is) and **exchange value** (how much it is worth in trade). Water has immense use value but low market price; diamonds have little practical use but command high prices.

This paradox puzzled classical economists and was unresolved until the development of **marginal utility theory** in the 19th century, which reframed value not in terms of total utility, but **the utility of the next unit consumed**.

Example

Imagine you're in a desert, dying of thirst. A bottle of water in that moment might be **more valuable to you than a diamond**, because its **marginal utility**—the value of that next bottle—is extremely high.

However, in everyday life, where water is abundant, the **next unit** of water has relatively little value. You may have gallons at home already, so one more glass isn't worth much to you.

Diamonds, on the other hand, are scarce and rarely encountered. Their **marginal utility** stays high because each additional diamond still holds significant perceived value due to its rarity and social symbolism.

Thus, while **total utility** (overall usefulness) of water is greater, **marginal utility** (added usefulness of one more unit) often explains why diamonds are more expensive in a marketplace.

Why It Works

The paradox works because it contrasts two types of value:

1. **Use value**: Based on the overall importance of the good (e.g., water is essential to life).
2. **Exchange value**: Based on market dynamics—what people are willing to trade for the good.

Before marginal utility theory, economists tried to ground value purely in **labour or inherent usefulness**, but those theories couldn't explain why non-essential goods like jewels could be more expensive than necessities.

The **resolution** came with economists like **William Stanley Jevons, Carl Menger**, and **Léon Walras**, who introduced **marginalism**. They realized that value depends not on the total amount of utility a good provides, but on **how much satisfaction or benefit the next unit adds**.

How It Works

Marginal utility theory posits:

- The **value of a good is determined by its marginal utility**—how much additional benefit a person gets from consuming one more unit.
- When a good is **abundant**, each additional unit adds little extra value (as with water in developed societies).
- When a good is **scarce**, each unit is more highly valued (as with diamonds).

This theory aligns prices with individual preferences, availability, and context rather than absolute necessity.

Application

The paradox and its resolution laid the groundwork for:

- **Modern microeconomics** and **price theory**
- Understanding **consumer choice and demand curves**
- Explaining **pricing anomalies** in labour markets, luxury goods, and natural resources
- Influencing **public policy**, especially in **resource pricing** and **environmental economics**

- Developing **cost-benefit analyses** that focus on marginal rather than total effects

---

Key Insights

- Value is **context-dependent**, not absolute.
- Scarcity, perception, and marginal utility determine what we're willing to pay.
- Essential goods may be cheap not because they're unimportant, but because they're **abundant**.
- The paradox shows how **economic intuition can clash with common sense**, requiring deeper theoretical tools to resolve.
- It emphasizes that **economic value is subjective**, shaped by individual preferences and situational factors.

70. Bolzano–Weierstrass Paradox

Theory Overview

The **Bolzano–Weierstrass Theorem** is a foundational result in real analysis, not a paradox in the formal sense. However, it can seem **paradoxical** or counterintuitive to those unfamiliar with the subtleties of **infinite sequences and limits** in mathematics. The "paradox" arises from its seemingly contradictory implications: **every bounded sequence has a convergent subsequence**, even if the sequence itself never settles or appears chaotic.

Formulated through the work of **Bernard Bolzano** and later **Karl Weierstrass**, the theorem states:

"Every bounded infinite sequence in $\mathbb{R}^n$ has at least one convergent subsequence."

This result seems paradoxical because it implies **order within apparent disorder**—that within any infinite, bounded mess of numbers, we can always find a **thread of stability**, a subsequence that converges to a real limit.

Example

Imagine the sequence:

$$a_n = (-1)^n$$

This is the classic alternating sequence: −1, 1, −1, 1, −1, ...

It **does not converge**—it oscillates forever. But according to Bolzano–Weierstrass, since this sequence is **bounded** (between −1 and 1), it must have a **convergent subsequence**.

Indeed, we can extract the subsequence of all the −1's:

$$a_2, a_4, a_6, \ldots = -1, -1, -1, \ldots$$

This converges to −1. Similarly, the sequence of all the 1's also converges to 1. So although the original sequence doesn't converge, **some parts of it do**.

In more complex examples (especially in higher dimensions or in seemingly erratic data), it might seem paradoxical that convergence is guaranteed at all. That's the subtlety that makes the theorem appear paradoxical to those unfamiliar with mathematical rigor.

Why It Works

The "paradoxical" effect of the Bolzano–Weierstrass Theorem arises from **our intuition clashing with the logic of infinity**. When we look at an infinite sequence that never settles, it feels like it should behave chaotically forever. The theorem surprises us by guaranteeing that **some part of the sequence behaves nicely**—not just sometimes, but **always**, as long as the sequence is bounded.

This result is grounded in the **completeness property of real numbers**, which ensures that limits of convergent sequences exist within the real number system.

How It Works

The theorem is proven by combining **boundedness** with the **nested interval** and **compactness** principles. In one dimension ($\mathbb{R}$), the idea is:

1. Divide the interval containing the sequence into two halves.

2. At least one half contains infinitely many elements of the sequence.

3. Repeat this halving process indefinitely, narrowing in on a limit point.

By choosing a term from the sequence in each narrowing interval, you can construct a **convergent subsequence**. This strategy generalizes to higher dimensions through **compactness of closed, bounded sets in $\mathbb{R}^n$**.

Application

The Bolzano–Weierstrass Theorem is essential in:

- **Real analysis**: Underlies the study of limits, continuity, and compactness.

- **Optimization and calculus**: Guarantees existence of limit points in iterative methods.

- **Functional analysis**: Helps in proving the compactness of operators.

- **Machine learning and numerical computation**: Ensures stability and convergence behaviour in iterative algorithms.

- **Signal processing and physics**: Where bounded oscillatory data may hide convergent behaviour.

Key Insights

- Infinite behaviour doesn't mean **total unpredictability**; **boundedness imposes structure**.

- The theorem formalizes the idea that within chaos, there's always **a pocket of convergence**.

- It's a powerful example of how mathematical reasoning **contradicts naive intuition**, especially regarding infinity.

- It lays the groundwork for more advanced concepts like **compactness** and **sequential compactness** in topology.

- The paradox isn't a contradiction in logic, but a challenge to our **intuition about infinite processes**.

71. Hairy Ball Theorem

Theory Overview

The **Hairy Ball Theorem** is a result from **algebraic topology**, a branch of mathematics that deals with properties of space preserved under continuous deformation. The theorem states:

"**There is no non-vanishing continuous tangent vector field on even-dimensional n-spheres.**"

In simpler terms, this means that **you cannot comb a hairy ball flat without creating at least one cowlick or bald spot**. More formally, for a sphere like the surface of the Earth (a 2-dimensional sphere in 3D space), it's impossible to assign a direction (vector) to every point on the surface such that the directions are **continuous** and **nowhere zero** (i.e., with no place where the vector disappears).

This theorem has both mathematical significance and a beautifully intuitive geometric visualization, and it has inspired various paradoxical interpretations in physics, meteorology, and computer graphics.

Example

Imagine trying to comb the hair on a perfectly spherical ball so that all hairs lie flat against the surface and point in a continuous direction across the whole sphere.

No matter how skilfully you comb, you will **always end up with at least one point where the hair stands up, whirls, or disappears**—a so-called "cowlick." That's the bald spot or singularity that the Hairy Ball Theorem guarantees.

A real-world example would be the **Earth's wind patterns**. If you tried to represent wind direction everywhere on the globe (ignoring elevation), the Hairy Ball Theorem implies that **there must always be at least one point with zero wind velocity**—like the eye of a cyclone or a still point in atmospheric motion.

Why It Works

The theorem works because of the **topological structure** of even-dimensional spheres. Unlike a torus (doughnut-shaped surface), which can have non-zero vector fields everywhere, a 2-sphere (like Earth's surface) has **topological constraints** that prevent smooth, non-zero vector fields.

It relies on a branch of topology called **homology theory**, which classifies spaces based on how their shapes can be deformed. The 2-sphere has a non-trivial topological invariant that ensures a zero must exist in any continuous vector field on it.

The intuitive reason is that trying to "flatten" all the vectors around a sphere will inevitably cause a conflict at some point—creating a zero vector or a discontinuity.

How It Works

Mathematically, the theorem is typically proven using **algebraic topology tools** such as the **Euler characteristic** and **Brouwer's fixed-point theorem**. For a 2-sphere, the Euler characteristic is 2, which implies (via the Poincaré-Hopf Index Theorem) that the sum of the indices of zeros of any vector field must equal 2. Thus, zeros (singularities) must exist.

In contrast, odd-dimensional spheres like the 1-sphere (a circle) or 3-sphere **can** support non-zero continuous vector fields.

Application

The Hairy Ball Theorem applies in various fields:

- **Meteorology**: Proves that somewhere on Earth, there must be a point with no horizontal wind.

- **Fluid dynamics**: Impacts models of rotating flows on spherical surfaces.

- **Computer graphics**: Affects texture mapping and shading on spherical models—there must be at least one point of distortion.

- **Robotics and motion planning**: Highlights the limits of orientation mapping on spherical joints or spaces.

Key Insights

- Even though the theorem is purely mathematical, it has **deep implications in physical systems** involving fields on curved surfaces.

- It illustrates how **topological constraints can impose real-world limitations**—e.g., there's no such thing as a global, non-zero, consistent direction on a sphere.

- The theorem underscores the **interplay between geometry, continuity, and topology**.

- It's a powerful reminder that **some problems aren't solvable not due to effort or tools, but due to the shape of the space itself**.

72. Borel's Paradox

Theory

Borel's Paradox, named after French mathematician Émile Borel, is a subtle and counterintuitive result in **probability theory**, especially in the context of **conditional probabilities on continuous spaces**. It exposes a paradox in how we condition probabilities on events of **measure zero** — events that, while possible in theory, have **zero probability** of occurring in a continuous probability space.

The paradox arises from the observation that **different methods of conditioning on the same measure-zero event** can yield **different, seemingly contradictory results**, depending on how that conditioning is carried out. This violates our intuitive assumption that conditional probabilities should be unique and well-defined, especially when applied to the same "event."

The paradox challenges naive applications of conditional probability, revealing that **context and method of conditioning matter** — especially when dealing with continuous distributions and geometric symmetries.

Example

Consider choosing a point at random on the surface of a sphere (say, the Earth). The distribution is uniform over the sphere — every point is equally likely. Now, suppose we want to compute the **conditional probability** distribution of the longitude, **given** that the point lies on the **North Pole**.

Naively, one might say: "Since the North Pole is a single point, it has no longitude — all longitudes converge there. So the longitude is undefined." But if you try to condition the uniform distribution on "the point is at the North Pole" (an event of measure zero), you get **different results depending on your coordinate system**.

Alternatively, suppose instead you condition on the point lying on **some meridian**, like longitude 0°. This is a **great circle** — still a measure-zero subset of the sphere. Depending on whether you condition in **spherical coordinates** (latitude and longitude) or using **Cartesian coordinates** and then transforming to spherical ones, you get **different conditional distributions** over latitude.

This violates the intuition that probability distributions should be invariant under coordinate transformations if the overall distribution is uniform and symmetric. Yet they aren't — and that's the paradox.

Why It Works

Borel's Paradox works because it confronts the **undefined or ambiguous nature of conditioning on measure-zero events** in continuous spaces. In discrete probability, conditioning is simple: you restrict the sample space and renormalize. In continuous spaces, especially geometric ones with infinite precision, such events can't be directly observed, and the way we **approach the conditioning** (through limits, coordinate systems, or approximations) affects the result.

The paradox highlights a deep point: **probability distributions are not always coordinate-invariant when conditioning on null sets**. Conditioning is not just about sets, but also about the structure and the paths by which you reach those sets.

How It Works
Formally, the paradox arises from conditioning via **regular conditional probability** and the **Radon-Nikodym derivative**, which are well-behaved on sets of positive measure but problematic on null sets. Conditioning on a zero-measure event is **ill-defined** unless approached as a limit of positive-measure sets — and even then, **the limit depends on the approach**.

This means that conditioning on "being on a meridian" or "at the pole" doesn't yield a unique result without specifying **how** you're arriving at that condition, such as from what direction or with what prior structure.

Application
Borel's Paradox has important implications in **Bayesian statistics**, **geometric probability**, and **machine learning**. It warns against blind application of conditional reasoning in continuous models, particularly in high-dimensional data analysis, spherical modelling (e.g., GPS or directional statistics), and **Bayesian inference** involving improper priors or singularities.

It's also relevant in **physics**, where probability densities on continuous manifolds (like phase space or configuration space) must be handled with mathematical rigor.

Key Insights

1. **Measure-Zero Events Are Tricky**: Conditioning on them can produce ambiguous or inconsistent results.

2. **Coordinate Systems Matter**: Probability isn't always invariant under change of variables when conditioning on null sets.

3. **Conditional Probability Requires Context**: The method of conditioning affects the outcome, especially in continuous spaces.

4. **Limits Must Be Handled Carefully**: Conditional probability should be defined through proper limits and regularization.

5. **Not All Intuition Transfers from Discrete to Continuous**: Classical conditioning rules can break down in infinite spaces.

Borel's Paradox serves as a powerful reminder that **probability theory, especially in continuous domains, demands precise definitions and awareness of underlying structure**, or risk falling into subtle, yet serious logical traps.

📖 Linguistic & Semantic Paradoxes

Language and meaning create contradictions.

73. Liar Paradox

Theory Overview

The **Liar Paradox** is one of the oldest and most famous paradoxes in logic and philosophy. It arises from a sentence that refers to its own truth value in a way that creates a contradiction. The classic version is:

"This sentence is false."

If the sentence is **true**, then what it says must hold—so it must be **false**. But if it's **false**, then what it says isn't true, which would mean it's **true**. This leads to an inescapable contradiction: the sentence is **true if and only if it is false.**

The paradox dates back to at least the 4th century BCE and is often attributed to **Epimenides**, a Cretan who allegedly declared, "All Cretans are liars." Later formulations, especially in formal logic, have used self-reference to expose limitations in systems of **truth, language, and logical consistency**.

The Liar Paradox is not merely a linguistic trick—it has deep implications for **foundational logic**, **semantic theory**, and the **limits of formal systems**.

Example

A simple case:

Statement A: "Statement A is false."

Try to evaluate whether Statement A is true or false.

- If it's **true**, then it asserts that it is **false**, which contradicts its truth.
- If it's **false**, then what it asserts is **not the case**, which means it must be **true**.

This cyclical logic traps us in a loop where the sentence flips between truth and falsehood—**a logical inconsistency** within the binary framework of classical logic.

Why It Works

The paradox works because it highlights the **fragility of self-reference** within truth systems. In classical logic, every proposition must be either **true or false**, and **not both** (the law of the excluded middle and the law of non-contradiction). The Liar Paradox directly challenges this binary logic.

It also reveals a deeper issue: that allowing a sentence to **refer to itself in terms of truth** creates instability. When truth becomes a subject **within** a language system rather than a concept **about** the system, paradoxes arise.

How It Works

The Liar Paradox hinges on three principles:

1. **Self-reference**: The sentence refers to itself.
2. **Bivalence**: Every proposition is either true or false.
3. **Compositionality**: The meaning of a complex expression is built from its parts.

The contradiction comes when you try to assign a stable truth value. Under classical logic, this leads to a **semantic collapse**. To address this, philosophers and logicians have developed several solutions or reinterpretations:

- **Tarski's Hierarchy**: Alfred Tarski proposed separating object-language (talking about facts) and meta-language (talking about truth), so that no sentence can refer to its own truth within the same level.

- **Kripke's Partial Truth Framework**: Saul Kripke suggested using **partial truth values**, allowing some sentences to be "undefined" rather than forcing binary truth.

- **Paraconsistent Logics**: These reject the law of non-contradiction, allowing some statements to be both true and false without collapsing the system.

- **Dialetheism**: A controversial view that accepts some contradictions as literally true—i.e., some sentences can be both true and false.

Application

The Liar Paradox has influenced:

- **Mathematical logic**: It helped inspire **Gödel's incompleteness theorems**, which use self-referential logic to show limits of formal systems.
- **Semantics and philosophy of language**: It has shaped debates on the nature of meaning, reference, and truth.
- **Computer science**: Related to halting problems and recursion issues in programming languages.
- **Artificial intelligence**: Raises questions about how machines might model or interpret truth and contradiction.

Key Insights

- Self-reference + truth = **potential inconsistency**.
- Not all language that *appears* meaningful is **logically stable**.
- Classical truth theory must be modified or stratified to handle semantic paradoxes.
- The Liar Paradox shows the **limits of formal systems** and pushes us to consider **alternative logical frameworks**.
- It remains a powerful tool for exploring **meta-linguistic complexity and logical rigor**.

74. Barber Paradox

Barber Paradox

Theory Overview

The **Barber Paradox** is a classic logical puzzle introduced by **Bertrand Russell** to illustrate the kind of **self-referential contradictions** that plagued **naive set theory**. It is a simplified, everyday-language version of **Russell's Paradox**, designed to make the core issue more accessible to non-mathematicians.

The paradox centres around a scenario involving a barber who is said to shave **all and only those men who do not shave themselves**. This innocent-sounding rule turns out to be **logically impossible** when you ask whether the barber shaves himself. The contradiction it exposes lies in **self-reference** and the violation of the principle of **well-foundedness**—the idea that sets or categories should not contain themselves.

Example

Here's the setup:

In a village, there is exactly one barber who shaves **all those men in the village who do not shave themselves**, and **only those**. The question is: **Does the barber shave himself?**

Let's examine the two possible answers:

1. **Suppose the barber shaves himself.**
   Then, according to the rule, he **must not shave himself**, because he only shaves **men who do not shave themselves**.

2. **Suppose the barber does not shave himself.**
   Then, by the rule, he **must shave himself**, because he shaves all men **who do not shave themselves**.

Both answers lead to a **contradiction**. So the original assumption—that such a barber could exist under these conditions—is **logically incoherent**.

Why It Works

The paradox works because it involves **self-application of a rule that negates itself**. The contradiction arises when a set (or category) includes itself **only if it does not include itself**, which is impossible. It's a form of **semantic loop**—a rule that, when applied to itself, breaks the very conditions it sets.

The strength of the paradox is in its **simplicity**. Unlike more technical paradoxes, it doesn't rely on mathematical notation or complex logical systems. Instead, it reveals the deep flaws in a system based on **unrestricted definitions**, using plain language.

How It Works

The logical structure is akin to **Russell's Paradox** in set theory:

- Define a set **R** = $\{x \mid x \notin x\}$, the set of all sets that do **not contain themselves**.

- Ask: **Is R ∈ R?**
    - If yes, then by definition, $R \notin R$.
    - If no, then by definition, $R \in R$.

This mirrors the barber scenario. Both paradoxes expose the failure of systems that **allow self-reference without constraints**, leading to **non-well-founded** or circular definitions.

To resolve these paradoxes, modern logic and mathematics introduce **type theory** or **hierarchical frameworks**, which forbid such self-referential constructions.

Application

The Barber Paradox has significant implications in:

- **Set theory**: It prompted the move from naive set theory to **axiomatic systems** like **Zermelo–Fraenkel (ZF)**, which avoid such contradictions.

- **Formal logic and semantics**: It illustrates the danger of **unrestricted comprehension**—the ability to define sets or categories with overly broad rules.

- **Computer science**: Especially in **type systems** and **recursive programming**, where circular definitions must be carefully managed.

- **Philosophy of language**: It informs debates on **reference, meaning**, and the structure of definitions.

Key Insights

- The paradox shows that **self-referential definitions** can easily lead to contradiction.

- It demonstrates that some conditions, while **linguistically coherent**, are **logically impossible**.

- It supports the need for **restricted logical systems** that avoid self-application or impose **hierarchies**.

- The Barber Paradox is not just a puzzle but a **conceptual warning** about the foundations of logic and mathematics.

- Ultimately, it teaches that clarity in rule-making must be accompanied by **constraints on self-reference** to maintain consistency.

75. Recursion Paradox

Theory Overview

The **Recursion Paradox** refers to a self-referential logical structure in which a process or definition refers back to itself in a way that creates a conceptual loop or infinite regress. In logic, mathematics, computer science, and philosophy, recursion is usually a **powerful tool** for defining complex structures from simpler ones. However, when **unbounded or improperly handled**, recursion can lead to **paradoxes**, contradictions, or systems that cannot be resolved or evaluated.

The paradox arises when a definition, process, or statement **relies on itself to be complete or meaningful**, without a base case or clear terminating condition. While recursion is essential in many areas of formal systems, the paradox warns that **not all self-reference leads to clarity**—some leads to infinite regress, undecidability, or inconsistency.

Example

A classic illustration of the Recursion Paradox comes from **language and logic**:

"This sentence refers to itself."

On the surface, this statement is harmless. But consider:

"This sentence is false."

Now, the sentence refers to itself in a way that **creates a contradiction**. If it's true, then it's false, and if it's false, then it's true. This is closely related to the **liar paradox**, and illustrates **self-reference without stable grounding**.

In **computer science**, a function like:

```
def paradox():
    return paradox()
```

is also a recursive paradox. It calls itself without a **base case**, resulting in an **infinite loop** or a **stack overflow**. There's no stopping point—no place where the function terminates and delivers a value. The recursion becomes paradoxical because it **never resolves**.

Why It Works

The Recursion Paradox works because **self-reference and circular definitions** disrupt classical notions of logic and truth. Systems built on foundational rules (like arithmetic, computation, or language) are expected to **bottom out**—to ground their definitions in something non-circular.

When they don't, we get paradoxes. These challenge the limits of formal systems and force us to confront **the boundaries of definability and computability**.

This paradox also relates to **Gödel's incompleteness theorems**, which demonstrate that any sufficiently powerful formal system can produce true statements that it **cannot prove**, often using self-referential constructions.

How It Works

The Recursion Paradox operates through three mechanisms:

1. **Self-reference**: The entity (sentence, function, rule) refers to itself.

2. **Lack of a base case or grounding**: There's no external anchor to terminate the recursion or give it meaning.

3. **Circular dependency**: Understanding or resolving the entity requires first resolving itself.

When these three combine, they **collapse the system into infinite regress or contradiction**.

Application

The Recursion Paradox has implications in:

- **Logic and philosophy**: Shows the limits of formal definability and truth statements.

- **Computer science**: Informs compiler design, recursion control, and algorithm design.

- **Linguistics**: Illuminates how recursive syntax can generate infinite language possibilities—but also complexity.

- **Cognitive science**: Self-modelling systems (e.g., human consciousness) are inherently recursive and may involve similar paradoxes.

- **Mathematics**: Recursion underlies number theory, proof systems, and algorithmic logic, with paradoxes shaping our understanding of computability.

Key Insights

- Recursion is powerful but **must be well-structured** to avoid paradox.

- Unbounded self-reference leads to **infinite regress or contradiction**.

- The paradox illustrates the **fragility of systems** that depend on internal consistency.

- Recognizing recursive paradoxes helps clarify **where rules and definitions need external grounding**.

- The paradox is central to understanding **limits of logic, language, and formal computation**.

76. Sorites Paradox (general form)

Theory

The **Sorites Paradox** (from the Greek *sōritēs*, meaning "heap") is a classic paradox in **philosophical logic** that explores the **vagueness** inherent in many natural language concepts. At its core, the paradox arises when we attempt to apply precise reasoning to a term or category that lacks a sharp boundary. The paradox is also known as the **Paradox of the Heap**, and it poses a fundamental problem for how we understand categories, gradation, and borderline cases.

The paradox is built on three intuitive premises:

1. A single grain of sand does **not** make a heap.

2. If n grains of sand do not make a heap, then $n + 1$ grains do not make a heap either.

3. Therefore, **no finite number of grains of sand makes a heap** — which is absurd, since clearly at some point we do have a heap.

The problem arises because we treat a **vague predicate** (like "heap," "bald," or "tall") as if it obeys **binary logic** — either true or false — when it may actually exist on a spectrum.

Example

Take the word **"tall."** Suppose we say that someone who is 4 feet tall is not tall. We also say that if someone is not tall, then someone one millimetre taller is also not tall. If we apply this logic iteratively, we are forced to conclude that no one — not even someone 7 feet tall — is tall.

This reasoning clearly leads to an absurd conclusion, yet it follows logically from seemingly harmless premises. The paradox is not about the *truth* of the conclusion, but about the **structure of reasoning** applied to a vague concept.

Why It Works

The paradox works because it exploits the **lack of clear boundaries** in vague concepts. We assume that there must be a precise point at which something becomes a heap, or a person becomes tall, but our language and cognition don't provide such points. We also assume that small changes (e.g., adding one grain or millimetre) should not alter categorical judgments — an assumption known as **tolerance.**

Combined with the principle of **transitivity** (if something is true for one case and the difference is negligible, it should be true for the next), this leads to the problem: small steps preserve the status, but large steps clearly cross thresholds.

How It Works

The paradox is often modelled using **fuzzy logic**, **supervaluationism**, or **contextualism** — frameworks that attempt to formalize vagueness. For example:

- **Fuzzy logic** assigns degrees of truth (someone might be "0.8 tall").

- **Supervaluationism** allows for truth-value gaps (some statements are neither true nor false).

- **Epistemicism** claims that there *is* a precise cutoff, but we don't or can't know it.

None of these solutions is universally accepted, but each tries to reconcile the intuitiveness of vague terms with logical rigor.

Application

The Sorites Paradox has real-world implications in **law, medicine, ethics,** and **artificial intelligence** — wherever decisions must be made on the basis of vague categories.

- In **law**, what counts as "reasonable force" or "adult age" may lack precise boundaries.
- In **medicine**, when does someone shift from "healthy" to "ill"?
- In **AI**, designing algorithms that classify ambiguous data (e.g., spam filters, image recognition) requires confronting vagueness head-on.

Key Insights

1. **Language Is Inherently Vague**: Everyday concepts lack sharp boundaries.
2. **Tolerance Leads to Trouble**: If small changes never matter, then big changes never do either — which is false.
3. **Binary Logic May Be Inadequate**: Not all categories fit into true/false boxes.
4. **Vagueness Demands New Tools**: Solutions like fuzzy logic or supervaluationism aim to handle borderline cases.

5. **Philosophy Meets Practicality**: Sorites-type reasoning affects real-world policies and technological design.

The Sorites Paradox is more than a puzzle — it's a lens into the **limits of classical logic** and the challenges of reasoning in a world full of shades of gray.

77. Grelling's Second-Order Adjective Problem

Theory

Grelling's Paradox, also known as **Grelling's Second-Order Adjective Problem**, is a **semantic** and **self-referential paradox** involving **adjectives that describe themselves**, or fail to. It was formulated by the German logician Kurt Grelling in the early 20th century as part of efforts to explore the foundations of language and logic, particularly inspired by the work of Bertrand Russell on set-theoretic paradoxes.

The paradox focuses on the distinction between **autological** and **heterological** adjectives:

- An adjective is **autological** if it describes itself. For example, "short" is a short word, so it is autological.

- An adjective is **heterological** if it **does not** describe itself. For example, "long" is not a long word, so it is heterological.

The paradox arises when we ask: **Is "heterological" heterological?**

Example
Let's analyse the term "heterological" using its own definition:

- Suppose **"heterological" is heterological**. That means it does **not** describe itself. But this is exactly what it's supposed to mean — that it doesn't describe itself. So if it's heterological, then it must be **autological**, which is a contradiction.

- Suppose **"heterological" is autological**. That means it **does** describe itself. But "heterological" means "does not describe itself," so this leads to the opposite of what autological implies — another contradiction.

Thus, in either case, we get a paradox. The adjective "heterological" cannot consistently be classified as either heterological or autological.

Why It Works
Grelling's Paradox works because it uses **self-reference** and a **semantic loop** to generate contradiction. It mirrors **Russell's Paradox**, which asks whether the set of all sets that do not contain themselves contains itself. Both paradoxes rely on **definitional self-inclusion** and the consequences of trying to classify a term using its own criteria.

What makes Grelling's Paradox especially elegant is that, unlike the Liar Paradox ("This sentence is false"), it does **not use explicit reference to truth or sentences**. It arises purely from **ordinary language**, applying adjectives to themselves — making the paradox sneakily subtle and striking.

How It Works
Grelling's Paradox reveals a fundamental problem in **semantic classification**: natural language allows expressions that refer to themselves in ways that disrupt binary categorization. The key mechanism is **second-order**

predication — describing properties of descriptions — which creates a loop that logic struggles to resolve within standard frameworks.

Formally, any attempt to assign a truth value to the predicate **H("heterological")** results in self-contradiction, indicating a failure in classical bivalent logic to handle semantic self-reference robustly.

Application
Grelling's Paradox has implications in **philosophy of language**, **formal semantics**, and **logic**, particularly in discussions of **self-referential systems**, **category theory**, and **truth predicates**. It helped motivate the development of **type theory**, where expressions are sorted into levels to prevent self-application — similar to how Russell addressed his own paradox.

In **computer science**, especially in programming language theory and formal verification, understanding and preventing self-referential inconsistency is essential. Languages that allow unrestricted self-reference may become logically inconsistent or computationally intractable.

Key Insights

1. **Self-Reference Breeds Paradox**: When a term refers to its own property, logical contradictions can emerge.

2. **Ordinary Language Can Be Unstable**: Natural terms like "short" or "descriptive" can create logical challenges when applied reflexively.

3. **Hierarchy Can Prevent Contradiction**: Type theories and stratified systems offer ways to avoid these paradoxes by preventing self-application.

4. **Semantics Is More Complex Than Syntax**: The paradox shows that even grammatically correct constructions can lead to semantic incoherence.

5. **Echoes Deeper Logical Issues**: Grelling's Paradox highlights the same foundational concerns that underlie Gödel's Incompleteness Theorems and Tarski's work on the indefinability of truth.

Grelling's Second-Order Adjective Problem stands as a testament to how language, when turned inward on itself, can defy the very logic we use to understand it — a profound insight into the limits of self-reference and classification.

78. Meaning Holism Paradox

Theory

The **Meaning Holism Paradox** arises from a theory in the philosophy of language and mind known as **semantic holism** or **meaning holism**, which holds that the meaning of a single word or sentence is **determined by its relations to the entire language system**. In other words, a word does not have meaning in isolation, but only in the context of other words, beliefs, and sentences in a speaker's overall conceptual network.

This view stands in contrast to **atomistic** theories of meaning, which suggest that individual words or concepts have meanings independently of their broader context. Holism emphasizes that linguistic meaning is **system-dependent**, often drawing from Quine's and Wittgenstein's ideas that "the meaning of a term is its use in the language."

The **paradox** comes when we try to apply this holistic theory of meaning consistently: if the meaning of any one term depends on all others, then **changing the meaning of one term would, in principle, change the meaning of every other term**. This leads to a dilemma: how can communication, translation, or even belief revision be possible if any local change alters the entire semantic structure?

Example

Suppose Alice says the word "dog," intending to refer to domesticated canines. Under meaning holism, the meaning of "dog" is not just tied to its dictionary definition but to its relationships with other words like "animal," "pet," "bark," "cat," etc., and to Alice's beliefs about these concepts.

Now, imagine Alice revises her belief about "animal" (perhaps she now thinks robots count as animals). Under a strict holistic framework, this change might affect the meaning of "dog," which is related to "animal," and in turn affect the meaning of "pet," "life," "movement," and so on. The **web of meaning** shifts with each conceptual tweak. This domino effect leads to the paradox: if all meanings are interdependent, how is **semantic stability** possible at all?

Why It Works

The paradox works because it reveals the tension between the **fluid, interconnected nature of meaning** (as proposed by holism) and the **practical necessity of stable reference** in communication. We clearly can talk, translate, and disagree — but if meaning holism were entirely correct and uncompromising, even minor conceptual differences between speakers would make shared meaning impossible.

This suggests that either (1) meaning holism is false, (2) communication is largely an illusion, or (3) holism must be **restricted** to allow for **partial overlap of meaning**.

How It Works

Meaning holism functions by rejecting that words have fixed meanings in isolation. Instead, it models linguistic understanding as a **web of interdependent nodes** — change one, and the others shift too. This creates problems for:

- **Compositionality**: how sentence meaning is derived from parts.
- **Translation**: if meanings are system-relative, translation becomes ambiguous.
- **Belief revision**: any change in belief could lead to global conceptual upheaval.

The paradox arises from pushing holism to its extreme: assuming total interdependence makes meaningful communication seem impossible, yet we obviously **do** communicate.

Application

The Meaning Holism Paradox influences debates in **cognitive science, AI language modelling, epistemology**, and **semantics**. It challenges the design of systems that model meaning computationally, such as large language models, which must represent word meanings without needing a total understanding of the entire language network.

In **philosophy of mind**, it complicates theories of belief attribution — if beliefs are holistically defined, attributing a belief to someone (e.g., "she believes dogs are animals") may require knowing their entire belief system.

Key Insights

1. **Meaning Is Relational**: Individual meanings depend on networks of beliefs and linguistic connections.

2. **Total Holism Undermines Communication**: If every meaning depends on every other, shared language use becomes implausible.

3. **Partial Holism May Be Necessary**: A balance between holism and atomism helps preserve both nuance and communicability.

4. **Belief Revision Becomes Risky**: Changing one belief could, paradoxically, change all others if holism is taken seriously.

5. **Practical Language Use Refutes Absolutism**: Despite holism's appeal, communication works, suggesting constraints on interdependence.

The Meaning Holism Paradox serves as a philosophical stress test, revealing the limits of theories that lean too far into conceptual interconnectedness — and reminding us that meaning, while systemic, must also be usable.

79. Vagueness Paradox

Theory

The **Vagueness Paradox** is a central puzzle in logic and philosophy, dealing with the **indeterminate boundaries** of certain concepts in natural language. It arises from the fact that many everyday terms — such as "tall," "bald," "heap," or "rich" — lack **precise cutoffs**. There is no exact number of hairs that makes someone bald or precise height that makes someone tall. This inherent indeterminacy leads to paradoxes when we try to apply classical logic, which assumes **bivalence** — that every proposition is either true or false.

At the heart of the Vagueness Paradox is the problem of **borderline cases**, where we cannot decisively say whether a term applies. If we insist on crisp boundaries, we are forced to draw arbitrary and unjustified lines. If we reject boundaries entirely, then we risk falling into contradictions or absurdities. This tension creates a paradox about how language functions and how truth values are assigned.

Example

Consider the word **"bald."** Suppose we start with a man who has a full head of hair and remove one hair at a time. Common sense tells us that removing a single hair doesn't make someone bald. Yet, if we apply this rule repeatedly, we are led to conclude that even a man with no hair at all isn't bald — which is clearly false.

This reasoning forms the **Sorites-style structure** of the paradox (from the Greek word *sōritēs*, meaning "heap"). It highlights the problem of vagueness: if we cannot say when someone becomes bald, can we say anything meaningful at all about baldness?

Why It Works

The paradox works by exploiting our **intuitions about tolerance** — the idea that small changes don't affect categorization — and our **commitment to classical logic**. Classical logic relies on principles such as:

- **Bivalence**: Every statement is true or false.

- **Law of the excluded middle**: For any proposition, either it or its negation is true.

But vague predicates defy these principles. If someone is a borderline case of baldness, we hesitate to call the statement "He is bald" either true or false. Yet classical logic allows no middle ground. This clash creates the paradox.

How It Works

The paradox is structured around three assumptions:

1. **Tolerance**: Small changes (like losing one hair) don't change category membership.

2. **Transitivity**: A series of small changes doesn't result in a significant difference.

3. **Definiteness**: There must be a specific point at which a vague term becomes applicable or not.

Together, these lead to contradiction. Either we accept tolerance and transitivity and reject definiteness, or we impose an arbitrary boundary and violate our intuitions.

To resolve this, philosophers have developed several approaches:

- **Epistemicism**: There *is* a sharp cutoff, but we can't know it.
- **Fuzzy logic**: Truth values range between 0 and 1, allowing for degrees of truth.
- **Supervaluationism**: Some statements are neither true nor false, but truth is preserved across all "precisifications" (ways of making vague terms precise).

Application

The Vagueness Paradox is crucial in **law, medicine, ethics, AI,** and **linguistics**. For instance, in legal contexts, terms like "reasonable force" or "undue influence" must be applied without exact definitions. In **AI**, training models to classify vague categories like "appropriate" or "relevant" requires accounting for gradations and uncertainty.

It also plays a key role in **semantic theory**, decision-making algorithms, and social policy, where clear categories are needed, but natural language resists them.

Key Insights

1. **Vagueness Is Ubiquitous**: Most everyday language includes vague terms without sharp boundaries.

2. **Classical Logic Struggles with Borderlines**: The demand for bivalence creates tension with linguistic practice.

3. **Tolerance vs. Precision**: Small changes shouldn't cause large categorical shifts, yet vagueness forces us to consider this.

4. **Solutions Require New Logics**: Fuzzy logic, super valuation, and epistemicism offer different trade-offs.

5. **Practical Decisions Must Navigate Gray Areas**: Legal, ethical, and computational systems must reconcile vagueness with clarity.

The Vagueness Paradox reveals the **limits of formal reasoning** in capturing the messy, imprecise nature of human concepts — challenging us to rethink how we define and use language.

80. Referential Opacity Paradox

Theory

The **Referential Opacity Paradox** is a problem in the **philosophy of language and logic**, concerning how we refer to things within certain kinds of linguistic contexts—especially **belief, knowledge, and other propositional attitude reports**. The paradox arises when **substituting co-referential terms** (that is, different expressions that refer to the same object) leads to a **change in truth value**, which seems to violate the principle of **substitutivity of identicals**.

In classical logic, if two terms refer to the same thing (say, "Clark Kent" and "Superman"), then you should be able to substitute one for the other in any sentence without changing its truth. However, in certain contexts — especially where someone's **mental states or attitudes** are involved — this substitution breaks down. These contexts are called **referentially opaque**, as opposed to **referentially transparent** contexts, where substitution preserves truth.

This creates a paradox: how can two terms refer to the same object but not be interchangeable in every context?

Example

Consider Lois Lane. She believes that:

(1) "Superman can fly."

This is true. Now, since **Clark Kent is Superman**, we might assume Lois also believes:

(2) "Clark Kent can fly."

But suppose she does **not** know that Clark Kent is Superman. In fact, she believes:

(3) "Clark Kent cannot fly."

Here's the paradox: "Clark Kent" and "Superman" refer to the same person. So, by the logical rule of substitutivity, any belief about Superman should also be a belief about Clark Kent. Yet Lois clearly distinguishes between them. This suggests that **reference alone is not sufficient** to explain how meaning works in propositional attitude contexts.

Why It Works
The paradox works because it challenges our assumptions about **semantic equivalence and identity**. In classical logic, if two expressions refer to the same entity, they should be **interchangeable salva veritate** (without changing the truth of the sentence). However, in everyday language, mental states are **sensitive to how something is described**, not just to what it is.

This sensitivity breaks the link between identity and substitutability, suggesting that the **mode of presentation** or the **sense** of a term (as Frege proposed) plays a crucial role in meaning — not just the referent.

How It Works
The paradox reveals the importance of **intensional contexts**, where what matters is not just reference but how things are conceived or described. In these contexts, replacing a name

with another name for the same object can change the truth-value of the sentence.

The standard way to resolve this paradox is to distinguish between **extension** (what a term refers to) and **intension** (the concept or sense it conveys). So, while "Superman" and "Clark Kent" have the same extension, they differ in intension — and this difference matters in belief reports.

This view leads to richer semantic models, such as those used in **possible world semantics** and **intensional logic**, where propositional attitudes are treated as relations to propositions, not just facts.

Application
The Referential Opacity Paradox has profound implications in **philosophy of mind, linguistics, logic,** and **artificial intelligence**. In AI and natural language processing, systems that model belief or intention must distinguish between different ways of referring to the same entity. Legal, ethical, and psychological analyses of intention and belief also rely on understanding these subtleties.

In **modal logic**, where necessity and possibility are involved, referential opacity is a central concern, especially when evaluating what could or must be true from different perspectives.

Key Insights

1. **Not All Contexts Allow Substitution**: Even co-referential terms can't always be swapped without altering meaning.

2. **Belief Is Sensitive to Description**: What someone believes depends not just on facts, but on how they conceive of those facts.

3. **Frege's Sense–Reference Distinction Matters**: Sense (intension) can't be ignored when dealing with mental state reports.

4. **Semantic Context Is Crucial**: Understanding language requires attention to the type of context—intensional vs. extensional.

5. **Challenges Classical Logic**: Referential opacity exposes the limits of traditional logic in handling language and belief.

The Referential Opacity Paradox highlights the complexity of meaning and reference, showing that understanding language — especially about beliefs — involves more than just tracking identities. It requires a grasp of how things are represented in the mind and in discourse.

81. Performative Contradiction Paradox

Theory

The **Performative Contradiction Paradox** arises in the **philosophy of language**, **pragmatics**, and **epistemology** when a statement contradicts the very **conditions required to assert it**. In other words, it's not that the content of the statement is logically false, but that the **act of asserting it** undermines or invalidates it. This is what makes it a **performative** contradiction: the *performance* of speech contradicts the *propositional content*.

This differs from logical contradictions, which involve incompatible propositions (e.g., "P and not-P"). A performative contradiction is paradoxical because the speaker's act of making a claim reveals that they **implicitly accept assumptions** that their statement explicitly denies.

It's often associated with **speech act theory** (J.L. Austin, John Searle) and explored in discussions about **rational discourse**, **ethics**, and **truth claims**.

Example

Consider someone saying:

"I am not speaking right now."

This is a performative contradiction. The act of **saying** this sentence presupposes that the speaker **is speaking**, even though the content denies it. The contradiction lies not in the sentence's grammar or logic, but in the clash between **what is said** and the **fact that it is said**.

Another example occurs in philosophy:

"There is no such thing as objective truth."

To assert this coherently, one must treat the statement as **objectively true**, thereby contradicting its content. The act of asserting truth about the **nonexistence of truth** undermines the statement itself.

Why It Works

The paradox works because it exposes the **tacit commitments** we make when we speak. Assertions come with **pragmatic presuppositions**: when you say something, you're not only conveying content, you're also engaging in a social act that assumes certain norms (like coherence, sincerity, truthfulness, or communicative intent).

When the content of an utterance denies the very possibility of that act or those assumptions, we encounter a performative contradiction. These paradoxes compel us to think more carefully about the **conditions for meaningful communication**.

How It Works

A performative contradiction typically involves three components:

1. A **speech act** (asserting, denying, questioning, etc.)

2. **Presuppositions** implicit in that act (e.g., belief in truth, the speaker's presence, rationality)

3. **Propositional content** that denies or negates those presuppositions

When the third clashes with the second, we get a contradiction — not in logic, but in **discourse function**.

In formal terms, this can be modelled using **pragmatic logic** or **discourse models**, which account for speaker intentions, context, and the role of utterances in interaction.

Application
Performative contradiction is used in **ethics, argumentation theory**, and **political philosophy**. For example, in **discourse ethics**, philosophers like Jürgen Habermas argue that any participant in rational debate implicitly accepts certain norms (like the value of truth and reason). Denying those norms within the debate becomes a performative contradiction — a **self-defeating position**.

In **law**, a defendant claiming "I do not recognize the legitimacy of this court" while appealing to the court's procedures can commit a performative contradiction. In **AI and human-computer interaction**, systems that simulate dialogue must navigate the pragmatics of speech, and contradictions between function and content can disrupt trust and coherence.

Key Insights

1. **Meaning Is More Than Content**: The act of saying something carries implicit commitments.

2. **Contradictions Can Be Pragmatic**: A statement can be logically consistent yet discursively self-defeating.

3. **Speech Presupposes Shared Norms**: Communication relies on unspoken assumptions like sincerity, truth, and rationality.

4. **Useful in Ethical and Rational Discourse**: Identifying performative contradictions helps evaluate arguments and expose incoherence.

5. **Highlights the Limits of Pure Logic**: Real-world discourse involves roles, intentions, and context beyond propositional truth.

The **Performative Contradiction Paradox** reveals that **language is action**, and some actions cannot succeed unless certain conditions are already accepted — even if the content denies them. It's a powerful reminder that speech is embedded in **practical, social, and normative contexts**.

🚀 Physics & Relativity Paradoxes

Stem from extreme or theoretical scenarios in physics.

82. Twin Paradox

Theory Overview

The **Twin Paradox** is a famous thought experiment in **special relativity**, proposed to illustrate the **counterintuitive effects of time dilation**. It involves two twins—one of whom embarks on a high-speed journey through space while the other stays on Earth. Upon returning, the traveling twin is younger than their sibling.

Though it appears paradoxical—since both twins could view the other as "moving"—the resolution lies in the **asymmetry** of their experiences, especially the effects of **acceleration and non-inertial frames**. The paradox is not a contradiction in Einstein's theory, but a challenge to our classical intuition about time and simultaneity.

Example

Imagine twin siblings, **Anna** and **Ben**. Anna stays on Earth while Ben boards a spacecraft and travels to a distant star at **90% the speed of light**, then turns around and comes back. Due to **time dilation**, a prediction of Einstein's theory of special relativity, **Ben's onboard clock ticks more slowly** relative to Anna's.

Suppose the journey takes **10 years in Ben's frame** (5 years out, 5 years back). Meanwhile, **on Earth**, more time has passed—say, **22 years**, according to calculations using the Lorentz transformation. When Ben returns, he finds that Anna is **12 years older** than he is.

To a non-expert, this feels paradoxical. Since motion is relative, why wouldn't Anna appear to be the one moving from Ben's perspective, making her the one who should age less?

Why It Works

The Twin Paradox works as a paradox because it **exposes the limits of classical reasoning** when applied to relativistic motion. Our everyday experience tells us that time is absolute and symmetrical. But special relativity replaces this with a more complex structure in which **simultaneity is relative**, and **the passage of time depends on the observer's frame of reference**.

At a glance, it seems each twin could argue the other is moving—so each should see the other age more slowly. However, the resolution lies in the **non-symmetrical paths**: Ben's journey involves **acceleration, deceleration, and a frame change** when he turns around. These break the symmetry of the situation.

How It Works

The paradox is resolved within special relativity as follows:

- **Anna remains in an inertial frame** (no acceleration), while Ben **switches frames** when turning around.

- Special relativity applies cleanly within each inertial segment of Ben's journey, and the Lorentz transformation accounts for time dilation.

- The key insight is that **Ben's frame is not equivalent** throughout the entire trip—his clock accumulates **less proper time** because of his trajectory through spacetime.

When calculated precisely using spacetime diagrams or the math of proper time integrals, the predictions match: **Ben is younger**, and there is no contradiction.

Application

The Twin Paradox is more than a thought experiment—it has real-world applications:

- **GPS satellites** account for both special and general relativistic time dilation to ensure accurate timekeeping.

- **High-speed particle experiments** (like muons traveling in accelerators) confirm that fast-moving particles experience time more slowly, as predicted.

- The paradox helps teach the **importance of non-inertial frames** in relativistic physics and fosters understanding of how time operates in Einstein's universe.

Key Insights

- Time is **not absolute**; it depends on velocity and path through spacetime.

- The paradox illustrates that **acceleration and changing reference frames matter**, breaking the symmetry that would otherwise confuse the outcome.

- Special relativity is consistent and **predicts measurable time differences**, confirmed by both theory and experiment.

- Our classical intuitions about time must be revised in light of **relativistic physics**.

- The Twin Paradox is a foundational tool for understanding **spacetime geometry, time dilation, and relativistic simultaneity**.

83. Zeno's Paradoxes (Achilles, Dichotomy, Arrow)

Theory Overview

Zeno's Paradoxes were developed by the ancient Greek philosopher **Zeno of Elea** around the 5th century BCE. Designed to defend the teachings of **Parmenides**, who argued that motion and change are illusions, Zeno's paradoxes challenge our understanding of time, space, and movement.

These paradoxes are not just ancient puzzles; they raise profound questions about the **continuity of space and time**, the **nature of infinity**, and how modern mathematics and physics reconcile intuitive contradiction with rigorous logic.

Zeno proposed over 40 paradoxes, but the most famous are:

1. **Achilles and the Tortoise**
2. **The Dichotomy Paradox**
3. **The Arrow Paradox**

Each paradox attempts to **demonstrate that motion is logically impossible**—or at least deeply counterintuitive—when space and time are divided infinitely.

Example

1. Achilles and the Tortoise

Achilles, the swift Greek hero, gives a slow-moving tortoise a head start in a race. Zeno argues that Achilles can never overtake the tortoise, because by the time Achilles reaches the point where the tortoise was, the tortoise has moved a bit farther. This continues infinitely: every time Achilles reaches the tortoise's last position, the tortoise has moved ahead, however slightly.

Implication: Achilles will never catch up.

2. The Dichotomy Paradox

To reach any destination, you must first travel half the distance. Then you must cover half the remaining distance, and so on. This process creates an **infinite number of tasks** to complete in a finite amount of time.

Implication: Motion can never begin, because there are infinitely many steps to take.

3. The Arrow Paradox

An arrow in flight is, at any single instant, **motionless**—occupying a fixed point in space. If every moment in time shows the arrow at rest, how can it ever be moving?

Implication: Motion is an illusion; it's just a sequence of still frames.

Why It Works

Zeno's Paradoxes work by exposing the **counterintuitive implications of dividing space and time into infinitely small parts**. In a world where space and time are infinitely divisible, strange things happen: infinite steps seem to take infinite time, and motion appears to break down into a series of unmoving states.

They cleverly exploit the **concept of infinity**, which ancient mathematics could not fully formalize. These paradoxes demonstrate how a naive understanding of infinity leads to logical traps.

How It Works

The paradoxes rest on two assumptions:

1. **Space and time are continuous and infinitely divisible**.
2. **A task involving infinitely many parts cannot be completed in finite time**.

Modern mathematics, particularly **calculus**, resolves these paradoxes using the concept of **convergent series**. For example:

- The infinite sequence of distances in the Dichotomy Paradox (½, ¼, ⅛...) adds up to a finite total: 1.
- The infinite steps Achilles must run through can be completed in finite time.

- The Arrow Paradox is resolved by understanding **instantaneous velocity**: motion doesn't require movement during indivisible instants but is defined as a **limit** over time.

Application

Zeno's Paradoxes have influenced:

- **Mathematics**: Helping shape concepts in calculus, limits, and series.

- **Philosophy**: Sparking debates about continuity, space, and time.

- **Physics**: Informing theories about spacetime in quantum mechanics and relativity.

- **Computer science**: In modelling algorithms and understanding computational limits involving infinite processes.

Key Insights

- Infinity can be **mathematically tamed**, but still challenges our intuitions.

- Motion is not contradictory when space and time are handled with **limit-based reasoning**.

- Zeno's Paradoxes remain essential teaching tools for exploring **conceptual foundations** in logic, physics, and math.
- The ancient questions they raise continue to resonate in **modern science and metaphysics**.

84. Einstein–Podolsky–Rosen Paradox

Theory Overview

The **Einstein–Podolsky–Rosen Paradox**, commonly known as the **EPR Paradox**, was introduced in a 1935 paper by **Albert Einstein**, **Boris Podolsky**, and **Nathan Rosen**. The paradox challenges the **completeness of quantum mechanics** by arguing that the theory allows for **"spooky action at a distance"**—a phenomenon Einstein found deeply unsettling.

At the heart of the EPR argument is **quantum entanglement**—a condition where two or more particles are linked in such a way that the state of one immediately affects the state of the other, regardless of the distance between them. The paradox was designed to show that if quantum mechanics is correct, then it must be **non-local**, meaning that an action in one place can have an instantaneous effect elsewhere—violating the principle of locality upheld by relativity.

Einstein and his colleagues concluded that **quantum mechanics must be incomplete**, suggesting that **"hidden variables"** might exist—unknown elements of reality that could account for the apparent non-locality.

Example

Imagine two particles are created together in such a way that their properties—say, their spins—are entangled. If particle A is sent to Alice and particle B to Bob, and Alice measures the spin of her particle, she finds it to be "up." Instantly, she knows that Bob's particle must be "down," no matter how far apart they are.

Here's the paradox: **before measurement**, neither particle has a definite spin—it's only upon observation that the spin becomes fixed. So how does Bob's particle "know" what result to give at the exact moment Alice makes her measurement? Either:

1. The particles had definite spins all along (hidden variables), or
2. Measurement on one particle **instantaneously affects** the other, no matter the distance.

Quantum mechanics supports the second option. Einstein, however, rejected this as "spooky action at a distance," and argued that **any complete physical theory must preserve locality and realism**—hence, quantum mechanics, as formulated, must be incomplete.

Why It Works

The EPR Paradox works because it exposes the **conceptual tension** between **quantum nonlocality** and **classical intuitions** about separability and realism. It challenges the assumption that objects have properties independent of measurement and that signals cannot travel faster than light.

The paradox doesn't show that quantum mechanics is wrong—but that its implications **defy classical logic**.

How It Works

The EPR argument rests on three principles:

1. **Locality**: No information or influence can travel faster than light.
2. **Realism**: Physical properties exist before they are measured.
3. **Completeness**: A theory is complete if it accounts for all elements of physical reality.

Quantum mechanics violates either locality or realism (or both) to maintain internal consistency. EPR argued this meant the theory must be incomplete.

But later developments, particularly **Bell's Theorem (1964)** and subsequent experiments, showed that **no local hidden variable theory can reproduce all quantum predictions**. The universe **is nonlocal**, at least in the quantum sense.

Application

The EPR Paradox has profound implications in:

- **Quantum information science**, leading to technologies like **quantum teleportation** and **quantum cryptography**.

- **Philosophy of physics**, challenging our notions of **causality**, **reality**, and **measurement**.

- **Experimental physics**, driving precision tests of quantum entanglement (e.g., Bell test experiments).

- **Quantum computing**, where entanglement is a core resource for parallelism and secure computation.

Key Insights

- The EPR Paradox questions the **completeness and locality** of quantum mechanics.

- Entanglement reveals that particles can be **deeply linked** beyond classical explanation.

- Later experiments favoured **quantum nonlocality**, disproving local realism.

- The paradox highlights how **quantum theory departs** from everyday logic but remains **empirically correct**.

- It helped spark the **quantum information revolution**, changing how we think about the nature of reality itself.

85. Schrödinger's Cat

Theory Overview

Schrödinger's Cat is a famous thought experiment devised by Austrian physicist **Erwin Schrödinger** in 1935. It was meant to illustrate what Schrödinger saw as the absurdity or incompleteness of the **Copenhagen interpretation** of quantum mechanics when applied to everyday objects.

At the heart of the paradox is the quantum concept of **superposition**—the idea that a quantum system can exist in multiple states at once, such as a particle being in two locations or having two different energies. According to the Copenhagen interpretation, this superposition persists **until the system is observed**, at which point the wavefunction "collapses" into a definite state.

Schrödinger's thought experiment poses the question: *What happens when a quantum superposition is entangled with a macroscopic object like a cat?*

Example

In the thought experiment, a cat is placed inside a sealed box along with:

1. A **radioactive atom** that has a 50% chance of decaying within an hour.

2. A **Geiger counter** to detect decay.

3. A **vial of poison** triggered by the Geiger counter if decay is detected.

If the atom decays, the Geiger counter activates, the vial breaks, and the cat dies. If the atom does not decay, the cat lives.

Now, until someone opens the box, **quantum mechanics describes the atom as being both decayed and not decayed**—a superposition. Because the Geiger counter and poison are entangled with the atom's state, and the cat with them, **the cat is also both alive and dead**—a macroscopic superposition.

Only when an observer opens the box and "measures" the system does the wavefunction collapse, and the cat is observed to be either alive or dead.

Why It Works

The paradox works because it highlights a **philosophical and practical tension**: Can the strange rules of the quantum world apply to large-scale, everyday objects? While the Copenhagen interpretation accepts wavefunction collapse upon observation, Schrödinger's Cat reveals that applying this logic to real-world entities like cats leads to an **unacceptable conclusion**: a cat both alive and dead until someone looks.

This apparent absurdity was meant by Schrödinger not to explain quantum theory, but to **criticize it**, or at least expose its interpretational limits.

How It Works

The paradox hinges on **entanglement and superposition**:

1. The atom exists in a superposition of decayed and not decayed.
2. This state becomes entangled with the detector, the poison mechanism, and ultimately the cat.
3. The result is a superposition of entire macroscopic states: the cat is both dead and alive.
4. Measurement causes **wavefunction collapse**, resolving the system into one of the two outcomes.

Different interpretations of quantum mechanics handle this differently:

- **Copenhagen**: Collapse occurs upon observation.
- **Many-Worlds**: The universe splits—one where the cat is alive, one where it is dead.
- **Objective Collapse Theories**: Collapse happens spontaneously or based on mass/complexity, not observation.

Application

Schrödinger's Cat has become a cornerstone for:

- **Quantum computing**, where quantum bits (qubits) exist in superpositions.

- **Philosophy of science**, particularly in debates over realism and the role of the observer.

- **Interpretations of quantum mechanics**, influencing theories like Many-Worlds, decoherence, and quantum Bayesianism.

- **Public understanding**, as a metaphor for the strange and non-intuitive nature of quantum theory.

Key Insights

- The paradox exposes the **limits of applying quantum theory to the macroscopic world**.

- It challenges the boundary between **observer and system**, and **quantum and classical**.

- It demonstrates how **entanglement scales**, connecting quantum events to real-world outcomes.

- Schrödinger's Cat is not just a physics puzzle—it's a **philosophical provocation** about what reality truly is.

- The thought experiment remains central to **debates on the interpretation of quantum mechanics**.

86. Quantum Zeno Effect

Theory Overview

The **Quantum Zeno Effect** is a counterintuitive phenomenon in **quantum mechanics** where **frequent observation of a system can prevent it from evolving**. Named after the ancient philosopher Zeno of Elea—whose paradoxes challenged motion and change—the Quantum Zeno Effect (QZE) draws a surprising parallel: **a quantum system that is constantly measured seems to "freeze" in its current state**.

First proposed theoretically in the 1970s by **Bailey, Misra, and Sudarshan**, the effect shows how **measurement**, a fundamental act in quantum physics, doesn't just passively record reality—it can actively influence the evolution of the system. The paradox lies in the idea that **watching a quantum system too closely can prevent it from changing**.

Example

Imagine an unstable particle that is expected to decay after a certain amount of time. If you measure whether it has decayed at infrequent intervals, you'll eventually observe the decay. But if you check continuously—rapidly and repeatedly—each measurement momentarily collapses the particle's wavefunction back into the **undecayed state**.

As a result, **the act of repeated observation inhibits the natural decay process**. In the extreme, this leads to the paradoxical conclusion: **the particle will never decay if it is observed continuously**, even though it is supposed to be unstable.

This "freezing" of quantum evolution due to frequent measurement is the essence of the Quantum Zeno Effect.

Why It Works

The QZE works because of the peculiar role of **measurement in quantum mechanics**. In classical physics, measuring a system doesn't interfere with its evolution. But in quantum physics, the **act of measurement collapses the wavefunction**—forcing the system into a specific state.

Between measurements, a quantum system evolves smoothly (as governed by the Schrödinger equation). But each measurement **resets this evolution**, bringing the system back to its original state if the outcome confirms no change. If this process is repeated rapidly enough, the system never gets a chance to evolve significantly, effectively "freezing" it.

This aligns with the principle that **probabilities of transition between quantum states depend on the time allowed for such transitions**. Infinitesimally small time intervals mean infinitesimally small transition probabilities.

How It Works

Here's a simplified sequence of the QZE:

1. A quantum system starts in state A.
2. Left undisturbed, it evolves naturally toward state B over time.
3. But if you measure the system at very short intervals to check whether it's still in state A:
    - Each measurement collapses the wavefunction back to A if the system hasn't transitioned.
    - Since little to no evolution occurs between rapid measurements, the transition to B is suppressed.
4. The more frequently you measure, the less likely the system transitions from A to B.

This "watching prevents changing" is the paradox at the heart of the QZE.

Application

The Quantum Zeno Effect has practical and theoretical applications:

- **Quantum computing**: Helps protect quantum information from decoherence through techniques like quantum error correction and dynamic decoupling.

- **Quantum control and measurement**: Enables precision manipulation of quantum states in labs.

- **Atomic physics**: Used in experiments involving cold atoms and trapped ions to extend quantum state lifetimes.

- **Philosophy of science**: Challenges assumptions about the nature of time, change, and the observer's role in physical reality.

It also serves as a striking demonstration of **how quantum systems behave differently** from classical ones under observation.

Key Insights

- **Observation in quantum mechanics is not neutral**; it can actively prevent change.

- The QZE shows how **frequent measurement inhibits quantum evolution**, a stark contrast to classical systems.

- It emphasizes the **nontrivial role of time and measurement** in quantum behaviour.

- The paradox illustrates a profound truth: **in quantum systems, how often you look affects what you see**.

- The effect has implications for **quantum control, information theory, and the philosophy of measurement**.

87. Information Paradox

Theory Overview

The **Information Paradox** refers to a fundamental conflict in physics regarding the fate of **information** that falls into a black hole. It arises from the apparent contradiction between **quantum mechanics**, which insists that information is conserved, and **general relativity**, which implies that information could be lost forever in a black hole.

This paradox became widely recognized after **Stephen Hawking**'s 1974 discovery of **Hawking radiation**—a quantum mechanical process through which black holes slowly emit particles and eventually evaporate. The problem? Hawking radiation appears **thermal and random**, carrying no information about the black hole's contents. If the black hole fully evaporates, what happens to the information about the matter that fell in?

In quantum theory, the **unitarity principle** dictates that all physical processes are reversible and that information cannot be destroyed. If black holes erase information, that principle is violated—threatening the foundations of quantum mechanics itself.

Example

Imagine you throw a book, a person, or even a galaxy into a black hole. According to classical general relativity, all this matter is compressed into a singularity and cannot be recovered. As the black hole emits Hawking radiation and eventually disappears, it leaves behind no trace of the information that once existed.

This creates a problem: if you knew everything about the initial state (e.g., the pages of the book), but all that remains after evaporation is unstructured thermal radiation, then the evolution of the system has become **non-unitary**. This implies a **loss of information**, which is forbidden by quantum mechanics.

Why It Works

The Information Paradox works because it exposes a **deep incompatibility** between two otherwise successful theories. General relativity allows for singularities and causal disconnection via event horizons, which seem to trap information permanently. Quantum mechanics, by contrast, is built on the assumption that information is **never destroyed**—even when it is scrambled or transformed.

What makes this a paradox rather than just a technical issue is that **both theories have been experimentally successful**, yet their predictions contradict each other in the extreme environment of a black hole.

How It Works

The paradox unfolds through three basic principles:

1. **Information falls into the black hole** along with matter.

2. **Hawking radiation** carries away energy, but appears to contain **no information** about the interior.

3. The black hole **evaporates completely**, seemingly leaving behind **no way to reconstruct** the original information.

Over time, the system transitions from a known state (matter and information) to a final state (featureless radiation), breaking **time-reversal symmetry** and violating quantum principles.

Efforts to resolve this include:

- **Holographic principle**: All the information is stored on the event horizon's surface.

- **Black hole complementarity**: Different observers (outside vs. inside) may have valid but non-overlapping accounts of what happens.

- **Firewall hypothesis**: Suggests a breakdown of spacetime at the event horizon to preserve information.

- **Unitary evaporation**: Newer models suggest Hawking radiation may encode subtle information over time, preserving unitarity.

Application

The Information Paradox has profound implications for:

- **Quantum gravity**: It's a key motivation for merging general relativity and quantum mechanics.

- **Theoretical models**: It has driven developments in string theory, AdS/CFT correspondence, and loop quantum gravity.

- **Cosmology**: It challenges how we think about the early universe and spacetime singularities.

- **Quantum computing**: It parallels debates about information preservation in quantum systems.

Key Insights

- The paradox illustrates a **fundamental clash** between the two greatest theories of physics.

- It raises questions about the **nature of space, time, and information**.

- Solving it may require **redefining reality**, perhaps through new physics beyond current models.

- Recent work suggests that **information may leak out gradually**, offering hope for resolution.

- It continues to shape the **future of theoretical physics**, marking a path toward the elusive theory of **quantum gravity**.

88. Wigner's Friend

Theory Overview

The **Wigner's Friend Paradox** is a thought experiment in **quantum mechanics** that explores the role of the observer in determining physical reality. It was proposed by physicist **Eugene Wigner** in 1961 and builds upon the famous **Schrödinger's Cat** scenario by introducing **nested observers**—one inside a quantum system and one outside of it.

The core question Wigner posed was: *If an observer (the "friend") makes a measurement on a quantum system inside a closed lab, what does another observer (Wigner), outside the lab, say about the state of that system?* The paradox reveals a deep inconsistency in interpretations of quantum mechanics, particularly around the idea of **observer-dependent reality** and **wavefunction collapse**.

Wigner's Friend forces us to ask whether **measurement causes collapse**, and if so, **for whom?** Can two observers assign **different realities** to the same event, both consistently within quantum theory?

Example

Imagine Wigner's friend is inside a sealed laboratory conducting a quantum experiment involving a single photon. The photon is in a superposition of two polarizations:

horizontal and vertical. The friend performs a measurement and records the result—say, "horizontal."

From the **friend's perspective**, the superposition has collapsed: the photon had a definite polarization when measured.

But from **Wigner's perspective**, standing outside the sealed lab and treating the entire lab (including the friend) as a quantum system, the whole system remains in a **superposition**:

The lab is in a state where the friend observed "horizontal" **and** in a state where the friend observed "vertical."

This leads to a contradiction: for the friend, the system has collapsed. For Wigner, it hasn't. So: **Whose reality is correct?**

Why It Works

Wigner's Friend works because it pushes quantum mechanics into the realm of **meta-observation**. It demonstrates that, within standard quantum theory, observers may not agree on what's real. This idea challenges classical notions of an objective, observer-independent reality.

It exploits the linearity and universality of the Schrödinger equation: if all physical systems, including observers, evolve quantum mechanically, then measurement does not necessitate collapse—it merely results in entanglement with the measuring apparatus. This leads to **multiple coexisting**

outcomes, depending on who's looking and from what vantage point.

How It Works

The paradox uses three main elements:

1. **Quantum superposition**: Before measurement, a system exists in multiple states simultaneously.

2. **Collapse postulate**: Measurement collapses the superposition to a single outcome.

3. **Observer as a system**: When treated as quantum systems themselves, observers don't collapse anything—instead, they become entangled with the measured system.

The result is that **reality becomes relative**—each observer may have a valid but different description of the same event. This has been tested in more modern variants like the **Frauchiger-Renner thought experiment**, which showed that applying quantum mechanics to observers leads to logical contradictions under certain assumptions.

Application

The Wigner's Friend Paradox has implications in:

- **Quantum foundations**: It challenges traditional interpretations like the Copenhagen interpretation.

- **Quantum computing and information**: It raises questions about when and how information becomes classical.

- **Philosophy of mind**: It intersects with debates on consciousness and whether subjective experience plays a role in reality.

- **Quantum gravity and cosmology**: Where multiple observers might have conflicting accounts of events in extreme regimes.

It has also influenced **interpretations of quantum mechanics**, such as the **Many-Worlds Interpretation** (which denies collapse altogether) and **Relational Quantum Mechanics** (which posits that facts are relative to observers).

Key Insights

- The paradox reveals that **measurement in quantum theory is deeply observer-dependent**.

- It blurs the line between subject and object, between measurer and measured.

- It suggests that reality may not be absolute, but **relative to observers**.

- It challenges the completeness and consistency of conventional quantum mechanics.

- Solving the paradox may require **redefining what we mean by "objective reality."**

89. Ether Paradox

Theory Overview

The **Ether Paradox** (or **Luminiferous Ether Paradox**) refers to the historical conflict in physics over the existence of a hypothetical medium called the **ether**, once thought necessary for the propagation of light. In the 19th century, scientists believed that just as sound waves need air and water waves need water, **light waves must propagate through some medium**—the "luminiferous ether."

This assumption led to a paradox when **experiments failed to detect any evidence of ether**, despite its presumed necessity. The paradox highlights the clash between **classical mechanics** and emerging ideas in **electromagnetism and relativity**, ultimately culminating in a profound shift in our understanding of space, time, and motion.

Example

The most famous test of the ether's existence was the **Michelson–Morley experiment** in 1887. It aimed to measure the Earth's motion through the ether (the "ether wind") by detecting changes in the speed of light depending on Earth's direction of travel.

The idea was simple: if Earth moved through the ether, light traveling in the direction of motion should move at a different speed compared to light traveling perpendicular to it. The experiment used an interferometer to detect such differences.

Result? No difference was found. Light's speed remained constant in all directions, contradicting the ether theory and presenting physicists with a major problem: if ether exists, why can't it be detected?

Why It Works

The Ether Paradox works because it forces us to confront the **limitations of assumptions** based on analogies from classical mechanics. Scientists tried to fit light into the same framework as other waves, assuming it needed a medium. This assumption, although logical at the time, produced a theoretical construct (ether) that had **no observable properties** and **no interaction with matter**, yet was somehow required for light to travel.

When light's behaviour contradicted the predictions based on the ether, the scientific community faced a deep conceptual problem. The paradox pushed physics toward **a radical rethinking** of motion, measurement, and the nature of space.

How It Works

The Ether Paradox arises from the following logic:

1. All known waves need a medium; light is a wave → therefore, light needs a medium.
2. This medium, the ether, must permeate all space and be stationary.
3. If Earth moves through this medium, it should affect light's speed.
4. But repeated experiments (Michelson–Morley and others) failed to detect such an effect.
5. Therefore, either the ether behaves in a way that's undetectable—or it doesn't exist.

To resolve the paradox, **Albert Einstein** proposed in 1905 his **Special Theory of Relativity**, which **eliminated the need for ether** entirely. He postulated that:

- The laws of physics are the same in all inertial frames.
- The speed of light in a vacuum is constant for all observers, regardless of their motion.

This bold move made the ether concept **obsolete** and paved the way for modern physics.

Application

The Ether Paradox played a key role in:

- **The development of Special Relativity**, which redefined concepts of space and time.

- **Modern physics**, including quantum electrodynamics and the understanding of light as both a wave and a particle.

- **Experimental design**, showcasing how a negative result (failure to detect ether) can lead to revolutionary theoretical advances.

It also shaped the scientific method, illustrating how **empirical evidence must guide theoretical frameworks**, not the other way around.

Key Insights

- Not all intuitive analogies (e.g., waves needing a medium) hold at the fundamental level.

- Experimental results, especially null results, can drive major scientific revolutions.

- The ether was a theoretical construct without empirical support—and that mattered.

- The Ether Paradox helped birth **relativity**, one of the most successful theories in science.

- It reminds us that in science, **abandoning a wrong idea** can be just as important as discovering a new one.

90. Delayed Choice Quantum Eraser Paradox

Theory

The **Delayed Choice Quantum Eraser Paradox** is a thought-provoking phenomenon in **quantum mechanics**, combining elements of **wave-particle duality**, **quantum entanglement**, and **observer effect**. It arises from a variation of the famous **double-slit experiment**, designed to test how the behaviour of particles (like photons or electrons) changes depending on whether their paths are "observed." The paradox centres around a strange implication: **a measurement made in the present can seemingly affect the past behaviour of a particle**, as if reality itself only becomes definite **after** the act of observation—even if that observation is delayed.

Originally developed by **John Archibald Wheeler** (as the "delayed choice" experiment) and later refined into the **quantum eraser** version by **Yoon-Ho Kim et al. (1999)**, this paradox challenges classical ideas of **causality** and **temporal order**.

Example

Imagine a modified **double-slit experiment** with a twist. A photon is emitted and encounters a beam splitter that can send it toward one of two slits. After passing through the slits, the photon encounters another setup where **its path information may or may not be "erased"** using entangled photons and beam splitters. Crucially, the decision to "erase" or retain which-path information can be made **after the photon has already hit the detection screen**.

Now, if the experiment is set up to **preserve which-path information**, the photon behaves like a particle—no interference pattern emerges on the detection screen. But if the which-path information is **erased**, even retroactively, an interference pattern appears—suggesting the photon "acted like a wave." It's as if the photon "knows" whether its path will be measured *in the future*, and changes its past behaviour accordingly.

Why It Works
The paradox works because it confronts our intuitive understanding of **time, cause and effect**, and **measurement**. In classical physics, effects follow causes in a linear fashion. But in the quantum eraser setup, the act of measurement appears to **alter the outcome of a past event**—though no actual signal travels backward in time.

Quantum mechanics doesn't violate causality in a conventional sense because **no usable information is sent backward**, but the correlations challenge our assumptions about **objective reality**. What we perceive as a fixed history may instead be **dependent on future choices**.

How It Works
Technically, the system involves **entangled photons**. One photon (signal) goes toward the detection screen, and its entangled twin (idler) travels to a detector where the which-path information may or may not be recorded or erased. The

interference pattern only emerges **after** sorting the signal photons based on the outcomes of their entangled partners.

From the quantum formalism, the system evolves unitarily (without collapse) until a measurement is made. The measurement effectively **selects a subset** of the total wavefunction, giving the appearance of retroactive change. It's not that the past is physically altered, but that **what counts as the "past" depends on the experimental context**.

Application

This paradox has implications for **quantum information theory**, **quantum cryptography**, and the **foundations of physics**. It supports interpretations like the **Copenhagen interpretation**, where measurement defines reality, or the **many-worlds interpretation**, where all outcomes happen in parallel and are later selected by observation.

Philosophically, it forces us to rethink the **nature of reality**, **time**, and the role of the **observer**. It also motivates experiments in **delayed-choice entanglement swapping**, pushing the boundaries of nonlocal correlations and time-symmetric models of quantum mechanics.

Key Insights

1. **Measurement Defines Reality**: Until observation, quantum systems exist in superposition—not in a defined state.

2. **Time Is Contextual in Quantum Physics**: Future actions can influence how we describe past events.

3. **Entanglement Enables Correlated Outcomes**: Even when separated in space or time, quantum particles behave as one system.

4. **Classical Intuition Breaks Down**: Our assumptions about cause, effect, and linear time don't fully apply at the quantum level.

5. **Reality May Be Observer-Dependent**: The experiment supports the idea that **what is real** depends on how and when we choose to observe.

The **Delayed Choice Quantum Eraser Paradox** doesn't imply backward causation in the classical sense, but it profoundly challenges the assumption that the past is fixed and objective — reminding us that in the quantum world, reality is more flexible and mysterious than it first appears.

91. Firewall Paradox

Theory

The **Firewall Paradox** is a modern puzzle at the intersection of **quantum mechanics**, **general relativity**, and **information theory**, specifically concerning the fate of information in black holes. It was introduced in 2012 by physicists **Almheiri, Marolf, Polchinski, and Sully (AMPS)** and is often referred to as the **AMPS Paradox**. The paradox arises from attempting to reconcile three well-established principles in physics:

1. **Unitarity**: Information is never lost in quantum mechanics.

2. **Equivalence Principle**: An observer falling into a black hole experiences nothing unusual at the event horizon.

3. **Quantum Field Theory in Curved Spacetime**: Hawking radiation is produced via entangled particle pairs near the horizon.

The paradox shows that these three assumptions cannot all be true simultaneously. If quantum information is preserved (unitarity), and Hawking radiation is truly thermal (as originally proposed), then something must give — and the suggestion is that a **"firewall"** of high-energy particles exists at the event horizon, violently breaking the smooth fabric of spacetime and contradicting the equivalence principle.

Example
Imagine a spaceship drifting toward a supermassive black

hole. According to general relativity, the crew shouldn't notice anything strange as they pass the event horizon — it's supposed to be smooth and uneventful (locally). However, the firewall paradox proposes that, instead, the crew would be **instantly incinerated** by a wall of high-energy radiation — the so-called **firewall**.

This arises because, in order to preserve information and avoid the so-called **black hole information loss problem**, the outgoing Hawking radiation must carry information about the infalling matter. But quantum mechanics forbids a single particle from being maximally entangled with two different systems — and in the traditional model, the Hawking radiation must be entangled both with the earlier radiation and with its infalling partner.

This leads to a contradiction known as the **monogamy of entanglement**, and to resolve it, the entanglement with the infalling partner must be broken — which would manifest as a **firewall** at the horizon.

Why It Works

The paradox works because it pits three deeply held physical principles against each other. If Hawking radiation is to carry away information (preserving unitarity), then its entanglement with infalling particles must be severed. But severing that entanglement implies a breakdown in quantum field theory near the horizon — hence, the firewall.

It forces physicists to **give up at least one cherished assumption**, but each option comes with severe consequences:

- **Give up unitarity?** Violates fundamental quantum theory.
- **Give up the equivalence principle?** Destroys general relativity's smooth spacetime at the horizon.
- **Give up quantum field theory?** Undermines one of the best-tested theories in physics.

How It Works

The AMPS argument uses a thought experiment involving **entangled qubits** near the black hole horizon and those radiated away. The paradox hinges on quantum information theory and the **Page time** — the moment when half the black hole's original entropy has been radiated away. After this point, any new radiation must be entangled with earlier radiation to maintain unitarity, which breaks the previous entanglement structure expected by quantum field theory — leading to a firewall.

Application

The Firewall Paradox has reshaped discussions in **black hole physics**, **quantum gravity**, and the pursuit of a **unified theory**. It has prompted research into ideas like:

- **ER=EPR** (Einstein-Rosen bridges = entanglement), proposed by Maldacena and Susskind.

- **Holographic principles** (like AdS/CFT correspondence), which explore how boundary theories encode bulk gravity.
- **Quantum error correction** and **entanglement wedges**, which reinterpret spacetime as emergent from quantum information.

Key Insights

1. **Information and Gravity Collide**: The paradox forces a choice between core principles of physics.
2. **Entanglement Limits Matter**: Quantum entanglement's structure constrains what spacetime can be.
3. **Event Horizons May Be Violent**: Contrary to relativity, horizons might not be smooth.
4. **New Physics Needed**: The paradox suggests current theories are incomplete or incompatible.
5. **Spacetime May Be Emergent**: It supports the view that geometry arises from quantum entanglement.

The **Firewall Paradox** reveals the cracks in our understanding of quantum gravity — and remains a leading challenge in unifying the laws of the very big with the laws of the very small.

🎲 Game Theory & Economic Paradoxes

Game mechanics or incentives misfire.

92. Grelling–Nelson Paradox

Theory Overview

The **Grelling–Nelson Paradox** is a self-referential semantic paradox involving **adjectives** and how they apply—or do not apply—to themselves. First proposed by **Kurt Grelling and Leonard Nelson** in 1908, the paradox is a close cousin to the **Liar Paradox** and **Russell's Paradox**. It centres on a clever distinction between two kinds of adjectives: those that **describe themselves** and those that **do not**.

More precisely, it challenges how language **classifies linguistic entities** when self-reference is involved. The paradox emerges from trying to apply a classification system to itself—leading to a contradiction in the same way that Russell's Paradox does for sets.

Example

Begin by defining two types of adjectives:

1. **Autological adjectives**: adjectives that **describe themselves**.
   Examples:
      - "Short" is short.

- "Polysyllabic" is polysyllabic.
- "English" is an English word.

2. **Heterological adjectives**: adjectives that **do not describe themselves**.
   Examples:
   - "Long" is not a long word.
   - "French" is not a French word.
   - "Monosyllabic" is not monosyllabic.

Now consider the adjective **"heterological"** itself. Ask:

Is "heterological" heterological?

Two possibilities:

- If **"heterological" is heterological**, then by definition, it **does not describe itself**. But if it doesn't describe itself, then it **must not be heterological**—a contradiction.

- If **"heterological" is not heterological**, then it **must describe itself**—meaning it **is autological**. But if it is autological, then it **does describe itself**, which contradicts the claim that it's not heterological.

Thus, either assumption leads to contradiction. This is the **Grelling–Nelson Paradox**.

Why It Works

The paradox works because it reveals the **instability of self-reference** in natural language. Much like Russell's Paradox, which arises when we try to define the set of all sets that do not contain themselves, the Grelling–Nelson Paradox applies the same logic to **adjectives and language**.

The twist is that this paradox uses **no explicit self-reference** like "this sentence..." Instead, it **implicitly becomes self-referential** through classification—making it particularly insidious.

This makes the paradox a challenge not just for logic but for **semantics**, **category theory**, and **linguistic philosophy**.

How It Works

The structure of the paradox is built on:

1. **Binary classification**: All adjectives are either autological or heterological.

2. **Self-application**: The classification applies to adjectives **as objects**.

3. **Contradiction from self-reference**: Applying the classification to the term "heterological" leads to a logical loop.

The result is a semantic impasse—**"heterological" can neither be heterological nor autological** without generating contradiction.

Application

Though linguistic in form, the paradox has broader implications in:

- **Philosophy of language**: Highlighting the limitations of natural language categorization.

- **Logic and mathematics**: Analogous to Russell's Paradox, prompting the need for **hierarchical type theories** to avoid self-referential definitions.

- **Computer science**: Especially in **programming languages** and **meta-languages**, where similar loops can cause logical or runtime errors.

- **Epistemology**: Demonstrating that even apparently clear classification systems can **break down under self-reference**.

Key Insights

- **Self-reference**, even when indirect, can destabilize seemingly sound categories.

- Not all terms can be cleanly classified within binary systems.

- Like other semantic paradoxes, the Grelling–Nelson Paradox reveals that **language has structural limits** when used to speak about itself.

- It supports the need for **meta-linguistic hierarchies** to handle self-referential terms safely.
- The paradox challenges assumptions about **definability and consistency**, forcing us to rethink how we frame linguistic categories.

93. Braess' Paradox

Theory Overview

Braess' Paradox is a counterintuitive phenomenon in network theory and transportation planning, discovered by German mathematician **Dietrich Braess** in 1968. It shows that **adding extra capacity to a network**, such as building a new road in a traffic system, can paradoxically **lead to worse overall performance**, increasing travel time for everyone.

The paradox occurs because individual agents (drivers, for example) make **self-interested decisions** about which route to take, aiming to minimize their own travel time. When everyone behaves this way, the collective outcome can be **inefficient** or even **worse than before** the improvement. This reflects a classic issue in game theory where **individual rationality doesn't lead to collective rationality**.

Example

Consider a simplified traffic network with two routes from point **Start** to **Finish**:

- Route 1: Start → A (5 minutes, fixed) → Finish (variable: 1 minute per car)
- Route 2: Start → B (variable: 1 minute per car) → Finish (5 minutes, fixed)

Assume 4,000 drivers want to get from Start to Finish. Without any shortcuts, traffic will split evenly:

- 2,000 take Route 1: 5 + 2 = **7 minutes**
- 2,000 take Route 2: 2 + 5 = **7 minutes**

Now, add a **shortcut**: a new, zero-time road between A and B.

Rational drivers re-evaluate:

1. Start → A (5 min)
2. A → B (0 min, new road)
3. B → Finish (variable time)

Now, drivers think: "Why take B directly from Start when I can go via A and take the zero-time connector?" Similarly, no one wants to take the longer Finish route directly from A when the B-Finish segment seems faster. This logic leads **all drivers to use the new shortcut**:

- Start → A (5 min) → B (0 min) → Finish (now 4,000 cars × 1 min = **4,000 minutes**)

Result? Travel time balloons to **5 + 4 = 9 minutes, worse than the original 7 minutes**, despite the added road.

Why It Works

Braess' Paradox works because it exploits the **disconnect between individual optimization and system-wide efficiency**. In the new network, each driver chooses a path that seems optimal for them personally, not realizing that **everyone else will do the same**, leading to congestion on what appeared to be the quickest route.

This reflects the core issue of **Nash equilibrium** in non-cooperative games: everyone acting in their own interest can lock the system into a **suboptimal state** that no one can unilaterally improve.

How It Works

The paradox arises under specific conditions:

- The system is **congested**, with time or cost dependent on the number of users.
- There is no centralized coordination—agents act independently.
- Adding a route offers an **illusion of increased choice** without accounting for dynamic effects.

The system reaches a new equilibrium that may be worse for everyone—**a form of negative externality**.

Application

Braess' Paradox has real-world applications in:

- **Urban planning and traffic engineering**: Closing roads or restricting access can sometimes **improve flow**, not worsen it.

- **Internet and communication networks**: Adding capacity or rerouting traffic without holistic coordination can degrade performance.

- **Public policy and infrastructure**: Encourages designing systems with **cooperative behaviour or regulation** rather than pure freedom of choice.

- **Power grids**: Unexpected overloads or inefficiencies can result from added capacity if not managed carefully.

Key Insights

- More options don't always mean better outcomes in complex systems.

- **Self-interest in networks can lead to globally inefficient results**.

- Systems often require **coordinated or regulated behaviour** to function optimally.

- Removing or restricting resources (like roads) can paradoxically **enhance efficiency**.

- Braess' Paradox illustrates how **systems thinking** is essential when managing shared infrastructure.

94. Arrow's Impossibility Theorem

Theory Overview

Arrow's Impossibility Theorem, also known as **Arrow's Paradox**, is a foundational result in **social choice theory** formulated by economist **Kenneth Arrow** in his 1951 doctoral thesis and later work, *Social Choice and Individual Values*. The theorem addresses the challenge of designing a fair and consistent method to **aggregate individual preferences into a collective decision**, such as in voting or group choice.

Arrow proved that **no rank-order voting system** can convert the preferences of individuals into a community-wide ranking **without violating at least one** of a set of seemingly reasonable conditions. This result reveals a profound and unsettling limitation: **there is no perfect democratic voting system** that always satisfies all fairness criteria when choosing between three or more options.

Example

Imagine a simple election with **three candidates**: A, B, and C, and **three voters** with the following preferences:

- Voter 1: A > B > C
- Voter 2: B > C > A
- Voter 3: C > A > B

Each candidate is ranked first by one voter, second by one, and third by one. Now try to create a collective ranking that reflects everyone's preferences while satisfying some fairness rules. It turns out that **any ranking you choose will violate at least one desirable condition**, such as fairness or consistency.

Why It Works

Arrow's theorem works because it is mathematically rigorous and logically airtight. It shows that even when you define clear, reasonable criteria for a fair voting system, those criteria are **mutually incompatible** under general conditions.

Arrow defined **five conditions** (simplified here):

1. **Unrestricted Domain (Universality)**: The system must work for all possible individual preference orderings.

2. **Non-Dictatorship**: No single individual should dictate the group's preferences.

3. **Pareto Efficiency**: If everyone prefers A over B, the group should also prefer A over B.

4. **Independence of Irrelevant Alternatives (IIA)**: The group's preference between A and B should depend only on individuals' preferences between A and B, not on a third option.

5. **Transitivity**: The group's preferences should be logically consistent (if A > B and B > C, then A > C).

Arrow proved that **no system can satisfy all five conditions** when there are **three or more options** and at least two voters.

How It Works

The proof uses formal logic and combinatorics. It shows that whenever you try to satisfy four of the criteria, the fifth fails. For example, satisfying Universality, Pareto, IIA, and Transitivity typically leads to a **dictatorial outcome**—only one voter's preference ends up deciding the group outcome every time, violating Non-Dictatorship.

This isn't just a flaw in one specific voting method—it applies to **all** methods that rely on ranking (like plurality, Borda count, instant runoff, etc.).

Application

Arrow's theorem has deep implications in:

- **Voting systems**: Encourages the study of alternative voting models like approval voting, ranked-choice, or deliberative democracy.
- **Economics**: Helps explain the challenges of aggregating consumer preferences into social welfare functions.
- **Political philosophy**: Influences debates on democracy, fairness, and legitimacy.

- **Artificial intelligence and multi-agent systems**: Shapes how autonomous agents reach consensus or make group decisions.

It also informs **public choice theory**, which examines how collective decisions are made in governmental and institutional settings.

Key Insights

- There is no "perfect" voting system that is both fair and rational under all conditions.
- Trade-offs are inevitable in any democratic decision-making process.
- Real-world systems must choose **which criteria to prioritize**, depending on context and values.
- The theorem doesn't say democracy is hopeless—it clarifies its **structural limitations**.
- Arrow's work earned him a Nobel Prize and remains central to understanding **collective rationality**.

95. Ellsberg Paradox

Theory

The **Ellsberg Paradox** is a foundational problem in **decision theory** and **behavioural economics**, first introduced by economist Daniel Ellsberg in 1961. It challenges the assumptions of **expected utility theory**, particularly the principle of **subjective probability**, which states that rational agents should always maximize expected utility based on their beliefs about uncertain outcomes.

Ellsberg showed that people systematically violate this principle when faced with situations involving **ambiguity** — that is, when the **probability of outcomes is unknown** or imprecise. Unlike **risk**, where probabilities are known (like in a fair dice roll), **ambiguity** introduces **uncertainty about the uncertainty itself**. The paradox illustrates **ambiguity aversion**, the human tendency to prefer known risks over unknown ones, even when doing so contradicts rational decision-making under expected utility theory.

Example
Imagine an urn containing 90 balls:

- 30 are red.

- The remaining 60 are either black or yellow, but in an unknown proportion.

You are offered a choice between two bets:

- **Bet A**: Win $100 if a red ball is drawn.
- **Bet B**: Win $100 if a black ball is drawn.

Most people choose **Bet A**, even though both bets involve a 1-in-3 chance if the black and yellow balls are evenly split. Now consider a second choice:

- **Bet C**: Win $100 if a red or yellow ball is drawn.
- **Bet D**: Win $100 if a black or yellow ball is drawn.

Now most people choose **Bet D**, despite preferring red over black in the first scenario.

This preference pattern is inconsistent with expected utility theory. In the first pair, choosing red implies you think black is less likely than red. But in the second pair, choosing black or yellow implies black is more likely than red. This inconsistency exposes the **Ellsberg Paradox**.

Why It Works

The paradox works by presenting **ambiguity and risk side by side** and observing that people consistently prefer **known risks** over **ambiguous situations**, even when expected values are the same or favour the ambiguous option.

This violates the **sure-thing principle** in expected utility theory, which says if you prefer option X over Y in one situation, you should still prefer X over Y when the situation is broadened in ways that don't change their relative desirability. Ellsberg's experiment shows that human reasoning often doesn't follow this rule.

How It Works
Mathematically, expected utility theory assigns utility values to outcomes and multiplies them by probabilities. But in ambiguous situations, subjective probabilities become unstable or undefined. People substitute **ambiguity** with **pessimism** or **conservatism** — acting as if the ambiguous outcomes are less favourable, even without evidence.

Ellsberg's insights led to the development of **alternative decision theories**, such as:

- **Maxmin expected utility** (Gilboa & Schmeidler): Choose the action that maximizes the minimum possible utility.

- **Choquet expected utility**: Use non-additive probabilities to account for ambiguity.

- **Prospect theory** (Kahneman & Tversky): Incorporates loss aversion and probability weighting.

Application
The Ellsberg Paradox has broad implications:

- In **finance**, investors often prefer assets with known risks over those with unknown volatility, even if returns are better.

- In **insurance**, people overpay for protection against ambiguous but rare events.

- In **public policy**, decision-makers may avoid uncertain policies even when statistical models support them.

It also plays a major role in **AI safety**, **legal reasoning**, and **military strategy**, where ambiguity must be navigated, not just risk.

Key Insights

1. **People Fear Ambiguity More Than Risk**: Known probabilities feel safer than unknown ones.

2. **Rationality Is Contextual**: Human decision-making isn't always aligned with formal utility models.

3. **Subjective Probability Has Limits**: When probabilities aren't known, preferences become inconsistent.

4. **Behavioural Models Are Needed**: Realistic decision theories must incorporate psychological responses to ambiguity.

5. **Uncertainty Has Layers**: Not all uncertainty is equal — ambiguity introduces a deeper level of doubt.

The **Ellsberg Paradox** shows that **rational choice models must evolve** to accommodate the complexity of human preferences, especially when knowledge is incomplete or imprecise.

96. St. Petersburg Paradox

Theory Overview

The **St. Petersburg Paradox** is a classic problem in **decision theory** and **economics** that reveals a conflict between **expected value theory** and **real-world intuition**. First posed by **Nicolaus Bernoulli** in 1713 and later explored by **Daniel Bernoulli**, the paradox questions how people should evaluate uncertain prospects when the **potential payout is infinite**.

The setup involves a simple coin-tossing game with an **exponentially increasing reward** structure. Mathematically, the expected monetary value of the game is **infinite**, yet most people would only pay a **modest amount** to play. This disconnect between **mathematical expectation** and **human behaviour** exposes limitations in using expected value alone to guide rational decision-making.

Example

Imagine this game:

- A fair coin is tossed until it lands heads.
- If the first head appears on the 1st toss, you win $2.
- If it appears on the 2nd toss, you win $4.
- On the 3rd toss: $8.

- On the nth toss: you win $\$2^n$.

So the payouts double with each additional tail before a head.

To calculate the expected value:

- Probability of first head on toss

$$1 = \tfrac{1}{2}, \text{ reward} = \$2 \rightarrow EV = \tfrac{1}{2} \times \$2 = \$1$$

- Toss 2:

$$\tfrac{1}{4} \times \$4 = \$1$$

- Toss 3:

$$\tfrac{1}{8} \times \$8 = \$1$$

- And so on…

Summing all these gives:

$$EV = \$1 + \$1 + \$1 + \ldots = \infty$$

So the **expected value is infinite**. Yet, most people would only pay **$20, $50, maybe $100** at most to play. Hardly anyone would pay $1,000, let alone infinity. This is the paradox: **Why won't rational agents pay anywhere near the expected value?**

Why It Works

The paradox works because it reveals the **gap between theoretical valuation and practical behaviour**. While mathematically sound, the infinite expected value doesn't align with **risk aversion**, **utility theory**, or **real-world constraints**.

People don't evaluate gains linearly. Winning $1 million doesn't feel **1,000 times** better than winning $1,000. Additionally, the probability of high payouts (like $1,000,000 on the 20th toss) is so small (1 in over a million) that most discount it heavily.

This leads to a more psychologically realistic evaluation: we weigh rewards based on **utility**, not raw value.

How It Works

Daniel Bernoulli proposed one of the first solutions: **Expected Utility Theory**. Instead of assuming people value money linearly, he suggested they derive **diminishing marginal utility** from it. In other words:

- $100 is not worth twice as much happiness as $50.
- Use a **logarithmic utility function**, such as $U(x) = \log(x)$.

When applying this function to the game, the expected utility becomes **finite**, aligning more closely with how people actually behave.

Modern solutions also consider:

- **Bounded rationality**: People can't process infinite scenarios.

- **Risk aversion**: Individuals prefer certain outcomes over risky ones, even with higher expected returns.

- **Real-world constraints**: No one offers or can pay infinite sums, so the setup is artificial.

Application

The paradox has influenced:

- **Economics and utility theory**: Leading to more nuanced models of human decision-making.

- **Behavioural economics**: Studying how people deviate from expected value predictions.

- **Insurance and finance**: Where risk-adjusted returns are more relevant than theoretical maximum gains.

- **Game theory and AI**: Where agents must weigh outcomes using utility, not raw value.

Key Insights

- **Expected value alone is insufficient** for modelling rational decisions.

- People operate under **bounded utility**, not unbounded monetary expectations.

- The paradox illustrates the need for **utility theory**, risk assessment, and psychological realism in economics.
- It shows that **infinite outcomes**, while mathematically valid, are often irrelevant to practical decision-making.
- The St. Petersburg Paradox remains a cornerstone in understanding the **limits of rational choice theory**.

97. Monty Hall Problem

Theory Overview

The **Monty Hall Problem** is a probability puzzle based on a game show scenario, named after **Monty Hall**, the original host of the television show *Let's Make a Deal*. The paradox illustrates how human intuition about probability can be deeply misleading, especially when **conditional probabilities** and **new information** are involved.

At its core, the puzzle challenges the assumption that, once some uncertainty is removed, all remaining choices must be equally likely. The Monty Hall Problem shows that **switching your choice increases your chances of winning**, even though most people intuitively believe the odds are 50/50 after one door is revealed.

Example

Here's the standard version of the problem:

1. You are on a game show. There are **three doors**.

2. Behind one door is a **car** (the prize), and behind the other two are **goats**.

3. You choose one door—say, **Door 1**.

4. The host, Monty Hall, who **knows** what's behind each door, opens one of the **other two doors**, revealing a **goat**.

5. He then gives you a choice: **stick with your original door or switch to the other unopened door**.

Question: Should you switch?

Answer: Yes. Switching gives you a **2/3 chance of winning**, while staying with your original choice leaves you with only a **1/3 chance**.

Why It Works

This works because the probability **does not reset** after Monty opens a door. Initially, there's a 1/3 chance the car is behind your chosen door and a 2/3 chance it's behind one of the other two. Monty's action—revealing a goat—**doesn't redistribute probability evenly**; instead, it concentrates the 2/3 chance onto the **only remaining unopened door**.

So:

- Stay: You win if your initial 1/3 guess was correct.
- Switch: You win if your initial guess was wrong—which happens 2/3 of the time.

This probability structure holds because Monty **always reveals a goat** and always **gives the option to switch**, making his action **predictable and non-random**, which is key.

How It Works

Let's break it down further:

- You pick Door 1 (1/3 chance of car).
- Monty reveals a goat behind one of the remaining doors.
- The other unopened door now has a **2/3 chance** of hiding the car, because:
    - If the car was behind Door 1 (1/3 chance), switching loses.
    - If the car was behind Door 2 or 3 (2/3 chance), Monty opens the remaining goat door, and switching wins.

Monty's action filters information from the system. His consistent rule of revealing a goat provides a **conditional clue**, not just random noise.

Application

The Monty Hall Problem has implications in:

- **Probability theory and statistics**: Shows the difference between **prior and conditional probabilities**.
- **Cognitive psychology**: Demonstrates **how intuition often fails** in probabilistic reasoning.
- **Machine learning and AI**: Helps illustrate the importance of **updating beliefs** as new information is acquired (Bayesian inference).

- **Game theory and decision science**: Teaches how strategy should adapt based on **structured rules and known behaviours**.

Key Insights

- Our **intuition often confuses conditional and uniform probability**.
- **Monty's knowledge and behaviour** are not neutral—they filter probability.
- Probability isn't just about counting outcomes—it's about understanding **how information updates likelihoods**.
- The paradox underscores the need to **analyse decisions through structured reasoning**, not gut feeling.
- It remains a powerful educational tool in demonstrating the subtlety of **rational choice under uncertainty**.

98. Cooperator's Reward Paradox

Theory Overview

The **Cooperator's Reward Paradox** emerges in game theory, evolutionary dynamics, and moral philosophy, addressing a counterintuitive result about cooperation:

In systems that reward cooperation, the individual who contributes the most to a collective good can sometimes receive **less benefit** than those who **cooperate less—or not at all**.

This paradox highlights the **fragile balance between fairness, reward distribution, and incentivization** in cooperative systems. It raises important questions about **how societies, groups, or evolutionary processes should structure rewards** to maintain and encourage cooperation—without unintentionally punishing the most generous contributors.

It's related to concepts such as the **free rider problem, public goods games**, and **moral hazard**, but it specifically centres on **outcomes for cooperators who go above and beyond**, yet are paradoxically **worse off** than those who contribute little.

Example

Consider a small team working on a group project. One member, Alex, puts in 80% of the effort—researching, writing, organizing—while others contribute only 20%

collectively. At the end, the team receives **equal recognition and reward**. Alex may feel disillusioned: despite doing most of the work, the reward was not proportionate to the contribution.

In some cases, **non-contributors may even benefit more**—for example, they conserved time and energy for other opportunities, while Alex exhausted theirs for no extra gain. Over time, the system may **discourage high-effort cooperation**, reducing group efficiency and long-term success.

In a broader economic or biological context, this models scenarios like **communal hunting**, **taxation**, or **shared investment** in public infrastructure. When rewards are **pooled and divided equally**, the most generous contributors may be inadvertently **disincentivized**, causing overall cooperation to decline.

Why It Works

The paradox works because it **clashes with our intuitive expectations** about fairness and merit. In theory, more contribution should lead to more reward. But when group rewards are **evenly split** or **not precisely tracked**, high contributors may actually **subsidize** lower ones.

Moreover, in evolutionary settings, cooperators expend energy for the benefit of the group, while **free riders reap the benefits without cost**, leading to an evolutionary advantage for selfish strategies—unless mechanisms like **punishment**, **reputation**, or **reciprocity** evolve to balance the scales.

How It Works

The Cooperator's Reward Paradox arises through:

1. **Asymmetric contributions** to a shared goal.
2. **Symmetric or poorly aligned rewards**.
3. A system that lacks adequate **feedback or correction mechanisms**.
4. The failure to **internalize externalities**—i.e., not all costs and benefits are accounted for by the actors involved.

In repeated interactions, this leads to **declining cooperation** over time unless systems are modified to reflect **contribution-based outcomes**.

Application

This paradox has relevance in:

- **Game theory**: Especially in iterated **Prisoner's Dilemmas** and **public goods games**.
- **Organizational behaviour**: Incentive structures in teams, firms, and institutions.

- **Economics and taxation**: Progressive tax systems can sometimes create disincentives for high earners if not carefully balanced.

- **Evolutionary biology**: Explains the emergence of cooperation and punishment in species.

- **Ethics and justice**: Raises questions about fairness, recognition, and moral responsibility in shared outcomes.

Key Insights

- Rewarding cooperation **ineffectively** can reduce overall cooperation.

- **Fairness is not guaranteed** in collective systems unless explicitly designed.

- Sustained cooperation often requires **transparent, feedback-based incentives**.

- Systems must balance **individual effort and group benefit** to remain stable.

- The paradox serves as a caution: **goodwill without structural support** may lead to burnout and disengagement.

99. Resource Paradox

Theory Overview

The **Resource Paradox** refers to the counterintuitive phenomenon where countries or regions with an abundance of natural resources—especially valuable commodities like oil, gas, or minerals—often experience **slower economic growth**, **weaker governance**, and **greater political instability** than countries with fewer natural resources.

At first glance, it seems logical that resource-rich nations should be wealthy and prosperous. However, in many cases, these resources become a **burden** rather than a benefit. This paradox challenges the assumption that natural wealth automatically leads to human development and long-term economic strength.

The term "resource curse" became popular in the 1990s, though economists and political scientists have observed its effects for decades. Key contributors to this body of research include Richard Auty, Jeffrey Sachs, and Andrew Warner.

Example

Consider **Venezuela**, a country with some of the largest proven oil reserves in the world. In the 20th century, oil wealth made it one of Latin America's richest countries. Yet over time, dependency on oil revenues, political mismanagement, corruption, and the collapse of global oil prices contributed to economic collapse, hyperinflation, and humanitarian crisis.

In contrast, **South Korea** and **Singapore**—countries with virtually no natural resources—have achieved remarkable economic success through industrialization, education, and innovation.

Why It Works

The paradox works because resource wealth can **distort economic incentives and political systems**. Easy access to revenue from resource exports reduces the need to develop diverse sectors like manufacturing or services. Governments may become less accountable to citizens because they don't rely on taxes—they rely on resource rents instead.

This often leads to:

- **Overvalued currency** (Dutch Disease), making other exports less competitive.
- **Corruption and rent-seeking**, as elites scramble to control lucrative resource sectors.
- **Neglect of human capital**, such as education and infrastructure.
- **Increased risk of conflict**, especially in ethnically or politically divided societies.

Resource abundance, instead of promoting long-term investment and development, can encourage **short-term exploitation and dependency**.

How It Works

The mechanism of the resource curse unfolds through several interlinked pathways:

1. **Economic Effects**: A booming resource sector can crowd out other industries, leading to a lack of economic diversification. This makes countries vulnerable to price shocks.

2. **Political Effects**: Resource wealth often consolidates power in the hands of elites, reducing democratic accountability. It can also fuel authoritarianism or corruption.

3. **Social Effects**: Inequitable distribution of resource revenues can lead to unrest or civil conflict, especially in regions feeling marginalized.

This does not mean resource wealth *must* lead to decline— but it highlights how easily mismanagement and institutional weakness can turn a blessing into a curse.

Application

Understanding the Resource Paradox is vital for:

- **Economic policy** in resource-rich developing nations, guiding decisions on taxation, diversification, and investment.

- **International aid and development** strategies that focus on building institutions rather than just leveraging natural wealth.

- **Conflict prevention**, especially in countries where control over resources is linked to political power.

- **Climate policy**, as countries shift from fossil fuels to sustainable models and must manage existing resource dependence.

Key Insights

- Natural wealth can be a **trap** without strong institutions and good governance.

- The paradox emphasizes the importance of **economic diversification** and **long-term planning**.

- **Accountability** and **transparent resource management** are crucial for turning natural resources into public benefit.

- Wealth from the ground does not replace **human capital** as the foundation of lasting prosperity.

- With foresight, the resource curse can be avoided—turning paradox into opportunity.

100. Von Neumann–Morgenstern Stability

Theory Overview

The **Von Neumann–Morgenstern Stability** concept arises in the context of **cooperative game theory**, introduced by mathematicians **John von Neumann** and **Oskar Morgenstern** in their foundational 1944 book, *Theory of Games and Economic Behaviour*. It is used to understand how coalitions form in games involving multiple players who can cooperate, share resources, or divide payoffs.

Their key contribution was the concept of a **"stable set"** (also known as a **solution set**), which defines a set of possible payoff distributions (allocations) that are **internally and externally stable**—meaning no coalition of players has an incentive to deviate from them. The paradox or problem arises from the fact that **multiple** such stable sets may exist in a game—or none at all—raising questions about predictability and fairness in cooperative arrangements.

Example

Consider three companies—A, B, and C—negotiating a joint venture. Working alone, each can earn $10 million. But together, their profits increase due to synergy. Any pair can earn $30 million, and all three together can earn $60 million.

Now comes the issue: how do they split the $60 million fairly?

- If A and B exclude C, they can still make $30 million, leaving C with nothing.
- If all three work together, fairness might suggest an even split ($20 million each), but A and B might argue for more since they can succeed without C.

The **Von Neumann–Morgenstern stable set** would consist of all payoff distributions where:

1. No coalition has an incentive to break away (external stability).
2. Each included payoff is better than alternatives outside the set (internal stability).

In this example, multiple possible distributions might satisfy these conditions, or the conflict among coalitions might make no stable set possible.

Why It Works

The model works by acknowledging that in **cooperative settings**, power lies in the ability to form or threaten coalitions. Stability reflects the **strategic balance** where no subset of players finds it advantageous to deviate. It's not about what is *morally* fair, but about what is **strategically sustainable**.

This stability concept provides a foundation for understanding **negotiation outcomes**, especially in economics, politics, and business.

How It Works

A **stable set** satisfies two criteria:

1. **Internal Stability**: No outcome within the set is dominated by another outcome in the set (no member of the set is strictly worse for everyone).

2. **External Stability**: Every outcome not in the set is dominated by at least one member of the set (there is no reason to prefer something outside the set).

These criteria attempt to model rational coalition behaviour in a world where players look for beneficial partnerships and anticipate defection risks.

However, paradoxically:

- Some games admit **multiple stable sets**, making outcome prediction difficult.

- Some games have **no stable set at all**, even though cooperation seems possible.

This unpredictability makes the concept both powerful and philosophically challenging.

Application

Von Neumann–Morgenstern stability is foundational in:

- **Economic coalitions**: Mergers, partnerships, or cartel formations.

- **Political science**: Forming governing coalitions or treaties.

- **AI and multi-agent systems**: Designing systems where autonomous agents negotiate or share resources.
- **Social sciences**: Modelling cooperation and fairness in groups.

It also serves as a precursor to more modern solution concepts like the **core**, the **Shapley value**, or **Nash bargaining**.

Key Insights

- Stability in cooperation is not guaranteed; even rational agents can fail to reach an agreement.
- A "fair" solution may not be stable, and a stable one may not feel fair.
- Strategic threats and alliances shape the feasibility of agreements more than objective merit.
- The theory reveals that **equilibrium in group cooperation** can be elusive, plural, or even non-existent.
- It highlights the **complex dynamics of collective decision-making** where incentives, not just outcomes, govern behaviour.

101. Dutch Book Paradox

Theory

The **Dutch Book Paradox** is a foundational concept in **probability theory, decision theory**, and **philosophy of rational belief**, demonstrating that if an agent's subjective probabilities (i.e., degrees of belief) violate the axioms of **coherent probability**, then it is possible to construct a series of bets that guarantees a **sure loss** for that agent, regardless of the outcome. Such a guaranteed loss is called a **"Dutch book"**, named after a hypothetical bookie who manipulates irrational bettors.

The paradox is often used to argue that rational belief systems must conform to the mathematical rules of **Bayesian probability theory**. If an agent assigns incoherent or inconsistent probabilities (for example, probabilities that don't add up to 1, or violate the law of total probability), then they are vulnerable to being "Dutch-booked" — that is, exploited through a clever set of bets.

Example
Suppose a bettor believes the probability of **Event A** is 0.6 and the probability of **not A** (¬A) is also 0.6. This is already a problem because the two should sum to 1. A clever bookmaker can now offer two bets:

- **Bet 1**: Pay $0.60 to win $1 if A happens.
- **Bet 2**: Pay $0.60 to win $1 if ¬A happens.

The bettor takes both, thinking they have good odds. But one of the events must happen, so the bettor **pays $1.20 total** and only gets **$1.00 back** — a guaranteed loss of $0.20, regardless of the outcome. This is a **Dutch book**: the bettor's inconsistent beliefs allowed them to be exploited.

Why It Works
The Dutch Book Paradox works because it reveals the **practical consequences of probabilistic incoherence**. If beliefs are not aligned with the basic axioms of probability, they can be manipulated into self-defeating behaviour. The paradox makes a strong case for the normative claim that **rational agents should obey probability theory**, especially if they're engaging in actions like betting, where beliefs are tied to stakes.

This has deep implications in **Bayesian epistemology**, where degrees of belief (credences) are treated as probabilities, and rational belief updating follows **Bayes' Rule**. The Dutch Book argument shows that deviating from this framework isn't just illogical — it's dangerous.

How It Works
The paradox typically assumes:

1. The agent assigns **subjective probabilities** to events.
2. The agent is **willing to bet** based on these probabilities.

3. The bets are **structured fairly**, meaning they reflect the agent's own beliefs.

If the agent's beliefs violate the **Kolmogorov axioms** of probability (non-negativity, normalization, additivity), then it's possible to construct a set of bets such that the agent is **guaranteed to lose money**, no matter what happens.

This provides a pragmatic justification for using formal probability rules: **coherence in belief protects against exploitation**.

Application

The Dutch Book Paradox has wide applications in:

- **Bayesian statistics**: Justifies coherent updating of beliefs through Bayes' Theorem.

- **Finance and insurance**: Prevents arbitrage and ensures fair odds in betting and risk assessment.

- **Game theory and AI**: Ensures rational agents act consistently and update beliefs properly in uncertain environments.

- **Philosophy of belief**: Supports the view that rational belief must follow probabilistic structure.

It also appears in **machine learning** and **automated decision systems**, where algorithms are expected to make decisions based on coherent probability distributions to avoid systematic errors or exploitation.

Key Insights

1. **Incoherent Beliefs Are Exploitable**: Violating probability rules opens the door to guaranteed losses.

2. **Probability Theory as Normative**: The paradox justifies why rational agents should adopt Bayesian principles.

3. **Subjective Probability Has Structure**: Even personal belief must conform to mathematical consistency.

4. **Coherence Prevents Arbitrage**: In betting, finance, and AI, coherence ensures stability and fairness.

5. **Irrationality Has Practical Costs**: The Dutch Book turns flawed thinking into measurable loss.

The **Dutch Book Paradox** elegantly demonstrates that **rational belief is not just a matter of logic — it's a matter of survival in systems of uncertainty**.

Philosophical & Ontological Paradoxes

Challenge fundamental ideas about existence, identity, or reality.

102. Ship of Theseus

Theory Overview

The **Ship of Theseus** is a classic philosophical paradox that explores questions of **identity, continuity, and change over time**. The thought experiment dates back to ancient Greece and was famously recorded by Plutarch. It asks:

If every part of a ship is gradually replaced with an identical part, is it still the same ship?

The paradox becomes even more complex when we add a twist: suppose all the original parts are stored and eventually reassembled into a ship. Which of the two— the gradually restored ship or the fully reassembled original—is the "real" Ship of Theseus?

This paradox challenges our intuitions about **what makes an object the same over time**. Is identity based on continuity of form? Of material? Of function? Or something else?

Example

Imagine a wooden ship named *Theseus*. Over the years, its planks rot and are replaced one by one with identical wooden planks. Eventually, none of the original material remains. Despite this, it has the same name, performs the same function, and looks the same.

Now, suppose someone collects all the discarded original planks and rebuilds the ship exactly as it was. You now have two ships: one with complete material continuity, the other with uninterrupted operational history. Which one is the real *Ship of Theseus*?

Why It Works

The paradox works because it reveals a tension between two **intuitive models of identity**:

1. **Continuity over time** – The ship that remained in use, even with replacement parts, maintains identity through functional and structural continuity.

2. **Original material** – The reassembled ship, using the original components, seems to retain the "essence" of the original.

By creating a scenario where both intuitions apply to different objects, the paradox exposes the **ambiguity in how we define sameness**. It doesn't break logic, but it destabilizes the assumptions we often take for granted about identity over time.

How It Works

The paradox hinges on **incremental change**. A single replacement doesn't affect the ship's identity, and if one replacement doesn't, then two, three, or even all replacements shouldn't either—until suddenly, you realize none of the original parts remain.

It's a variant of the **Sorites Paradox** (heap paradox): gradual changes lead to a significant transformation without a clear point of transition. When combined with the reassembly twist, it introduces a **challenge to uniqueness** in identity—how can both ships be "the same" when they clearly coexist?

Philosophers have responded in different ways:

- **Essentialism** claims identity is tied to some core essence.
- **Mereological views** focus on parts and their arrangement.
- **Four-dimensionalism** considers objects as extended through time, with all temporal stages being part of the whole.
- **Psychological or functional continuity**, in human analogues, is sometimes favoured over material composition.

Application

This paradox is widely applied in:

- **Philosophy of mind**: If your brain cells are gradually replaced, are *you* still you? What about uploading your mind to a computer?

- **Artificial intelligence and identity**: In AI and robotics, when do software or hardware updates result in a new system vs. the same one?

- **Law and ethics**: Questions of ownership and authenticity, such as with restored artifacts or modified organs.

- **Personal identity**: The paradox provokes thought about what constitutes the "self" amid constant physical and psychological change.

Key Insights

- Identity is **not absolute** but depends on how we define continuity—material, functional, historical, or psychological.

- Small changes may seem insignificant, but collectively they can challenge the very notion of sameness.

- The paradox reveals that **persistence over time** is more complex than it seems.

- There may not be a single "correct" answer—only different frameworks for thinking about identity.

- It's a powerful metaphor for **human change**, personal growth, and technological evolution.

103. Paradox of the Stone

Theory

The **Paradox of the Stone**, also known as the **Omnipotence Paradox**, is a classic philosophical problem that questions the coherence of the concept of **omnipotence**—specifically, the ability of a being (usually God) to do **anything**. It challenges the idea by asking whether an omnipotent being could create a stone **so heavy that even it cannot lift it**. If the being **can't create the stone**, then there's something it cannot do. If it **can** create the stone but **can't lift it**, again, there's something it cannot do. Either way, the being appears **not omnipotent**, creating a logical contradiction.

The paradox arises from attempting to apply **logical rigor** to a concept often treated as **metaphysically absolute**. It forces us to examine whether the very idea of "doing anything" is logically coherent—or whether omnipotence must be constrained by the rules of logic itself.

Example

Consider the following dilemma:

1. If an omnipotent being **can create a stone it cannot lift**, then there exists **a task it cannot perform**: lifting the stone.

2. If it **cannot create** such a stone, then again, there exists **a task it cannot perform**: creating the stone.

In both scenarios, there is something the being cannot do, which seemingly refutes the idea of omnipotence as "able to do all things."

Why It Works

The paradox works by **forcing a contradiction** within the definition of omnipotence. It uses **self-referential logic**, similar to the **liar paradox** or **Russell's paradox**, where a definition collapses under its own terms. By framing the task (creating a stone it cannot lift) as a test of omnipotence, it reveals a **logical boundary** to what "doing anything" can mean.

The paradox is also powerful because it mimics the kind of **hypothetical absurdity** we use to test the limits of abstract concepts—similar to how thought experiments test physical or moral theories.

How It Works

At its core, the paradox exploits **semantic ambiguity** in the phrase "can do anything." There are two possible interpretations:

1. **Absolute omnipotence**: The power to perform **any task whatsoever**, including logically contradictory ones.

2. **Logical omnipotence**: The power to do **anything logically possible**.

Most philosophers and theologians favour the second interpretation. Under logical omnipotence, the paradoxical task of creating a stone too heavy for the omnipotent being to lift is **not a real task**, but a **nonsensical pseudo-task**, like drawing a square circle. It's not a limitation on power to say such a task is impossible—because it is **incoherent** by definition.

Application

The Paradox of the Stone is widely discussed in **philosophy of religion**, particularly in debates about the attributes of God in monotheistic traditions. It's used to probe whether **omnipotence** is a logically coherent concept and whether divine attributes must be reinterpreted or limited for consistency.

It also has implications in **theology, metaphysics,** and **modal logic**, as it invites careful distinctions between different types of possibility (logical vs. metaphysical vs. physical).

In **AI and cognitive science**, analogous paradoxes help frame limits on intelligent systems—e.g., "Can an AI write a program it cannot debug?"—mirroring the self-referential tension found in the stone paradox.

Key Insights

1. **Omnipotence Must Be Defined Carefully**: Absolute omnipotence leads to contradiction; logical omnipotence avoids this.

2. **Not All Tasks Are Coherent**: Some challenges (like lifting an unliftable stone) are not "tasks" in any meaningful sense.

3. **Limits of Language**: Paradoxes often stem from misusing language to create impossible conditions.

4. **Self-Reference Creates Tension**: Like other logical paradoxes, this one arises from self-referential framing.

5. **Philosophy Clarifies Concepts**: The paradox shows how philosophical analysis helps refine vague or grand claims.

The **Paradox of the Stone** ultimately reveals that even the most powerful concepts—like omnipotence—require **logical boundaries** to remain coherent. Far from undermining power, such limits help us better understand what meaningful power truly entails.

104. Boltzmann Brain

Theory Overview

The **Boltzmann Brain Paradox** emerges from statistical mechanics and cosmology, particularly from ideas introduced by the 19th-century physicist **Ludwig Boltzmann**. Boltzmann sought to explain the second law of thermodynamics—that entropy tends to increase—by appealing to **probability**. He proposed that the universe's current low-entropy state (order) is just a **statistical fluctuation** within an otherwise high-entropy (disordered) universe.

Over time, this line of thinking led to a startling implication: if ordered structures are rare fluctuations in a sea of chaos, it should be vastly more likely for a **single conscious entity**—a disembodied brain with false memories (a "Boltzmann Brain")—to arise randomly than for an entire universe like ours to exist with all its structured order.

The paradox challenges our assumptions about **existence, observation, and probability**. If we accept Boltzmann's statistical model, we should conclude it's far more probable that *you* are a fleeting, spontaneously assembled brain floating in chaos, hallucinating reality—rather than a being in a vast, lawful universe.

Example

Imagine a universe that's reached thermodynamic equilibrium: all matter has decayed, and nothing remains but random particles fluctuating in chaos. Over infinite time, particles may randomly assemble into something momentarily structured—a working calculator, a chair, or a functioning human brain with fabricated memories.

The **most probable** of these would be the **simplest conscious systems**—a single brain, complete with sensory input and memories, but entirely deluded. According to Boltzmann's logic, this scenario is *far* more likely than the existence of a coherent universe like ours, because it requires fewer unlikely coincidences.

Why It Works

The Boltzmann Brain paradox "works" because it logically follows from a **naive interpretation of thermodynamics** applied to cosmology, particularly the idea that **random fluctuations** can temporarily create order. In a system where all configurations are equally likely over infinite time, the appearance of isolated brains is **more probable** than the emergence and evolution of an entire universe.

The paradox is not about physics being wrong—it's about what happens when we take **entropy-driven reasoning** to its extreme, without constraints on what is physically reasonable or observable.

How It Works

The Boltzmann Brain arises from this reasoning:

1. In an eternal, high-entropy universe, low-entropy states are random fluctuations.
2. The smaller and simpler the fluctuation, the more likely it is.
3. A single brain with false memories is a smaller fluctuation than an entire galaxy or universe.
4. Therefore, we should expect to be Boltzmann Brains—hallucinating everything—rather than real observers in a real cosmos.

But this leads to a contradiction: if most observers are Boltzmann Brains, and you're probably one, then your scientific reasoning (including the reasoning that led you to this conclusion) is likely false—**undermining itself**.

Application

Though theoretical, the paradox forces physicists and philosophers to **refine cosmological models**. Any viable model of the universe must account for the fact that we appear to be **stable, long-term observers** in a structured cosmos—not fleeting, disembodied minds.

In **modern cosmology**, this paradox motivates constraints on theories like eternal inflation or certain interpretations of the multiverse. Models that predict too many Boltzmann Brains are often considered **unacceptable**, as they contradict our most basic observational assumptions.

Key Insights

- The paradox highlights the dangers of **unchecked probabilistic reasoning** in cosmology.
- It emphasizes the importance of **observer selection**: not all theoretically possible observers are equal.
- If we take statistical mechanics literally, we risk conclusions that invalidate our own experience.
- To avoid this, cosmological models must ensure that normal observers (like us) are **overwhelmingly more probable** than Boltzmann Brains.
- The paradox reveals a deep tension between physics, probability, and consciousness.

105. Identity of Indiscernibles Paradox

Theory

The **Identity of Indiscernibles** is a metaphysical principle traditionally attributed to **Gottfried Wilhelm Leibniz**. It asserts that **no two distinct entities can have all their properties in common**. Formally, if object A and object B share all the same properties — including relational and intrinsic properties — then **they are not two things, but one and the same**. If they were truly distinct, there would have to be **at least one difference**, something that makes them discernible.

The **paradox** emerges when this principle is challenged by **possible counterexamples**, particularly in quantum mechanics and thought experiments involving symmetrical situations. The contradiction lies in situations where **two objects seem to be completely indistinguishable** yet are still treated as numerically distinct — suggesting that the principle may not hold universally.

Example
A classic example comes from **Max Black's thought experiment** in 1952. Imagine a universe that contains only two perfectly identical iron spheres, floating in space. These spheres have the **same mass, shape, composition, colour**, and are located at **equal distances from each other**, in a

completely symmetrical, featureless space. There is no external reference point, no way to say "this one is sphere A and that one is sphere B."

If these two spheres are absolutely indistinguishable in every property — spatial, relational, qualitative — then according to Leibniz's principle, they should be **one and the same object**. But intuitively, we feel they are **two**. This creates a paradox: **our metaphysical intuition** about identity and distinctness conflicts with the formal application of the principle.

Why It Works
The paradox works because it challenges a deeply intuitive but abstract metaphysical rule by **applying it to edge cases** where it breaks down. It exposes a gap between **ontological identity** (what something is) and **epistemic discernibility** (how we tell things apart).

It also functions by exploiting **symmetry**: if a system is perfectly symmetrical, and there's no way to distinguish one part from another even in principle, can we still say the parts are distinct? Or is "being distinct" an illusion caused by labelling?

How It Works
The paradox arises from assuming that **all identity must be grounded in qualitative properties** — that is, in measurable or perceivable differences. But in cases like Black's spheres or certain **quantum particles** (like electrons), we encounter

entities that appear to share every property and still count as multiple.

In **quantum mechanics**, identical particles (bosons or fermions) can be **completely indistinguishable**, yet their behaviour (e.g., obeying the Pauli exclusion principle) depends on their numerical distinctness. This suggests that identity in nature might not be tied solely to qualitative differentiation.

Philosophers have attempted various responses, including:

- **Rejecting the principle** in cases where numerical difference can't be grounded in qualitative terms.

- **Appealing to haecceities** ("thisnesses") — non-qualitative properties that make entities distinct.

- **Reinterpreting identity** in structural or relational terms, rather than intrinsic ones.

Application
The Identity of Indiscernibles Paradox is foundational in **metaphysics**, but it also influences **quantum theory**, **philosophy of language**, **logic**, and **ontology**. It plays a crucial role in debates about:

- **Object individuation**: What makes something a distinct object?

- **Quantum indistinguishability**: How can we describe particles that cannot be individually labelled?

- **Modal metaphysics**: How do we track identity across possible worlds?

It also informs **data modelling** and **AI**, especially in defining object uniqueness when attributes are identical.

Key Insights

1. **Identity May Not Depend on Properties**: Two things can be distinct without differing in any qualitative way.

2. **Symmetry Challenges Individuation**: Perfectly symmetrical scenarios reveal the fragility of the identity principle.

3. **Physics Undermines Classical Metaphysics**: Quantum theory suggests that numerical distinction need not follow classical rules.

4. **Individuation Is Contextual**: In many cases, identity depends on context or framework, not just features.

5. **Haecceities and Beyond**: Philosophers may need non-qualitative concepts to explain real-world distinctness.

The **Identity of Indiscernibles Paradox** reminds us that even the most intuitive metaphysical principles can break down under pressure, urging us to refine our concepts of identity in both philosophy and science.

106. Paradox of Tolerance

Theory Overview

The **Paradox of Tolerance** was introduced by philosopher **Karl Popper** in his 1945 work *The Open Society and Its Enemies*. It describes a situation in which unlimited tolerance may lead to the disappearance of tolerance altogether. That is, if a society tolerates **intolerance** without limit, the intolerant may ultimately destroy the tolerant society.

Popper's paradox is not a logical contradiction, but a social and moral dilemma: the challenge of maintaining an open society without enabling those who seek to undermine it. The paradox critiques the idea that tolerance must be absolute, and it proposes limits to tolerance in order to preserve a pluralistic society.

Example

Consider a democratic society that prides itself on free speech and open debate. Now imagine a group begins using that freedom to spread hate speech, incite violence, and promote authoritarian ideologies. If society **tolerates** this behaviour under the banner of free expression, that group might gain power and eventually **suppress the very freedoms** that allowed them to rise—freedom of the press, assembly, or religion.

History offers many examples of this, most notably **Weimar Germany** in the 1930s, where the Nazi Party used democratic processes to gain influence and then dismantled democracy itself. Popper's warning is clear: in order to **defend tolerance**, societies may be justified in **not tolerating** the intolerant.

Why It Works

The paradox works because it exposes a **blind spot** in liberal democratic thinking: the assumption that all viewpoints deserve equal space, regardless of their content. While tolerance is typically framed as a virtue, unlimited tolerance creates a **self-defeating loop** when it allows hostile ideologies to grow unchecked.

Popper argued that a tolerant society should reserve the **right to suppress** intolerant ideologies *if and only if* they pose a threat to pluralism and peaceful coexistence. This is not a call for pre-emptive censorship, but a conditional boundary based on behaviour and intent.

How It Works

At its core, the paradox reveals a tension between **principled freedom** and **pragmatic protection**. Societies operate on norms, and when one group actively works to erode the foundational values (like freedom, equality, and peace), tolerating them effectively enables **democratic erosion**.

Popper makes a crucial distinction: **intolerant speech can be tolerated**—unless it turns into **violent action or incitement**. In such cases, society must be willing to defend itself, even at the cost of suppressing some expressions. This doesn't mean abandoning tolerance, but rather defending it strategically.

Application

The Paradox of Tolerance has real-world relevance in debates about:

- **Hate speech laws**: Should neo-Nazis or extremist groups be allowed public platforms?

- **Social media moderation**: How should platforms deal with disinformation or violent rhetoric?

- **Democratic resilience**: How can democracies protect themselves from authoritarian manipulation?

Governments, tech companies, and civil society frequently face this dilemma. Limiting extremist speech or action isn't always straightforward, but the paradox serves as a **moral framework** for making difficult decisions about where to draw the line.

Key Insights

- Tolerance is not an absolute good if it enables its own destruction.

- A tolerant society must be **intolerant of intolerance** when it threatens peaceful coexistence.

- The paradox encourages us to defend open societies by being **vigilant**, not **passive**.

- Popper's warning is not anti-free speech, but a call to protect democratic values from those who would dismantle them using those very freedoms.

- In the real world, the paradox plays out in how societies balance **liberty** with **security**, and **pluralism** with **stability**.

107. Quantum Suicide

The **Quantum Suicide Paradox** is a thought experiment derived from quantum mechanics and the **Many-Worlds Interpretation (MWI)**. Proposed by physicist Hans Moravec and further discussed by Max Tegmark, the paradox explores what quantum theory implies about personal identity, death, and subjective experience.

At its core, Quantum Suicide tests whether, from a first-person perspective, a person can ever truly experience their own death in a universe governed by MWI. The paradox arises from the unsettling possibility that in some branches of the multiverse, an individual always survives—and thus may subjectively feel immortal.

Example

Imagine a scientist sets up an experiment similar to Schrödinger's Cat—but instead of a cat, **he himself** is the subject. A quantum device measures the spin of a subatomic particle. If the result is spin-up, the device does nothing; if it's spin-down, it triggers a mechanism that instantly and painlessly kills him.

Under the **Copenhagen interpretation** of quantum mechanics, the particle's spin is indeterminate until measured, and the scientist has a 50% chance of survival. But under the **Many-Worlds Interpretation**, the universe splits: in one branch, the scientist survives; in the other, he dies.

However, the **dead** version of the scientist is no longer conscious. From his own subjective point of view, he only experiences the universe in which he **continues to survive**. Repeating this experiment theoretically leads to **Quantum Immortality**: the observer never experiences death because their consciousness always "follows" the surviving version of themselves.

Why It Works

The paradox is built on the assumptions of the Many-Worlds Interpretation, which posits that all possible outcomes of a quantum event occur in separate, branching realities. There's no wavefunction collapse; every possibility happens.

From this viewpoint, your **subjective experience** only follows the path in which you remain alive. Death may occur in other branches, but you, the observer, are not there to experience them. This gives rise to the paradox: you might appear to survive **against all odds** in every situation—suggesting subjective immortality.

How It Works

The logic of Quantum Suicide relies on two pillars:

1. **MWI and Universal Branching**: Each quantum event creates branching realities. Your consciousness continues in the branches where it survives.

2. **Observer Continuity**: Consciousness is treated as continuous along one thread of survival. Death cuts off experience, so the only reality you experience is the one where you're alive.

In this way, even if there's a 0.0001% chance of surviving a dangerous experiment, your subjective experience will "find" that tiny thread—over and over again.

Application

Quantum Suicide remains a **philosophical and theoretical** construct rather than a practical application, for obvious ethical reasons. However, its implications stretch into several domains:

- In **philosophy of mind**, it challenges how we define identity and continuity of consciousness.

- In **ethics**, it raises difficult questions about risk, responsibility, and decision-making under multiverse assumptions.

- In **quantum theory**, it serves as a stark illustration of the implications of Many-Worlds taken to their logical extreme.

- In **popular culture**, it appears in science fiction narratives exploring immortality, alternate realities, or fate.

Key Insights

- Quantum Suicide explores what the Many-Worlds Interpretation means for **personal experience**.

- It suggests that while death is real in many branches, it is never experienced—raising the idea of **subjective immortality**.

- The paradox challenges our assumptions about probability, identity, and finality.

- It highlights the **philosophical tensions** between quantum mechanics and human consciousness.

- Though fascinating, it is **not a proof** of actual immortality—it's a conceptual probe into the deepest implications of quantum theory.

108. Many-worlds Paradoxes

Theory Overview

The **Many-Worlds Interpretation (MWI)** of quantum mechanics, proposed by Hugh Everett in 1957, suggests that all possible outcomes of quantum measurements actually **occur**, each in its own separate universe. Rather than wavefunction collapse (as in the Copenhagen interpretation), the universe *branches* at every quantum decision point.

The paradoxes associated with this theory arise not from contradictions in logic, but from **counterintuitive implications**. If all outcomes happen in some world, then what does it mean to observe a particular result? What is probability? How does free will or identity persist across countless versions of "you"?

These questions lead to a group of thought experiments often referred to collectively as the **Many-Worlds Paradoxes**.

Example: The Quantum Suicide Paradox

Imagine a scientist sets up a quantum experiment with a deadly mechanism: if a certain quantum event happens, he lives; if not, he dies. According to MWI, both outcomes occur—so in some branches, he dies, and in others, he survives.

From the **first-person perspective**, the scientist never experiences death—his consciousness continues in branches where he survives. This leads to the **Quantum Immortality** hypothesis: subjectively, you may always find yourself alive, even as copies of you die in other branches.

This challenges our intuitive understanding of death, consciousness, and survival. It also seemingly denies the finality of death, at least from a personal experiential viewpoint.

Why It Works

Many-Worlds Paradoxes stem from the rigorous mathematical foundation of quantum mechanics. The Schrödinger equation, which governs quantum systems, is deterministic and doesn't include wavefunction collapse. MWI takes this at face value and removes collapse altogether, solving several theoretical problems—like the measurement problem—at the cost of spawning a potentially infinite number of branching realities.

These paradoxes "work" because they extend the logic of the theory to its natural (if unsettling) conclusions. Rather than dismissing the implications as absurd, they force us to confront what quantum theory *actually says* when taken literally.

How It Works

In MWI, every time a quantum event with multiple outcomes occurs (like a radioactive atom decaying or not), the universe "splits" into distinct, non-interacting branches—each representing a different outcome. The wavefunction of the universe includes *all* these possibilities, and observers find themselves in one branch.

There is no probabilistic collapse; rather, each observer becomes entangled with a particular outcome. The Born rule (which gives the probabilities of outcomes) is then interpreted as the **measure** of how many versions of you experience each result.

Application

Though Many-Worlds is largely theoretical, its implications influence various fields:

- In **quantum computing**, MWI provides a conceptual framework for understanding quantum parallelism—why quantum computers can process vast possibilities simultaneously.

- In **philosophy of mind**, it raises questions about identity, personal continuity, and free will.

- In **ethics**, Quantum Immortality has prompted speculation about risk and survival, though most physicists reject it as a practical guide to decision-making.

Key Insights

- MWI avoids paradoxes like wavefunction collapse or observer-dependence by positing that *all outcomes exist*.

- The paradoxes are psychological and philosophical, not mathematical contradictions.

- It reframes probability: you don't have a chance of one outcome *happening*—instead, you will *experience* one, while others occur elsewhere.

- MWI pushes the boundaries of how we understand reality, showing that quantum mechanics may not just describe randomness—but an infinite, branching multiverse.

- Many-Worlds Paradoxes invite a profound shift in how we conceive of self, causality, and the nature of existence itself.

109. Gödel's Incompleteness

Theory Overview

Gödel's Incompleteness Theorems, published by Kurt Gödel in 1931, are among the most profound results in mathematical logic and philosophy. They demonstrate inherent limitations in formal systems—especially those powerful enough to express basic arithmetic.

There are **two theorems**:

1. **First Incompleteness Theorem**: In any consistent, formal system that is sufficiently expressive (capable of representing elementary arithmetic), there exist **true statements** that cannot be **proven within the system**.

2. **Second Incompleteness Theorem**: Such a system **cannot prove its own consistency** from within.

Together, these results shook the foundations of mathematics, ending the dream (promoted by thinkers like Hilbert) that all mathematical truths could be formally proven through a complete, consistent, and finite set of axioms.

Example

Imagine a formal system like Peano Arithmetic (a basic system for number theory). Gödel ingeniously constructs a mathematical statement that essentially says:

"This statement is not provable within this system."

If the system **proves** it, then it is **false**, because it says it is not provable—making the system inconsistent. But if the system **cannot prove** it, then the statement is **true** (since it correctly states its own unprovability)—meaning there's a true statement the system cannot prove.

This is a mathematical analogue of the **Liar Paradox**, but encoded with incredible precision into number theory using a method called **Gödel numbering**, which maps symbols and statements into arithmetic.

Why It Works

Gödel's argument works by creating a self-referential structure within a formal system. Instead of using plain language, he develops a way to talk about statements and their proofs **within arithmetic itself**. This allows the system to effectively "talk about itself."

He cleverly encodes the idea of "provability" using purely arithmetical constructs, thus turning metamathematical questions (about the system) into questions **inside** the system. Once this is done, the system can generate statements about its own properties—leading to the paradoxical but rigorous outcome.

How It Works

Gödel's method involves several steps:

1. **Arithmetization**: He assigns each symbol and rule of inference a unique number (Gödel numbering).

2. **Self-reference**: He builds a statement (now a number) that refers to itself using these numbers.

3. **Diagonalization**: A technique that allows a formula to apply to its own Gödel number—creating self-referential statements.

4. **Consistency Assumption**: The theorems rely on assuming the system is consistent (it doesn't prove both a statement and its negation).

Through this, he constructs a statement that the system cannot prove **if** it is consistent—thus proving the system is incomplete.

Application

Gödel's theorems have wide-ranging implications:

- In **mathematics**, they show that some truths can't be reached by proof alone, limiting the goals of formalism.

- In **computer science**, they inspired limits of computation (e.g., the Halting Problem, Turing machines).

- In **philosophy**, they challenge reductionism and raise questions about the nature of truth, knowledge, and mind.

- In **AI and cognitive science**, they've been (sometimes controversially) used to argue that the human mind is not just a machine—since we can "see" the truth of Gödelian statements, which formal systems cannot.

Key Insights

- No system of math can prove all truths about numbers if it is consistent.

- Any sufficiently powerful system can be used to construct statements it cannot resolve.

- Truth transcends proof: some truths are inherently **unprovable** within the system that expresses them.

- The theorems place **fundamental limits** on what logic and algorithms can achieve.

- They illustrate the **power—and fragility—of self-reference**, laying the groundwork for modern logic, language theory, and even AI limits.

110. Sorites (Vagueness)

The Sorites Paradox, also known as the *paradox of the heap*, arises from situations involving vague predicates—terms without clear boundaries. "Sorites" comes from the Greek word *sōritēs*, meaning "heap." The paradox reveals how small, seemingly insignificant changes can lead to surprising or absurd conclusions when dealing with vagueness.

Theory Overview

The paradox begins with a seemingly obvious premise: one grain of sand does not make a heap. It then adds: if one grain doesn't make a heap, then two grains don't either. By repeating this logic, we reach the conclusion that no number of grains, even 10,000, makes a heap. But clearly, at some point, a heap does emerge.

This paradox arises because of a **vague predicate**—"heap"—which lacks a precise cutoff point. The same logic applies to other vague terms like "bald," "tall," or "rich." If losing one hair doesn't make a man bald, then at what point does he become bald?

Example

Imagine a person with a full head of hair. You pluck one hair at a time, and after each pluck, you ask, "Is he bald yet?" Since one hair's loss doesn't seem sufficient, you keep saying "no." But eventually, the person is clearly bald—despite never identifying the exact moment the transition occurred.

Why It Works

The Sorites Paradox works because it exploits the **tolerance of vague terms** to small changes. Our language often operates in gradients, but logical reasoning tends to demand precise thresholds. The paradox exposes a tension between **natural language** and **formal reasoning**.

In everyday life, we rely on context to deal with vagueness. But in formal systems or legal language, this fuzziness leads to confusion or contradiction. The paradox forces us to confront how much imprecision we're willing to tolerate.

How It Works

There are several philosophical strategies for addressing the paradox:

1. **Epistemicism** argues that there *is* a precise boundary—we just don't know it.

2. **Supervaluationism** accepts that vague predicates have "borderline cases" and considers a statement true only if it is true under *all* acceptable precisifications.

3. **Fuzzy Logic** assigns degrees of truth (e.g., "0.7 true" for borderline baldness), rather than binary true/false values.

4. **Contextualism** holds that the meaning of vague terms shifts depending on use or discourse context.

Each approach preserves different intuitions about how language and logic interact.

Application

The Sorites Paradox has practical implications in **law, ethics, medicine, and artificial intelligence**, where binary decisions must be made using vague terms. For example, when is a person "legally blind"? At what point does someone become "disabled"? In **machine learning**, classification algorithms often struggle with fuzzy categories—e.g., identifying what counts as a "cat" in blurry images.

Key Insights

- Vagueness is intrinsic to natural language and human reasoning.

- Logical systems struggle with the tolerance to gradual change.

- There may be no clear solution—only better ways to manage fuzziness.

- The paradox challenges rigid categorization, prompting the development of alternative logics (like fuzzy logic) and more careful language use in formal systems.

111. Dialetheism

Dialetheism is the philosophical position that some statements can be *both true and false* simultaneously. This challenges one of the bedrocks of classical logic: the **Law of Non-Contradiction**, which asserts that no proposition can be both true and not true at the same time in the same respect.

Theory Overview

Dialetheism argues that not all contradictions are meaningless or signs of error. Instead, some contradictions—called *true contradictions* or *dialetheias*—may reflect genuine features of reality or thought. The concept is often used to explore semantic, logical, and metaphysical boundaries where traditional logic breaks down.

Philosopher **Graham Priest** is one of the foremost advocates of dialetheism. He developed a logic known as **paraconsistent logic**, which allows contradictory statements to coexist without rendering the entire logical system trivial (i.e., where everything becomes provable).

Example

Consider the **Liar Paradox**:

"This sentence is false."

If the sentence is true, then what it says must hold—so it's false. But if it's false, then it must be true. Rather than treating this as a breakdown or error, dialetheists accept the contradiction: the sentence is *both* true *and* false.

Why It Works

In classical logic, contradictions are explosive: from a contradiction, anything follows. Dialetheism avoids this explosion by using **paraconsistent logics**—systems that reject the principle of explosion. These systems are engineered to tolerate some contradictions without allowing them to infect the entire logical structure.

Dialetheism works not by replacing all logic, but by carving out space for contradictions that arise in specific, often self-referential contexts. It offers a more nuanced framework for reasoning about paradoxes, inconsistencies, and phenomena that defy binary truth values.

How It Works

Dialetheists employ **paraconsistent logic**, which changes how inference rules are applied. For example, from "A and not-A," classical logic would let you conclude any proposition B. Paraconsistent logic blocks this move, allowing "A and not-A" to exist without collapse.

This allows contradictory but nontrivial theories, particularly in contexts like set theory (e.g., Russell's Paradox), semantics (e.g., truth theories), and even legal reasoning or moral dilemmas where inconsistencies are tolerated or necessary.

Application

One real-world application lies in **legal theory**, where courts sometimes face cases that hinge on contradictory principles (e.g., justice vs. precedent). In software, paraconsistent logic can be used in **fault-tolerant systems** or **knowledge representation** where inconsistent data may still be useful.

In philosophical discourse, dialetheism provides tools to analyse paradoxes and challenge binary thinking. It has been explored in Eastern philosophies (e.g., some interpretations of **Buddhist logic**) and modern debates on truth and meaning.

Key Insights

- Dialetheism doesn't collapse into absurdity; it's a controlled embrace of contradiction.

- It questions whether *consistency* is always a virtue in reasoning.

- Not all contradictions are equal—some may reveal deeper truths about self-reference, vagueness, or linguistic boundaries.

- Dialetheism opens the door to a more flexible, layered understanding of truth.

Paradox of the Unexpected Gift

Here's an unexpected gift for you. Some additional Paradoxes. I hope you enjoy them. Dan

Bonus Chapter 1: **Berry Paradox**

Theory Overview

The **Berry Paradox** is a self-referential semantic paradox that arises from the interaction between **natural language and arithmetic**, particularly when attempting to define or describe numbers using phrases. It highlights the ambiguities and limitations inherent in definitions involving **descriptive complexity**—how concisely something can be described. First noted by G.G. Berry and made famous by Bertrand Russell, the paradox centres on the idea that certain descriptions—when referring to numbers—can lead to **logical inconsistency** or **circular reasoning**.

In essence, the Berry Paradox demonstrates that natural language allows for the construction of definitions that **refer to themselves or exclude themselves**, leading to a **self-referential loop** similar to the Liar Paradox. The crux of the paradox lies in defining numbers using phrases like "the smallest number not nameable in under eleven words," which itself becomes a name using fewer than eleven words.

Example

Let's walk through the classic example:

Consider the phrase:

"The smallest natural number not nameable in fewer than twelve words."

This phrase is **only eleven words long** and appears to **name** a specific number. But if the number it refers to **isn't nameable in fewer than twelve words**, and yet **this very phrase names it in eleven**, we reach a contradiction.

If the number is **nameable in eleven words**, then it **should not qualify** as the number being referred to. But if it **isn't** nameable in eleven words, then **how are we naming it now?**

This paradox hinges on **descriptive self-reference** and **the notion of definability within language**, especially when constrained by word count or complexity.

Why It Works

The Berry Paradox works because it exploits the **vagueness of language** and the idea of **definability by length**. It pushes our intuitions about naming, description, and number theory into conflict by using language to create a **semantic loop**. The contradiction does not arise from any error in arithmetic, but from an ambiguous use of language to define what "nameable" means.

It's related to **Richard's Paradox** and **Russell's Paradox**, in that it deals with **self-referential definitions** and **sets defined by exclusion** (e.g., the set of things that do not describe themselves).

How It Works

Key components of the paradox:

1. **Quantitative constraint on language**: Only phrases shorter than twelve words are allowed.

2. **Reference to definability**: The paradox defines a number in terms of its **non-definability** within a certain constraint.

3. **Self-reference**: The phrase indirectly refers to itself and breaks the very rule it sets.

4. **Contradiction**: A number supposedly not nameable in under twelve words is named in eleven, leading to a **logical contradiction**.

The paradox is not formal in nature but arises from the **interaction between meta-language and object language**—attempting to describe naming from within the same linguistic system.

Application

While the Berry Paradox is primarily philosophical, it has significant implications:

- **Computability theory**: It relates to **Kolmogorov complexity**, which studies the shortest possible description of an object or number.

- **Logic and mathematics**: Highlights limitations of **formal systems** and problems with naive set theory and definitions.

- **Artificial intelligence**: Demonstrates the difficulty of defining or constraining knowledge in **natural language** for machines.

- **Philosophy of language**: Emphasizes the blurry line between **syntax and semantics**, and the dangers of unqualified meta-level definitions.

Key Insights

- Not all paradoxes require falsehoods—**ambiguous definitions can cause real logical problems**.

- **Self-reference**, especially when combined with vague criteria (like word count), can easily lead to contradiction.

- The paradox reveals that **natural language is not well-suited for precise logical formulation** without strict formalization.

- It supports deeper insights into **computational complexity and description length**, connecting logic to information theory.

- Ultimately, the Berry Paradox serves as a cautionary tale in mathematics and philosophy: **careless or circular definitions can unravel the very logic they intend to clarify**.

Bonus Chapter 2: Moore's Paradox

Moore's Paradox is a philosophical puzzle about **belief and assertion**, first identified by the British philosopher **G.E. Moore** in the early 20th century. The paradox arises when someone makes a statement that is **logically consistent**, but nonetheless sounds **deeply absurd** when uttered sincerely. The classic form is:

"It's raining, but I don't believe that it's raining."

There's no contradiction in terms of **truth-value**—both parts could be true. It might be raining, and the speaker might, for some reason, not believe it. However, asserting such a statement **sincerely** seems paradoxical because it **violates the norms of rational belief and communication**.

This paradox is less about logical contradiction and more about the **pragmatic incoherence** of making certain statements while also claiming to hold specific beliefs.

Example

Consider someone saying:

"The meeting is at 3 p.m., but I don't believe that the meeting is at 3 p.m."

This might logically be the case—perhaps the person received accurate information but doesn't trust the source. However,

asserting the sentence as if it were a statement of knowledge creates confusion. **How can you assert something while simultaneously claiming not to believe it?** Belief is generally thought to underlie sincere assertions.

Another variation is:

"It's not raining, but I believe that it is."

Again, logically consistent, but psychologically puzzling. It seems to betray an **epistemic dysfunction**—how can one acknowledge that one's belief is false and still hold it?

Why It Works

Moore's Paradox works because it targets the **presuppositions** that govern our communication. When we assert a sentence, we imply that we **believe it to be true**. So when someone says, "It's raining, but I don't believe it," they're performing an act that pragmatically **undermines itself**.

This makes the paradox less about logic and more about the **norms of belief and speech**. We expect speakers to align what they assert with what they believe. Moore's sentences violate this expectation, creating a cognitive dissonance in the listener—even though the statement is not formally self-contradictory.

How It Works

The paradox relies on a clash between:

1. **Logical coherence**: The statement "P, but I don't believe P" is not contradictory.

2. **Pragmatic norms**: To assert P, one must **believe** P (norm of assertion).

3. **First-person authority**: When a person reports their own beliefs, they're presumed to have privileged access.

By asserting P and denying belief in P, the speaker **violates the epistemic commitment** usually required for assertions.

This disjunction between **semantics (truth)** and **pragmatics (belief and assertion)** creates the paradox.

Application

Moore's Paradox is important in:

- **Philosophy of mind**: It raises questions about self-knowledge, belief, and introspection.

- **Epistemology**: It challenges assumptions about the relationship between belief, truth, and rationality.

- **Linguistics and pragmatics**: It illuminates the rules that govern conversation and assertion.

- **Artificial intelligence**: Programming agents to recognize and avoid such inconsistencies in belief-reporting systems.
- **Mental health studies**: In understanding delusions or cognitive dissonance where beliefs and verbal assertions misalign.

Key Insights

- **Sincerity in assertion implies belief**—violating this norm leads to paradoxical speech.
- Moore's Paradox shows how statements can be **logically valid but psychologically incoherent**.
- It reveals the subtle interplay between **language, thought, and communication norms**.
- The paradox demonstrates that **not all inconsistencies are logical**—some are **pragmatic or epistemic**.
- It invites a richer understanding of how belief functions in everyday reasoning, and why **self-knowledge** is more complex than it appears.

Bonus Chapter 3: Münchhausen Trilemma

Theory Overview

The **Münchhausen Trilemma** is a philosophical problem in **epistemology**—the study of knowledge—which shows that it is impossible to provide any ultimate, non-circular justification for any truth claim. Named after **Baron Münchhausen**, a fictional character who claimed to have pulled himself out of a swamp by his own hair, the trilemma captures the **impossibility of justifying knowledge without relying on one of three unsatisfying options.**

The paradox was notably articulated by German philosopher **Hans Albert**, based on ideas from **Karl Popper**, and it remains a foundational challenge for theories of justification. The "trilemma" refers to the three possible types of justification, none of which escape serious philosophical criticism:

1. **Circular reasoning** (the claim refers back to itself),
2. **Regress ad infinitum** (each justification requires a prior justification, endlessly),
3. **Dogmatic stopping point** (asserting something as foundational without proof).

In short: **no belief can be justified in a way that escapes these three unsatisfactory outcomes.**

Example

Imagine you assert:

"I know that the Earth orbits the Sun."

You are then asked: "How do you know that?"

You might respond: "Because astronomers have measured it." If asked how you know their measurements are reliable, you might appeal to scientific method, and then to logic, and so on.

This leads to three problematic routes:

1. **Infinite regress**: You keep giving reasons forever, never reaching a foundational answer.

2. **Circular reasoning**: You eventually loop back and justify your belief using premises that assume the belief itself (e.g., trusting science because science says it's trustworthy).

3. **Axiomatic claim**: You stop and say, "Because that's just true," or "Because it's self-evident," which halts the justification arbitrarily.

No matter which path you choose, **you fail to provide an absolute, unquestionable justification**—thus revealing the paradox.

Why It Works

The Münchhausen Trilemma works because it exposes the **limits of rational justification**. Any attempt to justify a belief leads to one of the three unsatisfactory options. Each one undermines the supposed objectivity or certainty of knowledge:

- **Circularity** is logically invalid.
- **Infinite regress** makes justification impossible.
- **Dogmatism** violates the principle of critical inquiry.

This challenges the foundationalist idea that knowledge can be **built from indubitable truths**, showing instead that **all beliefs rest on unprovable assumptions** or structural gaps.

How It Works

The trilemma forces a thinker to confront the **structure of justification** itself:

- When asked to justify a belief, you must appeal to **another belief**.
- That belief, in turn, must be justified.
- This loop can only resolve through **repetition**, **suspension**, or **arbitrary grounding**—each with its own problem.

The paradox doesn't deny that knowledge is possible, but it casts doubt on the **possibility of absolute epistemic certainty**.

Application

The Münchhausen Trilemma has deep relevance in:

- **Philosophy**: Especially in debates about foundationalism, coherentism, and scepticism.

- **Mathematics and logic**: Gödel's Incompleteness Theorems echo similar themes of non-self-containment.

- **Science**: It questions whether scientific knowledge can be definitively grounded without circularity or brute assumptions.

- **Postmodern theory**: The trilemma supports the idea that all systems of thought are built on **arbitrary or contingent foundations**.

It also plays a role in discussions of **AI, rational argumentation**, and **philosophy of language**.

Key Insights

- The trilemma shows that **ultimate justification is structurally impossible**.

- Every knowledge system rests on **assumptions that cannot be fully justified**.

- It invites humility in claims to certainty and opens the door to **fallibilism**—the idea that all beliefs may be revised.

- Philosophers often choose between **coherentism** (circular but internally consistent belief systems) or **pragmatism** (justification based on usefulness rather than proof).
- The paradox is not a dead end, but a **reminder of the complexity of knowing**, encouraging more flexible, reflective epistemologies.

Bonus Chapter 4: Bootstrap Paradox

Theory Overview

The **Bootstrap Paradox** is a time travel paradox that occurs when an object, piece of information, or even a person is sent back in time and becomes trapped within a **causal loop**, with no discernible point of origin. The term derives from the expression "pulling oneself up by one's bootstraps," implying a **self-generating process** that seems impossible or circular.

The paradox raises fundamental questions about **causality, time, and the origin of information**. Specifically, it challenges the principle that everything must have a cause. In a bootstrap loop, cause and effect are so entangled that an item or idea appears to **exist without ever having been created**, defying our normal understanding of time and logic.

Example

One of the most famous examples involves **a time traveller** and **a book**. Imagine someone travels to the past and gives **Shakespeare's works** to a young William Shakespeare. Inspired, he copies the texts and eventually becomes famous for writing them.

Centuries later, a scholar travels back in time to study Shakespeare and brings the same complete works with him—delivering them again to Shakespeare. Thus, the writings exist in an **endless causal loop**, with **no true author**: Shakespeare didn't originally create them, nor did the time traveller—they simply **exist in time**.

Another version involves a **scientist who invents a time machine** after receiving blueprints from their future self. They build it, then later travel back and give the blueprints to their past self, completing the loop. The invention has **no original inventor**.

Why It Works

The Bootstrap Paradox works because it exposes a **logical and ontological inconsistency** in the concept of time travel, particularly in theories that allow closed time-like curves (CTCs). It brings attention to the fact that if **information or objects can loop through time indefinitely**, then they can **exist without a beginning**, violating our common-sense notions of cause and creation.

The paradox is especially unsettling because it is **logically consistent** within certain physical models (like general relativity), yet **philosophically troubling** due to its implications.

How It Works

The Bootstrap Paradox depends on:

1. **Time travel to the past** being possible.

2. **A closed causal loop**, in which a future event causes a past event that in turn causes the original future event.

3. **Lack of external origin**: The loop contains all the information or matter needed to sustain itself, but it has **no external cause**.

From a physics perspective, general relativity allows such loops in some solutions (e.g., Gödel's universe), though they raise issues of **entropy, determinism, and conservation laws**.

Application

The paradox is frequently used in:

- **Science fiction**: In stories like *Doctor Who*, *Predestination*, or *Tenet*, where time travel and causality loops are central plot devices.

- **Philosophy of time**: Challenging our assumptions about linear time and causality.

- **Physics**: As a theoretical concern in models involving wormholes, quantum gravity, or multiverse theories.

- **Information theory**: Posing puzzles about the origin and transmission of knowledge or data.

In computing, the paradox metaphorically illustrates situations where **output becomes input** in recursive or feedback systems, sometimes without a clear source.

Key Insights

- The Bootstrap Paradox questions whether **every effect needs a clear cause**.

- It suggests that time travel may lead to **ontologically problematic loops**.

- Even if logically consistent, the paradox **violates our intuitive understanding of time, memory, and identity**.

- It shows how **causal chains can become self-contained**, posing challenges to theories of knowledge, authorship, and originality.

- Ultimately, it forces us to rethink the nature of **existence and origin** in a universe where time may not be strictly linear.

Bonus Chapter 5: Lotteries Paradox

Theory Overview

The **Lotteries Paradox** is a philosophical paradox introduced by **Henry E. Kyburg Jr.** in 1961. It arises in **epistemology**—the study of knowledge and belief—and illustrates a conflict between three intuitively reasonable principles about rational belief. Specifically, it shows how **rational probabilistic reasoning** can lead to **logically inconsistent conclusions**.

The paradox centres on the tension between **high probability, individual rational belief**, and the logical principle that **beliefs should be closed under conjunction** (if you believe each of a set of things, you should believe their conjunction). While it may be rational to believe that **each individual ticket in a lottery will lose**, it is clearly irrational to believe that **all tickets will lose**, since **one must win**.

Example

Imagine a fair lottery with **1,000 tickets**, and only **one winning ticket**. You're told the draw is random, and every ticket has a 0.001 probability of winning.

For each individual ticket, it seems **rational** to believe it will **lose**—after all, the chance of any one ticket winning is very low. So you form 1,000 beliefs of the form:

"Ticket 1 will lose," "Ticket 2 will lose," ... "Ticket 1000 will lose."

Now, by the **closure of belief under conjunction**, you should also believe the **conjunction** of these beliefs: that **all tickets will lose**. But that's absurd—**you know that one ticket must win**. Therefore, your set of individually rational beliefs leads to a **collectively irrational conclusion**.

This contradiction is the **Lotteries Paradox**.

Why It Works

The paradox works by **exploiting the gap between probabilistic reasoning and logical consistency**. It shows that what seems rational at the **individual level** (believing each ticket will lose) becomes irrational at the **collective level** (believing all will lose). This creates a powerful challenge to our understanding of what counts as **reasonable belief**.

It's particularly striking because none of the steps feel obviously flawed:

1. High probability seems to justify belief.
2. Beliefs should ideally be consistent.
3. Beliefs should be closed under conjunction.

Yet accepting all three leads directly to contradiction.

How It Works

The logical mechanism of the paradox includes:

- **Probabilistic justification**: Believing something because it is extremely likely.

- **Conjunctive closure**: The principle that if you believe P and believe Q, you should also believe P & Q.

- **Consistency requirement**: A rational agent should not hold contradictory beliefs.

Together, these lead to an unsolvable triangle: you cannot hold all three principles without running into inconsistency.

To resolve the paradox, one of the principles must be **weakened or rejected**. Philosophers differ on which:

- Some argue against **closure under conjunction**, claiming that it's possible to rationally believe each individual claim without believing the whole set.

- Others question whether **high probability alone should warrant belief**.

- A third view is to maintain the logic and suggest we adopt **degrees of belief (credences)** instead of binary belief.

Application

The Lotteries Paradox has relevance in:

- **Epistemology**: Guiding theories of justified belief and rationality.

- **Probability theory**: Influencing how uncertainty is handled in formal systems.

- **Artificial intelligence**: Designing belief models in probabilistic agents.

- **Legal reasoning**: Where judgments based on high probability must still meet standards of certainty.

It also echoes challenges in **risk assessment**, where acting on many reasonable assumptions can lead to a clearly flawed conclusion.

Key Insights

- Rational belief can break down when scaled across many cases.

- The paradox challenges the assumption that beliefs are neatly **Boolean (true/false)** and suggests a **graded belief system** might be more realistic.

- It forces us to examine **how much probability is enough** to justify belief.

- Lotteries Paradox demonstrates the limits of applying simple logic to complex uncertain systems.

Bonus Chapter 6 : Observer's Paradox

Theory Overview

The **Observer's Paradox** is a conceptual dilemma that arises when the act of **observing or measuring** a phenomenon inevitably **alters** the very thing being observed. Originating in fields like **sociolinguistics, psychology,** and **quantum physics**, this paradox underscores the difficulty of studying natural behaviour without **influencing** it.

In **sociolinguistics**, the term was popularized by **William Labov**, who faced the challenge of studying how people naturally speak in everyday situations. When people know they're being recorded or observed, they often **change their speech**—becoming more formal, guarded, or self-conscious—thus producing **inauthentic data**.

The paradox poses a fundamental challenge in any discipline that aims to **study authentic, unfiltered behaviour**, because the presence of an observer, or even awareness of being watched, can **contaminate** the results.

Example

Imagine a researcher studying how teenagers speak casually with their friends. The goal is to record natural, everyday speech patterns—slang, accents, informal grammar. But as soon as the researcher sets up a camera or recorder, the teenagers become aware of being monitored and start **speaking more carefully**.

This means the researcher ends up recording **not the real behaviour**, but a **performance**, shaped by the social context of being watched. Even if participants are told to "just act normal," their awareness of observation changes the dynamic.

The same occurs in psychology labs (where subjects behave differently under observation), or in wildlife documentaries (where animals may flee or act cautiously when approached by humans). In quantum physics, a version of this is seen in the **Heisenberg uncertainty principle** or **wavefunction collapse**, where measuring a particle's position affects its momentum and vice versa.

Why It Works

The paradox works because **human behaviour is context-dependent**. The act of being observed becomes part of the context, influencing actions, language, and choices. Humans are deeply social creatures, and **self-monitoring increases under scrutiny**. Observation introduces **new incentives**, like managing impressions or adhering to perceived expectations.

This also applies to **non-human systems** where measurement involves interaction. For example, observing subatomic particles involves bouncing photons off them—which **physically alters** their properties.

How It Works

The mechanics vary across fields, but the core structure is:

1. A researcher or observer sets out to **measure or observe** a natural phenomenon.

2. The **subject becomes aware** of this observation (explicitly or implicitly).

3. This awareness causes a **change in behaviour or state**, skewing the results.

4. The resulting data reflects a **modified version** of reality—shaped by the act of observation.

In social sciences, this often manifests as **observer bias** or **participant reactivity**. In physics, it reflects the **intrusive nature of measurement tools** in systems governed by uncertainty.

Application

The Observer's Paradox is relevant to:

- **Sociolinguistics**: Pioneering techniques like "participant observation" or hidden microphones.

- **Ethnography and anthropology**: Developing rapport to reduce the subject's self-consciousness.

- **Experimental psychology**: Using blind and double-blind designs to limit bias.

- **Quantum mechanics**: Refining our understanding of measurement, superposition, and reality.

- **User testing and design research**: Accounting for altered user behaviour in controlled studies.

Key Insights

- Observation is **never truly neutral**—it often becomes part of the phenomenon itself.

- Authentic behaviour is hard to isolate when subjects are aware of being watched.

- The paradox urges researchers to **minimize their footprint** through subtle methods or **long-term immersion**.

- In science, it reveals the limits of **objectivity** and the need for models that **account for the observer**.

- Ultimately, it challenges us to ask: **Can we ever observe without participating?**

Bonus Chapter 7: Black Hole Information Paradox

Theory Overview

The **Black Hole Information Paradox** is one of the most profound and unresolved problems in theoretical physics. It emerges from an apparent conflict between **quantum mechanics** and **general relativity**—two of the most successful yet incompatible pillars of modern physics. The paradox centres on a critical question:

What happens to information that falls into a black hole?

According to **quantum mechanics**, information cannot be destroyed. Every physical process is, in principle, **reversible**, and the evolution of quantum states is **unitary**—meaning no information about a system's initial state is ever lost. However, according to **general relativity**, black holes can evaporate via **Hawking radiation**, a process discovered by Stephen Hawking in 1974. The radiation appears **thermal and random**, revealing no information about the matter that formed the black hole or fell into it.

This leads to a paradox:
If a black hole evaporates completely and only releases **featureless radiation**, the **information about its contents is lost**, violating quantum theory.

Example

Imagine a star collapses into a black hole. Later, you throw a book into it—a complex object full of information (letters, atoms, quantum states). Over time, the black hole emits Hawking radiation and eventually disappears.

Now the problem:

- **Where is the information contained in the book?**
- If it's gone forever, **quantum mechanics breaks**.
- If it comes out in the radiation, **how can random radiation carry that information**?
- If it remains in some remnant or another universe, it raises questions about **causality and predictability**.

None of these options are satisfying under current physics, creating a true paradox.

Why It Works

The paradox is so powerful because it **pits two well-tested theories against each other**. Quantum theory insists on information preservation. General relativity—via classical black hole mechanics and Hawking's calculations—suggests otherwise.

It reveals the **incompleteness of our understanding of gravity at quantum scales**. Hawking's semi-classical model treats quantum fields in a classical spacetime, an approximation that may fail near singularities or during evaporation.

The paradox is also robust: it doesn't depend on specific details of the black hole, the information content, or the observer—it's a **general and unavoidable conflict**.

How It Works

The key elements:

1. **Hawking radiation** results from particle-antiparticle pairs near the event horizon. One falls in; the other escapes.
2. This radiation appears **thermal**, encoding no discernible data about what fell into the black hole.
3. Over time, the black hole **loses mass** and eventually vanishes.
4. If the evaporation is complete and no information escapes, **unitarity is violated**.

Potential resolutions include:

- **Information is encoded subtly in the Hawking radiation** (via correlations).
- **Black holes don't fully evaporate**—a remnant stores the information.
- **Information leaks out via quantum gravitational effects** (e.g., via "soft hair" or holography).

- **The holographic principle**: the information of 3D objects is encoded on a 2D surface (e.g., the event horizon), possibly preserved even after evaporation.

Application

This paradox drives much of modern research in:

- **Quantum gravity**: Including string theory, loop quantum gravity, and holography.
- **Black hole thermodynamics**: Entropy and information models.
- **Quantum computing**: As a testbed for quantum information theory.
- **Theoretical cosmology**: Exploring the nature of spacetime, singularities, and the multiverse.

It led to proposals like the **AdS/CFT correspondence** (a holographic duality) and newer ideas like the **ER=EPR conjecture** (wormholes as entangled states).

Key Insights

- **Information cannot be destroyed**—a core principle of quantum mechanics.
- Black holes challenge our understanding of how information and space interact.

- The paradox suggests that **spacetime and gravity must be fundamentally quantum**.
- Progress may come not from reconciling the two theories directly, but from **rethinking the nature of space, time, and information itself**.
- It exemplifies how **theoretical paradoxes drive deep advances in science**.

Bonus Chapter 8: Paradox of Fiction

Theory Overview

The **Paradox of Fiction** is a philosophical puzzle that questions how people can have **genuine emotional responses** to characters, events, and situations they **know are not real**. First articulated by **Colin Radford** and **Michael Weston** in the 1970s, the paradox arises from a seemingly simple observation:

We often feel fear, sadness, joy, or anger toward fictional characters and narratives, even though we know they don't exist.

This leads to a triad of claims that appear individually plausible but collectively contradictory:

1. **We have genuine emotional responses to fictional entities.**
2. **To have genuine emotions, we must believe the objects of those emotions exist.**
3. **We know fictional entities do not exist.**

The paradox emerges from trying to accept all three claims at once. If we don't believe fictional characters exist, how can we feel real emotions toward them? Yet clearly, we do.

Example

Consider watching *Romeo and Juliet*. As Juliet awakens to find Romeo dead, many viewers feel sadness, empathy, even grief. But we all know that **Romeo and Juliet are fictional characters**—no real people have died. Still, the emotions felt during the scene are **real and powerful**.

Or take horror films: viewers often feel **genuine fear** watching a monster chase a protagonist, despite knowing full well it's **just a movie**.

This psychological realism conflicts with the philosophical assertion that emotions must be rooted in belief. If you don't believe something is true, how can it evoke a real emotional response?

Why It Works

The paradox works because it **challenges the assumption** that emotions are always tied to **belief in reality**. This is a reasonable assumption in day-to-day life: we fear tigers because we believe they can hurt us. But fiction introduces **a gray zone**, where **imagination** substitutes for belief, yet emotions remain intense and authentic.

The emotional engagement we experience while engaging with fiction reflects a **complex interplay between imagination, empathy, and suspension of disbelief**. We seem to engage with fiction using a special cognitive mode—one that allows emotional investment without literal belief.

How It Works

Philosophers have proposed several responses:

1. **Imaginative Theory** (Kendall Walton): Emotions toward fiction are not real emotions but **"quasi-emotions"**. When watching a horror film, you're not really afraid, but you're **imagining being afraid**, within the context of the story.

2. **Thought Theory**: Emotions can be triggered by **thoughts** or **representations**, even without belief. For instance, we can fear hypothetical scenarios or feel sad thinking about a tragic possibility, without believing it's real.

3. **Emotional Continuity View**: Fiction taps into **real human concerns**—love, loss, justice—so the emotional responses, while directed at fictional situations, are grounded in **real-world emotional frameworks**.

Each theory modifies or drops one of the three core premises to dissolve the paradox.

Application

The Paradox of Fiction is relevant in:

- **Aesthetics and art criticism**: Understanding how art elicits real engagement.

- **Narrative psychology**: Studying how fictional stories influence behaviour, beliefs, and emotional development.

- **Media and cultural studies**: Exploring why people bond with characters, grieve over fictional deaths, or change opinions after watching a film.
- **Therapeutic contexts**: Leveraging fiction (e.g., bibliotherapy or cinema therapy) to evoke and process real emotions in a safe environment.

Key Insights

- Fiction engages us not despite its falsity, but **because it resonates with universal emotions**.
- **Imagination is emotionally potent**, even when belief is suspended.
- The paradox invites us to rethink what **emotions require**—perhaps not truth, but **emotional relevance**.
- Fiction provides a **simulation space** where we can safely explore moral dilemmas, relationships, and fears.
- The paradox underscores the unique cognitive richness of **storytelling** and its central role in human experience.

Bonus Chapter 9: Dostoevsky's Paradox

Theory Overview

Dostoevsky's Paradox refers to the philosophical tension between **absolute freedom** and **the human need for moral boundaries, structure, or meaning**. This paradox is drawn from the works and themes of **Fyodor Dostoevsky**, the 19th-century Russian novelist and thinker, whose novels grapple with existentialism, free will, suffering, and the consequences of rejecting God or objective morality.

The paradox can be distilled from a line in *The Brothers Karamazov*—arguably one of Dostoevsky's most famous works—where one character claims:

"If God does not exist, everything is permitted."

This statement reflects the heart of the paradox: **If there is no divine authority, no objective morality, and humans are free to choose their values—can meaning, virtue, or society endure?** Dostoevsky explores whether humans can **bear the burden of total moral freedom**, or whether it leads to chaos, nihilism, and despair.

Example

In *Crime and Punishment*, the protagonist **Raskolnikov** commits murder under the belief that **he is above conventional morality**—that some individuals, like Napoleon, are justified in stepping outside moral norms for the sake of higher goals. He believes that without divine or objective moral laws, **power and intellect define morality**.

But after the act, Raskolnikov is consumed by guilt, paranoia, and existential suffering. Despite his rational justification, his **inner conscience** and sense of **moral reality** torment him. Dostoevsky uses Raskolnikov to show that **freedom from morality does not result in liberation, but in psychological and spiritual collapse**.

Why It Works

The paradox works because it pits two deep human drives against one another:

1. The desire for **freedom, autonomy, and rebellion** against imposed systems—be they religious, moral, or political.

2. The need for **structure, meaning, and moral certainty** to live cooperatively and meaningfully.

Dostoevsky's characters often explore this boundary. When people are told they can do whatever they want, some are crushed by the **weight of moral responsibility**; others descend into **nihilism or cruelty**. Thus, the paradox questions whether **freedom without limits** is sustainable—or even desirable.

How It Works

The core mechanics involve:

- **Removing external moral authority** (e.g., God, religion, societal codes).

- Giving individuals **absolute moral autonomy**.

- Observing the consequences: either the creation of a new, internalized moral system—or descent into **disorientation, guilt, or immorality**.

Dostoevsky suggests that humans crave **moral anchoring**, even when they intellectually reject traditional frameworks. His paradox doesn't argue for blind faith, but rather that the **absence of any shared moral centre** is deeply destabilizing.

Application

Dostoevsky's Paradox is relevant in:

- **Existential philosophy**: Especially in the works of Camus, Sartre, and Kierkegaard, who grapple with meaning, choice, and absurdity in a godless universe.

- **Modern ethics**: Raises questions about relativism, secular morality, and whether society can sustain moral norms without metaphysical grounding.

- **Psychology**: Seen in the effects of moral dislocation, guilt, and the need for purpose in identity formation.

- **Political theory**: Explores how ideologies that reject traditional values must construct new forms of collective meaning—or risk collapse.

Key Insights

- Absolute freedom, while attractive, may become a **burden too heavy** for the human psyche.
- Without shared moral grounding, individuals may struggle to find **meaningful purpose** or act ethically.
- Dostoevsky warns that rejecting traditional morality doesn't erase its emotional or existential consequences.
- His work suggests that **moral structure is not only social but deeply personal and psychological**.
- The paradox reflects the timeless struggle between **freedom and responsibility**, and the dangers of mistaking liberation for meaninglessness.

Bonus Chapter 10: Money Pump Paradox

Theory Overview

The **Money Pump Paradox** is a thought experiment in **decision theory and rational choice theory** that demonstrates how a person with **intransitive preferences**—preferences that are inconsistent in a circular way—can be **exploited repeatedly** for a loss, effectively having their money "pumped" away.

It illustrates a powerful principle: **if an agent's preferences are not logically coherent (i.e., transitive), they can be manipulated into making a series of decisions that leave them worse off.**

In rational decision-making, **transitivity of preferences** is considered a foundational requirement. If you prefer A over B, and B over C, then rationality requires you to prefer A over C. If this condition fails, your choices can form a **preference loop** that others can exploit, leading to a paradoxical situation where your own decisions undermine your well-being.

Example

Suppose you have the following intransitive preferences regarding three goods:

- You prefer **A over B**
- You prefer **B over C**
- But you also prefer **C over A**

Now, imagine someone offers to trade:

1. You start with **C**.
2. You pay a small fee to trade C for B (because you prefer B over C).
3. You pay another fee to trade B for A (you prefer A over B).
4. Then, you pay again to trade A for C (you prefer C over A).

You've now gone full circle and are back where you started—**with item C and less money**. This loop can repeat indefinitely, draining your resources. The person exploiting your preferences is effectively running a **"money pump."**

This illustrates the paradox: your preferences lead to a consistent, voluntary set of actions, yet cumulatively result in **net loss without any gain**—violating the principle of rational self-interest.

Why It Works

The paradox works because **intransitive preferences break rational coherence**. Even though each trade feels like a small improvement, the system as a whole is **cyclical and self-defeating**. The person doesn't notice the contradiction because they treat each decision **locally**, not globally.

The concept forces a critical examination of how **preferences must be structured** to avoid exploitation. It demonstrates that **rational agents must have consistent preferences**, or else their decision-making processes can lead to absurd and damaging outcomes.

How It Works

Key mechanics of the Money Pump Paradox include:

1. **Intransitive preferences**: The core condition for the paradox to occur.

2. **Small transaction costs**: Each trade comes with a minor fee, ensuring that the loop results in loss.

3. **Cyclical decision-making**: Each preference-driven trade leads to a loop that can be endlessly exploited.

4. **No awareness of the loop**: The agent never recognizes the broader pattern and believes each decision is rational on its own.

In rational choice theory, **transitivity** is often baked into utility functions to avoid this kind of irrational behaviour. If utilities are well-defined and transitive, no money pump is possible.

Application

This paradox is highly relevant in:

- **Behavioural economics**: Real people often display **context-dependent or inconsistent preferences**, making them vulnerable to marketing and pricing tricks.

- **Consumer choice theory**: Retail strategies sometimes exploit shifting preferences (e.g., bundling, framing).

- **Artificial intelligence and decision systems**: Ensuring that algorithms or agents don't loop through preference cycles that waste resources.

- **Ethics and policy design**: In helping design systems that protect people from exploitative cycles (e.g., in gambling or microtransactions).

Key Insights

- **Rational decision-making requires internal consistency.**
- Intransitive preferences make one vulnerable to **exploitation through logical cycles**.

- Each seemingly rational local decision can result in **irrational global outcomes**.

- The paradox highlights the importance of **structural integrity in preference systems**, not just immediate choice.

- It serves as a cautionary tale in both economics and philosophy: even small inconsistencies can lead to **catastrophic outcomes** when magnified over time.

I hope you have enjoyed this book as much as I have enjoyed researching it.

On the next page you can find the other books in this series.

My best to you, Dan

OTHER BOOKS IN THIS 100 SERIES – SCAN HERE

100 COGNITIVE AND MENTAL MODELS TO HELP YOUR CAREER: Mental Shortcuts for Smarter Choices, Sharper Thinking, and Success

-

ANOTHER 100 MENTAL MODELS TO HELP YOUR CAREER - VOLUME 2: Another 100 Powerful Mental Models for Clarity, Confidence, and Climbing the Career Ladder

-

100 HEURISTICS AND HEURISTIC MODELS: The Hidden Rules of Smart Thinking Used by Experts, Entrepreneurs, and Machines

-

100 GAME THEORIES AND DECISION MODELS FOR RATIONAL DECISION MAKING IN COMPETITIVE SITUATIONS: 100 Winning Strategies for Rational Thinking in High-Stakes Scenarios

-

100 BUSINESS STRATEGIES PROVEN TACTICS FOR GROWTH, INNOVATION AND MARKET DOMINATION: Actionable Strategies to Scale, Disrupt and Lead in Any Industry

-

100 LEADERSHIP MODELS AND STRATEGIES FOR EFFECTIVE DECISION-MAKING FOR ORGANIZATIONAL SUCCESS: Empowering Your Leadership, 100 Proven Strategies and Models to Enhance Decision-Making & Drive Success

-

100 BUSINESS GROWTH HACKS AND STRATEGIES TO GROW PROFIT AND INCREASE YOUR COMPETITIVE ADVANTAGE: Proven Techniques to Scale Faster, Boost Revenue, and Dominate Your Market with Actionable Growth

-

100 ECONOMIC THEORIES DEMYSTIFIED : A Guide To The World's Most Influential Economic Ideas From Keynesian Economics To Debt-deflation Theory

-

100 PASSIVE INCOME STREAM SIDE HUSTLES, MASTERING SIDE HUSTLES AND SMART INVESTMENTS: How to Make Money While You Sleep and Secure Your Financial Future

-

WHILST YOU ARE HERE , WHY NOT SCAN THIS TO SEE IF THERE ARE ANY MORE BOOKS PUBLISHED YET

OR FOLLOW ME AT @DANDANMUSICMAN ON X AND @DANDANMUSICMANUK ON INSTAGRAM

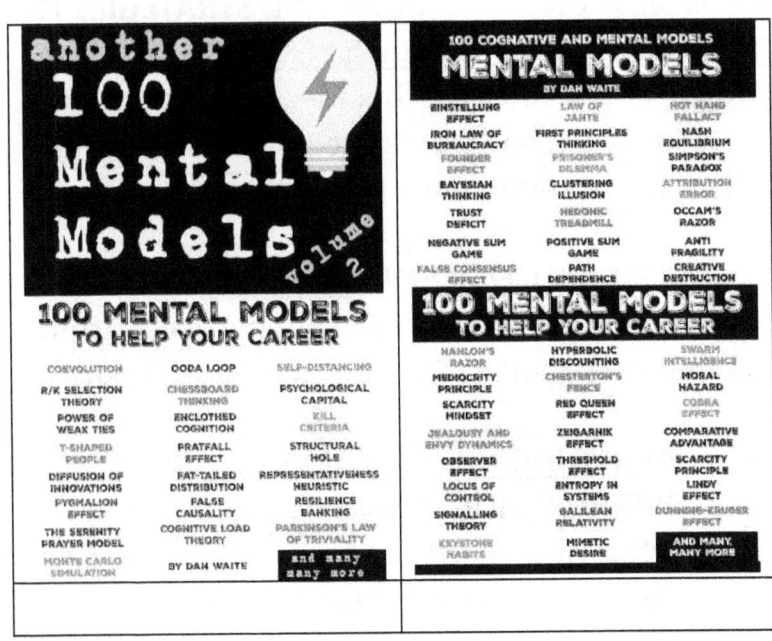

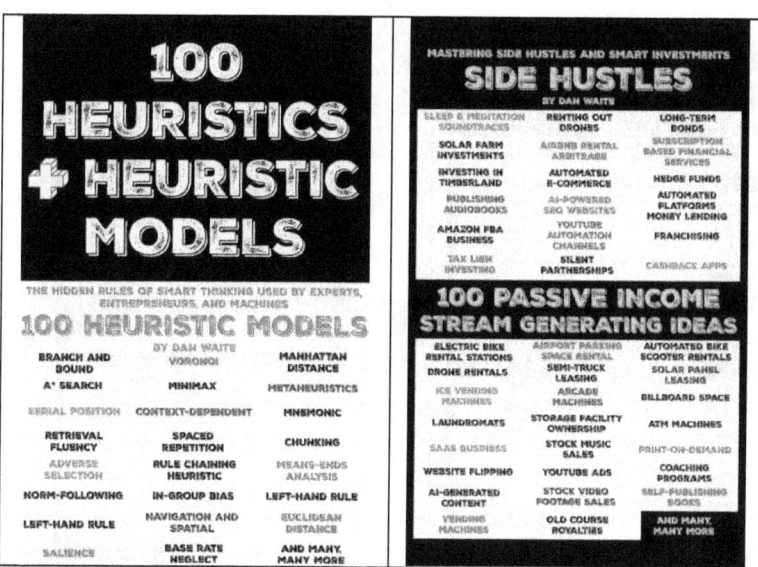

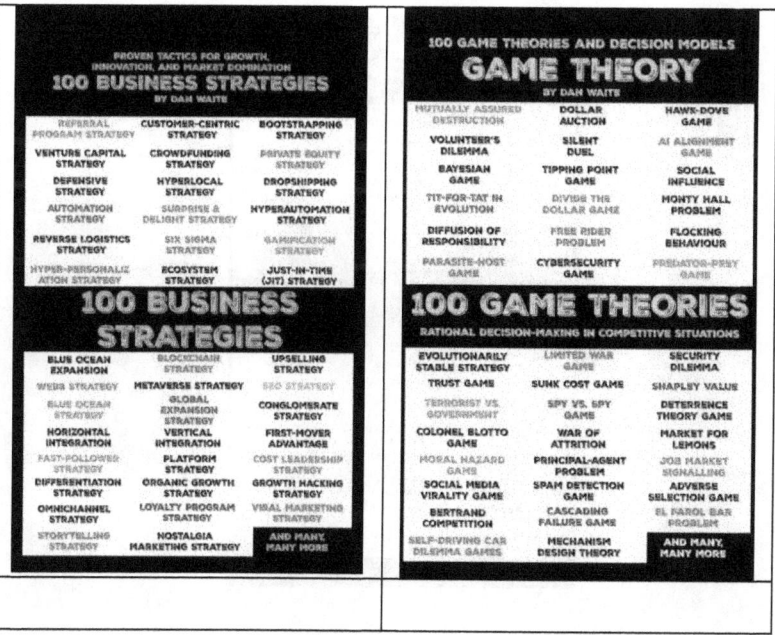

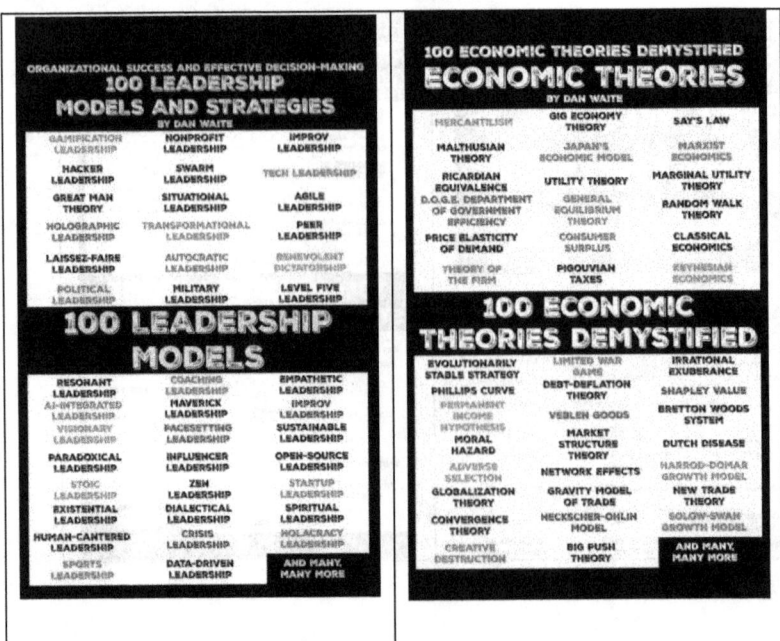

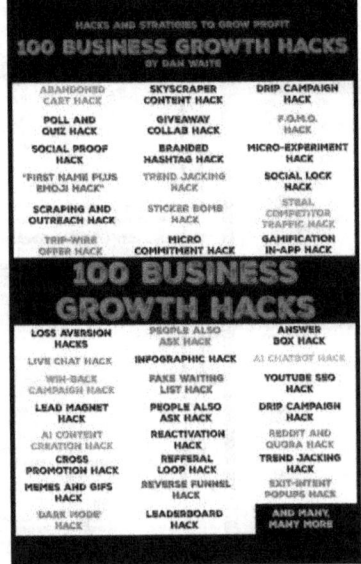

www.ingramcontent.com/pod-product-compliance
Lightning Source LLC
Chambersburg PA
CBHW071957150426
43194CB00008B/907